Jose Mourinho: The Art of Winning

What the appointment of Jose Mourinho says about Manchester United and the Premier League

ANDREW J. KIRBY

This is a Red Sportswriting Publication

Web: https://paintthistownred.wordpress.com/red-sportswriting-2/

First published in eBook form by Endeavour Press.

ISBN: 1537012363
ISBN-13: 978-1537012360

DEDICATION

For the kids, Leon 'Georgie' Kirby and Peggy 'Mour-Nina-oh' Kirby, who I hope to take to games soon…

For my Dad, Ray 'Georgie' Kirby, who never misses a match.

For my Mum, 'Pat-Rice Evra' Kirby, who goes to more games than me at the moment.

And for my partner, Heidi, who puts up with all this nonsense.

ALSO BY THIS AUTHOR

Fergie's Finest: Sir Alex Ferguson's First x11 (Endeavour Press, May 2013)

The Pride of All Europe: Manchester United's Greatest Seasons in the European Cup (Endeavour Press, June 2014)

Louis van Gaal: Dutch Courage (Endeavour Press, August 2015)

JOSE MOURINHO: THE ART OF WINNING

JOSE MOURINHO IN QUOTES

"The world is so competitive, aggressive, selfish and during the time we spend here we must be all but that."
Jose Mourinho

"I am Jose Mourinho and I don't change. I arrive with all my qualities and my defects."
Jose Mourinho

"Please don't call me arrogant, but I'm European champion and I think I'm a special one."
Jose Mourinho

"When I go to the press conference before the game, in my mind the game has already started."
Jose Mourinho

"Violence may be necessary for the successful stabilisation of power and introduction of new legal institutions. Force may be used to eliminate political rivals, to coerce resistant populations, and to purge the community of other men strong enough of character to rule, who will inevitably attempt to replace the ruler. The ends justify the means."

Niccolo di Bernardo dei Machiavelli

CONTENTS

INTRODUCTION

Lionel Messi and Cristiano Ronaldo apart, the biggest, most marketable stars in world football today are the managers. The 2016-17 edition of the FA Premier League is being billed as the most exciting yet, and that's not because of the influx of star players after the European Championships in France. Though some eye-catching names have joined the league, none have the cache of a Messi or a Ronaldo. None have the standing of a Jose Mourinho or a Pep Guardiola either. And so it is on the manager's shoulders that the responsibility for delivering the customary Premier League spectacle falls.

They are the *galacticos*.

Indeed, just before I started writing this Introduction I was listening to Danny Kelly on talkSPORT's Breakfast Show previewing the 2016-17 Premier League season. He barely mentioned the players. It was all about the managers: Mourinho, Guardiola, Antonio Conte, Jurgen Klopp, Claudio Ranieri. Kelly was slavering at the thought of all the mind games which would ensue; he barely gave a thought to the actual football. He admitted as much himself, when he suggested we were heading towards a future in which *there would be no football*; we'd just sit and watch the managers patrolling their stage-like technical areas for 90 minutes before the real drama of the post-match press conferences began.

Kelly had his tongue firmly implanted in his cheek of course. But there was more than a grain of truth in what he said.

We've come a long way, baby.

I've been reading a lot about Sir Matt Busby recently. Maybe it has something to do with Jose Mourinho being appointed manager of Manchester United. Call it harking back to better, more innocent times. Mourinho is in many ways the *anti*-Busby. Busby was a man of great integrity and humility; he was a man of the people. Mourinho, as Scott Hunt wrote for *Mancunian Matters,* "is bold, brash, bullish. At times he resembles a bulldog in Armani." German newspaper *Bild* described him as a "manager-lout." You might say he wouldn't know integrity even if it was a ball, smashed at him at full pelt off the right boot of Paul Scholes, and he's never even been in the same postcode – the same *universe* - as humility. And despite his posturing, he is most definitely not a *man of the people.* He is a beast of the media.

To many fans it might seem sacrilegious even to mention Busby and Mourinho in the same sentence, however without Sir Matt, and men of his ilk, there would have been no Jose Mourinho. Indeed, by looking back on Busby through the rosiest-tinted of spectacles, by painting him as some kind of stand-in persona for all things moral in a time of innocence, we may be doing him a disservice. For, remember, there was steel in Busby's character too. He wasn't without a few Mourinho-like traits either. The following quote might have been taken from a biography of Jose Mourinho – perhaps one penned by his acolyte, the journalist Harry Harris; after all, Harris has written *at least five* such books. Perhaps it might have referred to

Mourinho's prodigious years at Porto, when he became the youngest boss to secure the Champions League for his club. But it is not. It is taken from *Manchester United: The Betrayal of a Legend* by Michael Crick and David Smith. The book was published back in 1990.

"Call it confidence, conceit, arrogance, or ignorance, but I was unequivocal about it. At the advanced age of thirty-five I would accept only if they would let me have all my own way. As the manager I would want to manage. I would be the boss."

This is what I mean by Busby finding the path for men like Mourinho (and Sir Alex Ferguson) to follow, later. Busby took the United job on the condition that the role of manager was taken seriously; that he be allowed more influence within the club; that he could truly be *in charge*.

"Such an attitude, which of course is quite normal today, was highly unusual in 1945," wrote Crick. "The fact that United had continued since 1937 with the secretary, Walter Crickmer, as the part-time manager was some indication of how the directors saw the job. Team selection was officially the responsibility of the directors, and for many years after Busby's arrival the first item on the weekly board agenda was the selection of club sides for forthcoming fixtures. Indeed, until 1947 Busby would attend board meetings solely to discuss playing matters and then, the minutes often record, 'The manager having conducted his business retired from the meeting.' Only with Busby absent, would the directors discuss the minutes of the previous meeting and the club's financial affairs. Slowly, however, Busby gained influence."

Similarly, it was only in 1947 that the England appointed their first manager-proper in Walter Winterbottom. Before that, the national team was selected by the FA 'International Selection Committee'. Grudgingly, football men came to be trusted with football matters. They still weren't allowed within a mile of the business side of things, of course: there was still very much an upstairs/downstairs feel to the game in those days. Club boards and committees comprised local business owners, mostly upper class men who looked down on football men and their working class backgrounds; men like Busby, who came from mining stock. But, now men like Busby and Winterbottom had their feet in the door, there was no turning back and slowly, slowly, and then quickly, quickly, everything changed. Now decisions to appoint managers no longer football decisions. And the men who manage are no longer solely 'football managers'. They have to be so much more.

Managers must be psychologists. Tactical thinkers. Psychiatrists. Wind-up merchants. Machiavellian manipulators. But above all else they must be communications experts.

In his book *The Manager: Inside the Minds of Football's Leaders*, Mike Carson wrote: "In Britain, the people with the task and privilege of leading football at the front line are the managers. In fact, their role has only a little to do with management, and much more to do with leadership. The men who lead in the upper reaches of professional British football – especially in the (…) Premier League – are truly extraordinary. The work they do is intensive, personal, technical and critical – critical to the success of their teams, the growth of their clubs and the happiness of many. It is also subject to intense public scrutiny: their every move – whether witnessed, surmised or merely imagined – is subject to widespread analysis in almost every forum imaginable, from bar rooms through offices to internet blogs and live television and radio broadcasts."

Football managers of the old-school variety probably wish football management were more about football than it is *the other gubbins* (as they'd probably have it). They'd prefer to turn their backs on the media. Close their doors to representatives from the official sponsors.

Stop their players from appearing in advertisements. But football management has changed, and at the highest level it is a complex mix of different challenges which have very little to do with the actual business of playing the game. Managers who do not understand this soon find there is no place for them in the game. Managers who do are highly sought-after.

Busby, I reckon, would have changed with the times. Though in many ways he was old-school, he was also pragmatic. Sir Alex Ferguson was the same. They were men who weren't afraid to assume control of everything that went on within *their* club. They may have accepted some of the changes reluctantly – the overweening influence of the media, for example – but in the end they would use those changes to their own ends. Just like Jose Mourinho does now.

"The role of a leader in Premier League football is fascinating, complex and tough," wrote Carson. "Fantasy football leagues may convince us that it's about buying players and selecting a team. In reality it is about creating winning environments, delivering on enormous expectations, overcoming significant challenges, handling pressure and staying centred throughout."

Tough is right. The old adage used to be that goalkeepers were crazy; now, surely, it applies to managers instead. Who'd want to be a manager today? Even in 1979, in a rare *New Musical Express (NME)* piece on football, the writer Monty Smith described the role of an elite level manager as "a two-ulcer job", one which required a "peculiar temperament". He quoted Eamon Dunphy (ex-United player turned media pundit and author, (from his book *Only A Game)* "If you look rationally at the football season it is a series of hellish tests, Saturday after Saturday."

Now, this is doubly true. Becoming a manager in the 2010s - signing up to undertake that "two-ulcer job" - surely only appeals to those who like white- knuckle, adrenaline-sports. Maybe it is not a coincidence then, that according to Harry Harris: "Mourinho's favourite hobby is quad-biking, and he enjoys skiing and snowboarding."

But where things have moved on is the big games, the *duels* involving the biggest managerial heavyweights, don't take place on Saturdays as Dunphy said. Not any more. No: instead, they are the main feature on a Sky Super Sunday or else they are the headline act on the Monday Night Football show. If these clashes do – by happy chance – get scheduled for a Saturday, you can count on the fact they won't be at 3pm as per English football tradition. No, they'll be early doors: 12:30 or 12:45. Not exactly prime kick-off times for the traditional match-going fan. But the traditional match-going fan is no longer the Premier League's target audience. No, the target audience are Sky, or BT Sports TV subscribers here, and the 'global' fan-base beyond.

Sky and the Premier League have found the ideal way of marketing elite-level English football to consumers across the world. They have packaged it as the equivalent of a very long-running, complex, and immersive box-set drama series. They make it unmissable. You simply *have* to tune in to catch the latest instalment or else you'll fall behind; you won't know what's going on; you won't be current when it comes to those discussions around the water-cooler, or on Twitter and Facebook.

The managers – with all their foibles, their conflicts, their antagonisms - are key figures in selling the Premier League to subscribers. They are, as Mike Carson wrote "central characters in the drama. Sir Alex (Ferguson) is clear as to why this is: 'The media do this because today they are a beast that isn't interested any more in what happened in the 32nd minute of the match. If you go back in time, it was a chronicle of football. What you've got now is a dominant interest in reaction. It's about how to sell a newspaper, and the manager is the focus of that because they know he is the one person that can be sacked. So there is a strong focus on the success or failure of a manager. It goes with the role as the most important member of the club.""

The most important member of the club. We've come a long way, baby, since Sir Matt was shut out of his own boardroom.

Managers are now the pre-eminent figures in ensuring that the Premier League remains the most popular in the world. Even if it does not offer the highest quality football or the best supporters it offers the best *drama* and intrigue. Like a box-set, the action revolves around a relatively small set of major characters (there can be only 20 managers at a time; though former managers keen to get back into the game often appear as extras; ghosts at the banquet). The narrative – what keeps people hooked - hangs off the heavyweights and they are complex figures; the Tony Sopranos of the piece. They are often dark, like Mourinho. They compel us to watch, and keep watching. They force us to sit through the adverts (in which they sometimes appear). To buy subscriptions. To bet. We have to know what happens next, and next. There is always a next.

The players are mere scenery. Background music. (And sometimes that is a good thing: what with all the media training they have to undergo these days, it's not often they have anything interesting to say, unless they are flogging a new, updated version of their – ghost-written - autobiography.) The managers are the protagonists, particularly Mourinho. Like all main characters in stories, Mourinho has been on 'a journey'. We have watched his character arc unfold before our very eyes. From the funny, charming and sharp-suited, dark and handsome stranger who so confidently announced himself to the world, through his shaven-head and strangely vulnerable-looking spells where his haunted eyes told you of his belief that the whole world was against him, through his chest-thumping, Blue gilet-clad spells, to the older but not necessarily wiser, grey-haired Red Devil we have today. From hero to anti-hero, we've watched him laugh and cry (after he was initially turned down for the United job after Fergie's retirement). We've grown bored of his antics and wanted him out; then hungered and pleaded for his great comeback. We still don't fully understand him, for he is more complex than that, but we've always watched, always listened.

For this devil always has the best lines.

"Mourinho's words are arguably his greatest weapon," said Scott Hunt, for *Mancunian Matters*. "They surround him like a mist and make him nigh on impossible to pin down or get on top of. He manages to create a bubble around him and his players that seems impenetrable and instils an 'us against the world' mentality at his clubs. It makes him unpopular. Hated by Italian and Spanish media for his outlandish comments and outrageous behaviour, Mourinho returned to England where the media are a little more in love with 'the special one'. The British people have bought into Mourinho the myth. He is an enigma and we hang on his every word."

As Andrew Murray wrote in August 2016's *FourFourTwo* magazine: "There's a very good reason why Manchester United chose Mourinho. He's box office. His name alone still holds immense cache and can attract the best players in the world, despite the club facing a second season in three without Champions League football."

As you'll have already gathered, this football book isn't always about football. Like all the best box-set series it features a wide-range of different narratives and themes. Within these pages we'll cover courtroom drama and the X-men; celebrity and stock markets; top-knots and linen baskets; psychology and branding; voyeurs and little horses; Darth Vader and Dirty Den. And for that I apologise. But there's no way around it; these days even *football* isn't all about football any more, just as Danny Kelly surmised. Football is the side-show; Mourinho is the main event.

Let me take you back to 2004-05. One of the most well-remembered adverts of that time was from Marks & Spencer: the almost pornographic way the camera lingered over their chocolate pudding; Dervla Kirwan's breathy voiceover claiming: "this is not just a chocolate pudding, this is a Marks & Spencer chocolate pudding". (See, I told you this book wasn't always about football.)

2004-05 also marked the start of Jose Mourinho's managerial career in England, and ever since then the Portuguese has made it his mission to prove that there are football managers and there are *super* football managers. Super Coaches. He has brought different dimensions to the role of manager, and he has helped changed the role; helped make it as much about image and brand as it is about picking a team. This book will analyse the role of Super Coaches in elite level football today, and evaluate Jose Mourinho's standing amongst this group.

On 27th May 2016, 17 years and one day after United won the three trophies which comprised the famous Treble, Jose Mourinho signed a three-year contract with arguably England's biggest football club and certainly English sport's biggest *brand* in Manchester United, with an option to stay at the club until at least 2020. By then, those who have perfect 20:20 vision in hindsight will be able to look back and judge whether the Portuguese's reign at Old Trafford has been a success; whether he has been able to step into the shoes of Alex Ferguson, a manager who was definitely not just a manager but a bonafide leader and legend. One thing is clear: right now the club has never been as far away from a Treble in those 17 years as it is now. So Jose has his work cut out for him.

At the same time, Jose Mourinho himself is for the first time facing questions about his own recent record. Sure he won the Premier League in his second season with

Chelsea he won the Premier League and League Cup, but before that he had gone two seasons (including one at Real Madrid) pot-less, and in the season *after* it, Chelsea's defence of their titles was so poor, and so riven with internal strife, that Mourinho was sacked by December. For a man with a record like his, two trophies in four years is not 'special'.

It is clear that it is make-or-break time for both Mourinho and Manchester United in terms of their reputation. We've reached a crossroads for both as to what kind of club and manager they'll be seen as in history. This book, then, will also examine whether the 53-year-old can lead United out of the relative wilderness. And it will ask what price will United have to pay for employing a man renowned for his winning-at-all-costs pragmatism, for his often divisive presence, for his frequent histrionics.

"To his detractors," wrote Harry Harris, "Mourinho is a man prepared to sacrifice style to win, with exuberance, mind games and disrepute charges – a flawed genius. To the players who worship him and talk of incredible relationships, to his proven CV, he is a genuine genius."

And yet, he is a manager with a reputation for short-termism. His managerial CV shows he works in clear, three-year cycles: in the first, team-building and identifying a common enemy; in the second, conquering all before him; and in the third, bust, as the players start to grow tired of his 'genius' for pissing everyone off. Mourinho is a 'specialist', a carnivore, hungry to win and get his teeth into opponents and rivals, but United legends are so much more than that – the Sirs, Fergie and Busby, saw a bigger picture; they were omnivorous. They built legacies. Dynasties. If Jose Mourinho is truly to become a legend at Old Trafford, after a rather nomadic existence as a manager, he must become more than he is. This book considers whether he can still develop as a manager and start to become more long-termist in his views.

It also contemplates the groundswell opinion on his appointment amongst United fans. Can we truly forget his Old Trafford touchline-dash and his Chelsea years? Is it a case of *once a blue always a blue*, or is it, *once a blue always a Red*, as it was with Wayne Rooney?

And make no mistake about it, Mourinho *was* a blue. Even when Mourinho was no longer Chelsea manager – he was manager at Madrid – he talked up their forthcoming Champions League final against Bayern Munich like this: "Of course I want the Blues to win, even though I have a lot of respect for the reds. I have a blue rib, still." And: "In my career I had two great passions, Inter and Chelsea, and Chelsea is more important for me."

What many Reds have concluded is that – at this time – we have little choice than to accept Mourinho's appointment, blue rib or no. Our board, famous for its dithering, has this time acted in a timely, decisive fashion and brought in the best they could get.

Sir Alex Ferguson, the most successful manager of all time at United, was famous for his watch-tapping displays on the touchline, trying to grab a little more Fergie-Time in which the Reds could snatch an unlikely equaliser or winner. On Jose Mourinho's wrist is a typically fancy "sapphire crystal delaCour" watch, on the back of which reads the following inscription: "I am not afraid by the consequences of my decisions."

United haven't quite entered Fergie-Time yet – we won the FA Cup last year – but we need to start clawing our way back onto our perch quickly, before we are left behind. So in the short-term, Mourinho's appointment makes sense. But in the longer term, he needs to realise that as well as being unafraid of the consequences, he also needs to be unafraid of change. He needs to *become* Manchester United. He needs to grow a red rib. The question is: will he?

Time is ticking.

1

"AN EARTHQUAKE, PROVOKED." WHAT EFFECT WILL THE MOURINHO SHOW HAVE ON MANCHESTER UNITED AS A FOOTBALL CLUB?

There used to be a weird rumour about Luis Nani, the enigmatic Portuguese winger: apparently the centre-piece of his front room was a life-sized marble statue of himself, wearing the jester's hat he'd donned to celebrate Manchester United's 2008 Champions League final win, in which he'd netted one of the vital penalties in the shoot-out against Chelsea.

The rumour was, of course, so much bunk. But you could see – sort of – why so many people had bought it. Nani had put in some downright weird performances in a Red shirt and he seemed a downright strange bloke, too. What's more Nani bears a striking resemblance to the King of the Weird, Michael Jackson, and old Wacko wasn't averse to the odd statue of himself, was he? (And how about that Michael Jackson statue which used to stand outside Craven Cottage for bizarre?)

But yeah, the story was bollocks. As it turned out, football fans should have been looking to another Portuguese forward with Manchester United for such an incredible display of vanity. Though both Nani and Cristiano Ronaldo had trod the same path from Sporting Lisbon to Manchester United, and they both played similar attacking roles in the side, Ronaldo always did things bigger and better than his counterpart. Ronaldo didn't just go for a statue. No, he had a whole CR7 *museum* built in his home-town of Funchal, Madeira.

Another fellow Portuguese, Jose Mourinho, has often been accused of similar levels of narcissism. Only, instead of a statue or a museum, Mourinho had a cardboard cut-out. "A life-sized cardboard cut-out stood in Jose Mourinho's office at Valdebebas, Real Madrid's training ground north-east of the city," wrote Sid Lowe in *Fear and Loathing in La Liga*. "It was him sprinting across the Camp Nou turf, finger in the air, celebrating at the end of the 2010 Champions League semi-final."

But Mourinho didn't have the cut-out installed in his office out of any self-love; because he could never grow tired of looking at his own handsome visage. No, Jose had the cut-out installed as a permanent reminder of his own story and as a *mission statement* for his future. For the cut-out showed him celebrating "the moment Internazionale reached their first European Cup final in almost forty years," but more than that it showed the moment he knocked "Barcelona out and end(ed) their dream of reaching a second successive Champions League final."

Mourinho had been scorned by Barcelona. That was his story and also his *raison d'etre*. And in Madrid, his brand. For this was "the moment that Mourinho became Real Madrid's hero... and their coach. His audition could not have gone better. (...) Someone at Barcelona turned the sprinkler system on. (…) He arrived in Madrid on a mission: *to knock Barcelona off their perch."*

All that was missing was the deleted expletive and it could have been Fergie.

Mourinho and Real Madrid started out as a match made in heaven. They bonded over their mutual loathing of Barcelona. They forged an identity together based on the fact Madrid were not Barcelona. But in the end, as we will see in some of the other chapters in this book, that identity became confused – as all identities do, when they are purely constructed on *what they are not.*

In 2012-13 things began to fall apart for Mourinho in the Spanish capital. He'd won a great battle against Barcelona, not only in winning the La Liga title race over them, but also in driving their hero, *the cule* Pep Guardiola out of the club and out of town; into exhaustion and into exile in New York, where he took a sabbatical. Mourinho had gotten to him *that much.* But, as Lowe noted: "When Guardiola departed, it felt like Mourinho had been left orphaned; his adversary overturned, victory achieved for now, he no longer had a nemesis, a target, someone with whom to wage war. So he waged war with his own club."

His position became untenable. The seas were stormy and behind the scenes, Jose set his agent, Jorge Mendes, to start casting his net around, hoping he'd net something big: a life-raft perhaps. The big one was Manchester United. It was rumoured that Sir Alex Ferguson might be finally hanging up his hair-drier at the end of the season.

And so, in that same office; the cardboard cut-out of the victorious Mourinho galloping across the Camp Nou turf like some latter-day David Pleat now sun-bleached – the gloss of it gone - and tatty around the edges, Jose Mourinho sat down at his desk and he crossed his fingers and he made some calls, mostly to his sports agency Gestifute.

'I'm a celebrity,' he might have said, 'get me out of here.' Fuck this Bushtucker Trial - Real Madrid - for a game of soldiers.

He didn't get the answer he wanted and so, in an increasing state of desperation, he made some more. By the time he jabbed his thumb on the *END CALL* button for a final time, he was sobbing loudly. He was crushed.

His life-raft had been cruelly whipped away from him right at the last. He was being left to drown in Spain. Manchester United had offered the job to David Moyes. The Glaswegian was going to succeed Sir Alex Ferguson. Mourinho was crushed. He was shocked. He was sick as a dead parrot. (Some United fans could sympathise: though we didn't blub like babies at the news, many were underwhelmed to say the very least.)

In September 2013, with Mourinho now back in the Stamford Bridge hot-seat and wee Davie Moyes already finding the United throne too big to settle into properly, *The Guardian* reported the inside story of Jose Mourinho's astonishing reaction to being passed over for the United job. The primary source was a book - *Prepare to Lose: the Mourinho Era*, by Diego Torres, a writer for *El Pais*.

According to Torres, David Moyes' appointment not only made poor Jose cry, it also "provoked an earthquake": "Mourinho felt let down by Sir Alex Ferguson, who had recommended Moyes to the United board. (…) Mourinho … thought that Ferguson was, besides his ally, also his friend and godfather. He was convinced that they were tied by a relationship of genuine trust. He thought that his fabulous collection of titles constituted an 'endorsement' unreachable to any other contenders. When he knew that Ferguson had chosen Moyes, the Everton coach, he was struck by a terrible disbelief. Moyes hadn't won absolutely anything!"

And so, all those phone calls. "Torres said that Mourinho was on the phone constantly to his sports agency

Gestifute. 'Mourinho wouldn't stop calling them. His 'interlocutors' had heard him sob loudly and they were spreading the word. The most feared man in the company was crushed.'"

"Mourinho, according to the book, was sure that Ferguson would call with an explanation but he heard nothing. He recalled reading comments from the United director Sir Bobby Charlton pouring scorn on the idea of him getting the job. 'He was tormented by the memory of an interview of Sir Bobby Charlton in the Guardian in December. His judgments gave him a big uncertainty. 'A United coach wouldn't do what he did to Tito Vilanova', stated Charlton, evoking the finger in the eye, when asked if he saw Mourinho as a successor for Ferguson. In regards to the admiration that Ferguson professed towards him, the veteran footballer implied that it was a fable: 'He doesn't like him that much'."

"In the morning he called Mendes so that he urgently got in touch with United. Until the end he wanted his agent to pressure the English club as an attempt to block any operation. It was an act of desperation. They both knew that Mendes had put Mourinho in the market a year earlier."

"The book says that 'Mendes had already been told in the autumn of 2012 that Ferguson's first option was Pep Guardiola. He had been explained the reasons. In Gestifute, the message from a United executive rumbled like a drum: 'The problem is that when things don't work for Mou, he doesn't do club politics. He does Jose politics.'"

Mendes and Gestifute dismissed the story about Mourinho's tears. It was bunk, they implied, just like the story of Luis Nani and his amazing technicolour statue with the jester's hat. Indeed, when "Mourinho went on to take up the offer of a second term at Chelsea from the owner, Roman Abramovich (…) in June (2013) he claimed to have known of Ferguson's plans to stand down but said he was always intent on returning to Stamford Bridge: 'I knew that Ferguson was retiring many months ago,' he said. 'I would have turned down every job in the world – the Manchester United job, every one – for Chelsea.'"

In September 2013 Mourinho's adviser Eladio Parames was forced to deny the story yet again. " 'This story does not have any sense,' he is quoted by the Portuguese newspaper *O Jogo*. 'It is completely false. It has no head or tail.'"

Ah, but it had legs, didn't it? And it ran and ran. Though he'd pronounced himself 'the happy one' upon his unveiling at Stamford Bridge, after "renewing what he described as his marriage vows," Jim White observed: "even as he was presented with the razzmatazz of a Hollywood star to 250-plus journalists and more than fifty television crews filling the Harris Suite at the Bridge, there was nobody gathered in the room who really believed he would be seeing out the four-year contract he had just signed. In truth, not even him."

Happy One? There were times during his second spell at Chelsea, at which Mourinho looked thoroughly disillusioned with it all. And that was *before* he waged a war with the club - and specifically its employees – during his disastrous third season at the helm. You got the sense he wanted to be somewhere else. Yes, he won the Premier League title during his second season – as he does with most of his clubs – but a lot of the time it looked like Mourinho had grown weary of playing 'Mourinho'. He probably sensed what was around the corner just as much as we all did (spontaneous combustion; the Eva Carneiro row; losing the dressing-room).

When he finally was granted the object of his heart's desire, the United job, Mourinho said: "I think I prefer to forget the last three years." This was in answer to a question regarding United's diminished status since Sir Alex Ferguson's retirement, and the less than satisfactory

Moyes and Van Gaal regimes. But it could just as easily have referred to his *own* recent history.

Mourinho was finally where he wanted to be.

Samuel Luckhurst wrote an excellent piece in the *Manchester Evening News* in which he forensically pieced together Mourinho's many flirtations with United over the years, tracking them back even before his time at Real Madrid, and his tears in the office. "Strategically," said Luckhurst, "Mourinho began his audition to succeed Ferguson over seven years ago. Ahead of United's 2009 Champions League round-of-16 tie with Internazionale, he granted MUTV an exclusive interview and, in a light-hearted exchange, reporter Hayley McQueen asked Mourinho if he would like to succeed Ferguson."

"'I'd have to wait 20 more years,' he laughed. When asked if he was prepared to wait that long, he replied: 'No problem.'"

"At Old Trafford for the return leg, Mourinho had a smile as wide as a Cheshire cat as he sat in the away dugout and posed for some United fans taking pictures of him. It was his Sally Field moment: 'I cannot deny the fact that you like me, right now. You like me!'"

Four years later United faced Mourinho's new team Real Madrid at the same stage of the competition, and Mourinho, in his role of ring-master and drummer-upper of TV subscriptions described the game as 'the match the world is waiting for'. Luckhurst noted Mourinho had "come to understand, during his self-imposed exile from English football, the gargantuan size of United." (And indeed, in his inaugural speech as United supremo Mourinho constantly spoke of United as a "giant" club.)

"The world was waiting not just to watch the game but Mourinho," continued Luckhurst. "Earlier that campaign (the Champions League of 2012-13), he celebrated Cristiano Ronaldo's group stage winner against (Manchester) City with an exultant knee slide. Over the two legs against United, Mourinho was professional and measured as he continued his quest to win Real's *decima*." And "in the second-half (of the second-leg) at Old Trafford, his audition was as masterful as it was magnanimous. Mourinho consoled a disbelieving Nani after his dismissal, capitalised on Ferguson's fury, cheerleading - and midfield blind spot - by introducing Luka Modric to win the tie and then endeared himself in a post-match interview."

"'Independent of the decision, the best team lost. We didn't deserve to win but football is like this,' Mourinho said."

Hindsight shows us that at that point, Mourinho probably thought there was a very good chance he'd be standing in Fergie's place on the Old Trafford touchline the following season, and perhaps managing Nani (maybe advising him to go for a cardboard cut-out next time rather than a full-on marble statue: these things aren't easy to move if you've been kicked out the door, all the way to, say, Fenerbache).

But as it was, the swings and roundabouts of the managerial merry-go-round instead sent him all the way back to Chelsea. Do not pass go. *Maybe collect a hefty image rights deal.*

Mourinho v United, 2013-14

Jose Mourinho's first Premier League game in his first spell at Chelsea was at Stamford Bridge. Manchester United were the opposition. In Mourinho's second spell at Stamford Bridge he had to wait a little longer, but not much: Chelsea faced Manchester United at Old Trafford in the third game of the season. However, as Phil McNulty reported for BBC Sport: "the much-anticipated meeting (…) ended in anti-climax as Old Trafford witnessed its first goalless draw in the Premier League since May 2009."

United fans didn't know it then, but there were plenty more in the post.

But in 2013, bore-draws and goalless first halves of football were the exception, not the rule: there had been 77 Premier League games since that last 0-0 when United secured the title against Arsenal in 2009.

The best player on display at Old Trafford on the night of the Chelsea game was undoubtedly – and ironically - Wayne Rooney. The United number 10 was – uniquely - serenaded by both sets of fans during the game. Blues fans sung his name because it was well-known Jose Mourinho had made Rooney his top summer transfer target. The England striker was unsettled – had been ever since Sir Alex Ferguson's parting shot: that claim that Rooney had demanded a transfer (for about the hundredth time).

Rooney, of course, stayed.

The other interesting point of note regarding the match was Jose Mourinho's team selection. Firstly, he played with no recognised striker on the field. Phil McNulty noted that this "was perhaps more of a comment in his lack of faith in his strikers as Fernando Torres and Romelu Lukaku were left on the bench and Demba Ba was not in the squad."

One of the most damaging accusations which was thrown at Jose Mourinho during his second spell at Chelsea was that his ability to judge a player had become blurred. Romelu Lukaku was eventually moved out of the club; sent out on successive (and successful) loan spells before being sold to Everton, where he of course came back to haunt his former club. Though he at times looks cumbersome and his first-touch often goes further than colleagues can shoot, Lukaku at a lot of other times looks exactly like the striker Chelsea have been crying out for ever since Didier Drogba passed his peak.

And though Kevin De Bruyne did start the game at

Old Trafford, *he* didn't last much longer at Chelsea either. He made just three starts for Chelsea before being moved on to Wolfsburg in the January transfer window. A season later, De Bruyne was named footballer of the year in Germany and then he was being moved on again. This time for an astonishing £*55 million*. Manchester City were, of course, the club who stumped up the cash in 2015 – a full £37 million more than Mourinho had received for De Bruyne back in 2014. The Belgian will have a point to prove in Manchester derbies in 2016-17. But then again, so will everybody. And everybody will be overshadowed by the Pep n' Jose Show.

Along with Torres, Demba Ba and Lukaku, another player who missed out at Old Trafford was Juan Mata, the "Spain star who has illuminated Stamford Bridge" (McNulty) and reigning Chelsea player-of-the-year. Mata is a Barcelona-type player, known for his passing and technique rather than his pace and power: he is Iniesta-*lite*. We all know what Mourinho thinks about Barcelona and their style. Most of us also know what a Mourinho-type player is. They are physically imposing but able to cover the ground quickly; they do not shirk their defensive duties. Pretty much the opposite of Mata, then.

Mata's Chelsea colleagues used to call him Johnny Kills (*Juan* is John in Spanish and *Mata* is kills). And Mourinho effectively killed Mata's Chelsea career in the first half of the 2013-14 season. He started only half of Chelsea's Premier League games before the turn of the year and Mourinho made it known that he'd be happy to listen to offers for the Spaniard during the January transfer window.

So in the end it wasn't Rooney – the man who'd at one time seemed most likely – who trod the path between London and Manchester. It was Mata. United shelled out a then club record fee of £37.1 million for the player and Mourinho pronounced himself happy with the deal, mainly on account of he'd managed to secure a huge fee for a player who was a long way from first-choice, but also because he'd managed to sell to a team who weren't a direct competitor.

Yes, by then David Moyes' United were well off the pace in the Premier League and in the end they fell even further behind. Whether Mourinho was right in selling Mata (when he was so obviously wrong with Lukaku and De Bruyne) is open to some debate. Mata has become something of a fan-favourite at Old Trafford, largely thanks to his vital FA Cup Final equaliser in 2016, and his aping another fan-favourite Diego Forlan, in scoring a brace against Liverpool at Anfield (Mata's in the 2014-15 season, under Louis van Gaal). United fans still sing about Diego now; despite the fact he was forlorn for most of his time at the Theatre of Dreams. If, as is suspected, Mourinho eventually moves Mata on again now the Portuguese is at the helm at Old Trafford, it is debatable whether fans will continue to sing the Mata song (to the tune of 'Da Doo Ron Ron', made famous by The Crystals, the ever so slightly exaggerating: *"Who's the greatest player in the Premier League, It's you Juan Juan Juan, it's you Juan Juan."*) The reason things like an FA Cup Final equaliser and an Anfield brace have taken on such significant status amongst fans is because generally, the past three years have been *un*-memorable. We haven't competed for league titles (hell, we got all giddy in 2015 when we topped an embryonic league table for a *week)*. If Mourinho helps United claw their way back onto their perch, the three post-Ferguson years might well be air-brushed out of our minds altogether, and only that (twelfth) FA Cup win will trouble the history books.

Still, you got the impression Mata was where *Mourinho* wanted to be, and when United met Chelsea again later in the season at Stamford Bridge, Reds fans felt obliged to remind the Portuguese of that 'fact'. Samuel Luckhurst observed: "Mourinho was heckled with chants of 'You wanted his job' from the travelling Manchester United supporters that chilly January afternoon in 2014. Mourinho offered them a merry wave as Chelsea supporters crowed 'Where's your Fergie gone?' David Moyes, stoic throughout on the touchline, would last three more months."

In truth it was a sorry United who staggered into Stamford Bridge that night and an even sorrier one that limped out of it. The Reds started the game without last season's difference-maker extraordinaire, Robin van Persie – in truth they were barely *with* him during Moyes' pathetic, chocolate-fireguard title 'defence' – and his fellow striker Wayne Rooney. In their absence they were powder-puff up front. The midfield was easily brushed aside by their Chelsea counterparts, particularly new (re)-signing Nemanja Matic (now there was a real Mourinho-type player. The defending was shambolic. Veteran Samuel Eto'o helped himself to the simplest hat-trick of his career – all three goals stemming from ridiculous United mistakes – before Javier Hernandez bagged the dictionary definition of a consolation goal. Even as he collected the ball from the back of the Chelsea net and rugbied it back to the half-way line so the Blues could kick-off and maybe United could go at them again, everyone knew there was absolutely no way the Reds were going to get back into the game. And so it proved.

And if the Reds started the game without their supposed 'world class' striking duo, they ended it without their captain: Nemanja Vidic saw red for a lunge at Eden Hazard which was borne of pent up frustration. The challenge was the dictionary definition of a player just having had enough; just wanting it to end; just wanting that jinky winger to please, stop taking the piss.

Vidic received an automatic three-match ban. United would now be down to the bare bones for their 'vital' League Cup semi-final second leg against Sunderland. They were trailing 2-1 from the first leg. United were champions of England, and in five short months that was how low we'd now set our sights.

And it was about right, given the squad we had and the way Moyes had them playing. In his match report, Phil McNulty wrote that the "mitigating circumstances" of the Chelsea defeat – Van Persie and Rooney's injuries – "cannot disguise the brutal truth that United's current squad is simply not in shape to mount a title challenge and is inferior to that at Arsenal, let alone Chelsea and Manchester City."

It wasn't all Moyes' fault in fairness. It was years of lack of serious investment in the squad finally bearing fruit. It was the undertow of the Glazer regime finally washing our patched-together squad into the rocks. Sir Alex Ferguson had, through will alone, managed to drive this lot to the title last year, but surely nobody else could have done it, and in fact, Fergie himself has to take *some* responsibility for the team he handed over to Moyes. While he insisted it was up to standard – and of course, he could point to the fact he'd won the league with them – there were simply too many below-par players or else worn-out players; players who'd given their all for that final Fergie hurrah in May 2013 (Van Persie springs to mind) and who now had nothing left in the tank.

Still, despite the fact "Moyes' United were about as threatening as Nick Powell up front, but Mourinho's diplomacy was telling," wrote Luckhurst. "'Today, we play against the champions,' he said in his programme notes ahead of the fixture. 'We don't play against a team that is 11 points away from the leaders, we play versus Manchester United.' In the claustrophobic press room at full-time, Mourinho insisted Chelsea were fortunate to be 2-0 up at the interval and opined, after Javier Hernandez had reduced the arrears, 'they were coming'. Mourinho even refused to dismiss the worst United side in 25 years as title contenders."

Despite everything he'd witnessed, he still couldn't

bring himself to disparage the hopeless United team his Blues had faced. He couldn't admit that, in past times, Chelsea against United used to be a case of immovable object meets unstoppable force, but it was now a case of brick meeting window. He wouldn't crow, not now. Not while he was still auditioning.

Mourinho v United, 2014-15

The next time Jose Mourinho met Manchester United was on 26th October 2014. In many ways, he faced a very different club to the one he'd faced almost ten months earlier, in January. The Red Devils had finished the 2013-14 season with something of a whimper, in seventh place in the Premier League. It was an abysmal title defence: the Reds never even threatened to compete with the top guns and in the end fans had had to resort to 'supporting' Manchester City, just so Steven Gerrard and Luis Suarez's Liverpool wouldn't become champions.

Manager David Moyes – Fergie's 'Chosen One' – had been sacked on April 22nd, a year to the day since Sir Alex's Reds had been confirmed as champions for the twentieth time. That was the day it was confirmed United couldn't qualify for the following season's Champions League, after an embarrassing capitulation to Moyes' former club Everton at Goodison Park. That was some measure as to how quickly our stock had fallen in the intervening 12 months. Indeed, by the end of the season it was confirmed that next year would be the first in 25 we wouldn't be competing in *any* European competition. We hadn't even scraped into the Europa League.

Almost the only bright spark to the whole miserable season for United fans – a Patrice Evra wonder-strike against Bayern Munich in the Champions League aside – had been the way we finished it, with club stalwarts

Ryan Giggs, Nicky Butt, and Phil Neville in our dugout, as caretaker manager and assistants respectively. After that, we were just glad it was all over.

The boys from the Class of '92 might have provided some continuity for the club. They were a touchstone to the Ferguson years and the famous Treble. But they were also largely untested as managers and coaches and the United hierarchy wouldn't contemplate such a gamble on awarding them the jobs in the long-term. They wanted a guarantee that Champions League football – and all its attendant monetary trappings – would be back at Old Trafford with a break of only one season. The board wouldn't risk everything on Giggs, Neville, *et al*, and instead they plumped for a Super Coach.

Enter Louis van Gaal, Mourinho's former mentor from their Barcelona days. The Dutchman was announced as manager on 19th May 2014 and he immediately hit a high-note by appointing Giggs – who'd just hung up his boots after a glorious, star-studded career – as one of his assistants. It was assumed Van Gaal was grooming Giggs to take over from him eventually, but things didn't quite work out like that. Still, in those early months of the Van Gaal regime, there was some cause for renewed optimism amongst Reds fans, not least as we watched from afar as he saw out his contract with the Dutch national side by coming *this close* to winning World Cup glory with them. He reached the semi-finals, where the Netherlands were beaten on penalties by Argentina. That he'd led his team - patently the worst Dutch squad to compete in a major competition in living memory – so far boded well for the future. And after last season United fans were under no illusions as to the quality of our own squad.

Even before he arrived in Manchester Van Gaal set about reshaping Manchester United's playing resources. Some we were sorry to see go: Rio Ferdinand, Nemanja Vidic and Patrice Evra were all becoming creaky, but they'd been wonderful servants to the club and it was sad to see them move on to pastures new. Others, we couldn't wait to see the back of (Anderson, Zaha, and to a lesser extent Hernandez and Nani). In August and September, the Dutchman started getting rid of the dead wood which had stunk out the place, and United said goodbye to nine players on loan – only two of which would ever return to Old Trafford; and four were transferred. To be fair to Van Gaal he'd given these guys a chance. He'd fielded most of them in an early season League Cup tie against Milton Keynes Dons, a match United were *supposed* to win. Only they didn't. They were battered 4-0. Angel Di Maria, who was looking on as a box-fresh signing, secured on the very same day – 26th August – must have wondered what the hell he was getting himself in to.

Di Maria signed for a fee of £59.7 million from Real Madrid, breaking the club record transfer fee and the record transfer fee paid by a British club in one fell swoop. He was a bonafide superstar; he'd been the man of the match in the 2014 Champions League final, when his Real Madrid beat city rivals Atletico 4-1 (after extra time) to win their tenth crown, the fabled *decima*. He was a *galactico*, or, as the English tabloids would have it, a *Gaal-actico*.

The near- £60 million United splashed on the flying Argentine took United's total outlay in the summer transfer window to £130 million. Under the tenure of the usually parsimonious Glazers, United had never spent anything like as big: they'd certainly never countenanced Ferguson and Moyes breaking open such a hefty war-chest. But that showed the level of the club's desperation to secure Champions League football – and TV revenue, and a place at Europe's top table - the following year. For the first time in a long time, the Reds were bringing in (supposedly) proven quantities, not 'ones for the future'. This wasn't only a U-turn for United, it was also one for Van Gaal, who didn't necessarily have a reputation for buying in genuine world stars, rather for improving players and developing a team ethic which was over and above the individual. But desperate times and all that…

And the spending didn't end there. On transfer deadline day in came two more: Daley Blind, who'd excelled in the Netherlands journey to the semi-final of the 2014 World Cup; and Radamel Falcao, the man who was supposed to be the icing on the cake. Dubbed *El Tigre*, at Porto and Atletico Madrid he'd forged a reputation as one of the deadliest strikers in world football. That form bagged him a £45 million transfer to Monaco, where his annual salary was reported to be around £12 million. But at Monaco, he suffered an anterior cruciate ligament injury for six months. It wasn't clear yet that he could recapture the form which had catapulted him to the world's attention. Still, United took a gamble on him. He signed, initially on loan, in the hope his career could be rehabilitated at the club. It was an expensive gamble, sure, but one which seemed to reap instant rewards when it was revealed that champions Manchester City had also been interested in him but he'd chosen Old Trafford instead. Like Di Maria before him, he was a statement signing. United were back.

Only, it didn't quite work out like that. United's early season form was patchy to say the least. Van Gaal had to wait for his fourth league match of the season before he saw his first win (a 4-0 thrashing of QPR). The players – old and new – struggled to get their heads around the Dutchman's rigid 3-5-2 system and his insistence on possession football. After ten matches the Red Devils were in ninth place in the Premier League. They'd recorded just two wins. It was their worst start to a season since that of 1986-87, when Ron Atkinson was United manager.

The ninth game of the season was against Mourinho's Chelsea at Old Trafford in front of a crowd of 75,327, the vast majority of whom were starting to get decidedly twitchy. Some were even beginning to mutter that the fare served up was worse than it had been under David Moyes. But this was Chelsea, top of the league, and for one night only, the fans showed a United front and got behind the team. I started this section by stating that when Jose Mourinho met Manchester United on 26th October 2014 in many ways he faced a very different club to the one he'd faced almost ten months earlier, in January. But in many ways he faced a club which was still the same: still treading-water; still not in direct competition with the Blues; still struggling to forge an identity post-Ferguson.

Chelsea were both the same and different to the previous season also. After finishing in third place in the Premier League in 2013-14 Mourinho had made only minor adjustments to his squad. He was now at the point of tapping in the final pieces of the jigsaw whilst Van Gaal was still at the point of trying to discover exactly what the picture on the box displayed. Mourinho spent heavily – of course – but his spending was targeted, it wasn't scatter-gun. He brought in the ex-Arsenal midfielder Cesc Fabregas from Barcelona for £27 million and then the striker he'd so craved the previous season, the man who'd shoot him to the league title, Diego Costa, for £32 million from Atletico Madrid. Both hit the ground running: Fabregas' creativity sparked the Blues to seven wins in eight matches. They'd scored for fun in those games: bagging six at Everton, four at home to Swansea, and three against Burnley and Aston Villa. In eight games they'd netted 23 times. So much for the boring, functional football tag so many commentators foist upon Mourinho teams. Diego Costa had contributed with nine goals already. He'd scored within 17 minutes of his league debut, and then couldn't stop scoring: he was on fire.

But Costa was injured for the Old Trafford clash, and in his stead Mourinho called upon "the old warrior" (McNulty) Didier Drogba to step up to the plate. Even though Drogba's last goal for Chelsea was back in March

2012 against Stoke City – like Mourinho he'd been away from the club a while, supposedly easing down the gears on his playing career and this was his first start in two and a half years - there was an air of inevitability that he'd score against United. Even though prior to the game Drogba had a poor record against United – just three in 19 games – Reds fans were convinced he'd score. Even though he looked tired and leggy now, it was bound to be him. Because? Well, because Drogba – like John Terry and Frank Lampard - was the very embodiment of Mourinho's footballing philosophy on the pitch. And Mourinho liked grabbing the headlines at Old Trafford.

Drogba scored. Of course he did. In the 53rd minute his header from a corner took a slight deflection off Robin van Persie and found the United net. And from then on, it was obvious to everyone present that Chelsea would win. For just as Drogba's goal was inevitable, so were Mourinho's tactics following it. The Blues retreated to the edge of their own penalty area. They spoiled. They sat back, hoping to grind out the win. Over half of the team were cautioned (they drew six yellow cards and one red card). Van Persie missed three chances. This was fast becoming the same old United; though we were still unbeaten at Old Trafford, our appalling form against our rivals ever since Sir Alex Ferguson had retired had inured us to defeat in the big matches. That was simply the way things were now. In Fergie's time, we'd never have been so pessimistic. There was always the chance of a goal in Fergie Time, after all. But surely not here, surely not tonight. Surely not against a team as well-organised as Maureen's mob.

As the Blues invited United on to them as the game ticked towards its conclusion, the crowd at the Theatre of Dreams roared them on all the same, as much for habit's sake as anything else. We knew the script: toil, toil, and toil again but never seriously trouble the opponent's goal.

Robin van Persie didn't know the script. He'd

barely played under Moyes because of injury and maybe attitude too. He was perhaps still under the impression that this was a top of the table clash and not a match-up between first and eighth. And at last he stole Drogba's headlines with a 94th minute, Van Gaal Time equaliser at which "Old Trafford exploded in celebration". Meanwhile, as Phil McNulty reported for BBC Sport: ""Blues manager Jose Mourinho turned away in disgust (...), frustrated that the victory his side deserved for controlling long periods had slipped away in a chaotic conclusion."

"For United manager Louis van Gaal," he wrote, "there will be pleasure in showing the resilience and fighting spirit of old to earn a point - but also the reality that Chelsea showed him how much ground they still have to make up, despite that £150m outlay this summer."

The Dutchman hadn't found a team yet, but he had stumbled upon a new never-say-die spirit within the squad. And, more importantly, he'd broken the first ground in helping United set aside our inferiority complex when pitted against our traditional Premier League rivals. Under David Moyes, the Reds had succeeded in recording only one victory in eight against Liverpool, Manchester City, Chelsea and Arsenal. They beat the Gunners 1-0 at Old Trafford. Otherwise it was a tale of misery. A home draw and a heavy away defeat against Chelsea; two losses against Liverpool; two embarrassments against Manchester City, in which the aggregate score was 7-1 to the lazer blues. The defeats in themselves would have been hard enough for fans to stomach, but Moyes' attitude around those games (stating that Liverpool were favourites prior to their Old Trafford meeting, and talking up Manchester City as being "a level above" United and admitting we "should aspire to" their level) made us taste bile.

Van Gaal's United might have followed up the last-gasp draw against Chelsea with a loss at Manchester City in the next game, but the Dutchman showed none of the

Moyesian defeatism in his pre- and post-match press conferences. And in late November, a smash-and-grab win at Arsenal showed there was some improvement. That game was the second in a six-game winning streak which saw United climb to the (relatively) lofty heights of third in the table. The sixth game in that streak saw us beat Liverpool 3-0 at Old Trafford.

A run of draws followed, however, as the Reds plateaued. Goals were proving harder to come by. The loss of Di Maria due to a hamstring injury over December and the busy Christmas period hamstrung the side's creativity and particularly its pace. He returned in January, but didn't seem the same player we'd seen in autumn. By the turn of the year, Falcao had scored only two league goals. Of the other *Gaal-acticos,* only Daley Blind was proving a consistent performer, and inconsistent performances showed in inconsistent results. Van Gaal tried time and again to re-integrate his superstars into the side, but time and again they did not live up to expectations. By the end of February, United's customary loss at Swansea saw their place within the top four (and hence amongst the next season's Champions League qualifiers) for the first time under real threat. And there was a torrid spell of matches on the horizon. Over the next six games, they'd have to face Newcastle, Chelsea, and Liverpool away, and Tottenham and Manchester City at home. Both Tottenham and Liverpool were direct rivals for the vital fourth place. There was no longer any room for error for Van Gaal's men.

The Red Devils did the first part right on the night of Wednesday 4th March, up at St. James' Park. But it took a late, late show from Ashley Young – almost in Van Gaal time – to bag all three points for United. And in truth, result aside, it was an uninspiring display from the Reds. There was no spark, no creativity, and very little passion. Di Maria in particular was woeful – substituted before the half-hour by Van Gaal. Certainly there was nothing in the performance to suggest what was to come during the rest of a magnificent March and amazing April (which coincided with the birth of my daughter, Peggy – for a while United hadn't done anything but be brilliant during the first weeks of her life and I wondered whether she might be a lucky charm for the Reds as well as for my family).

At Newcastle, United had finished the game with only two of Van Gaal's expensive new signings on the pitch: Blind and Herrera (and in truth Herrera had been identified by David Moyes; only Edward Woodward's dithering had prevented the Spaniard from joining United much earlier). Against Tottenham, United would include only those two of the Dutchman's *Gaal-acticos* after Di Maria's suspension following a sending-off in a 2-1 FA Cup defeat to Arsenal. It was a continuation of the Argentine's personal *annus horribilis* as he received his marching orders for pushing the referee in the back, but to many fans that was seen as a blessing in disguise. It had made for a painful watch, seeing such a gifted player struggle so. (Falcao was nowhere to be seen.)

Without him, against the odds, the 2014-15 Manchester United vintage suddenly became reminiscent of the sides we used to watch. The Reds simply blitzed Tottenham. They were 3-0 and out of sight by half-time. I had to rub my eyes and wonder whether I was dreaming (which was surely conceivable, considering my daughter had been born just hours earlier).

Next up, Liverpool. And Van Gaal wouldn't tinker with a winning side no matter that Di Maria was available for selection after serving his suspension. He wouldn't ring the changes now. He was confident. Before the game, he was decidedly un-Moyesian with this typically arrogant statement: "Anfield is not a very easy ground for United but now I am manager here, maybe I can change that."

But that confidence was not without foundation.

That first half at Anfield was the most controlled display of dominant football I have seen from United at Liverpool in many a year. We were simply streets ahead of them; a better *team*. Juan Mata scored after 14 minutes and the Reds didn't look back. The game wasn't without its moment of high comedy either. Angel Di Maria wasn't the only 'world superstar' not to make the starting eleven for his club: Steven Gerrard had been left champing at the bit after being benched by Brendan Rodgers. But he was introduced at half-time in order to try and wrest control of the game back from United. He lasted just 42 seconds before he was sent-off for a stamp on Ander Herrera, who was on imperious form for United. Ten minutes later, United made it 2-0 with one of the best goals you could ever hope to see in Liverpool: Juan Mata again, this time with a delicious scissor-kick volley which sent the 2,800 away fans behind the goal into delirium. Liverpool pulled one back, through Sturridge, to make for a nerve-wracking last 20 minutes, but the Red Devils held on to record a fantastic victory.

Before the game at Anfield United fans had wondered whether Van Gaal was maybe getting ahead of himself. But now it looked like he was being proved right. It did seem that for much of the season we'd been waiting for United to click. Amongst the squad, there was *a team*. Van Gaal – at last - discovered it, and all it took was for him to discard his *Gaal-acticos* and instead concentrate on that nucleus of players who could perform consistently, game to game.

The Reds were starting to churn out results. Next up, United recorded a routine 3-1 win against Aston Villa at Old Trafford in the Easter sunshine; United so comfortable Van Gaal felt assured enough to bring on Di Maria and Falcao near the end. The next game would be the real test: the 70th Manchester derby. City at home. The lazer blues were a point behind the Reds at the start of play but United's recent record against the noisy neighbours was atrocious. They'd won just one out of the last seven; City winning the other six. Even at Old Trafford, United had an appalling record: they'd lost the past three Manchester derbies at the Theatre of Dreams, conceding 11 goals and scoring just two. Included amongst that was the nadir, *that* 6-1 for City.

But unlike Moyes, Van Gaal was confident. He did not twist. He stuck. Again, the team-sheet showed barely any changes. Again, the *Gaal-acticos* were left to warm the bench. And although Sergio Aguero, that habitual derby scorer, netted early for City, the Reds wouldn't let this setback knock them off their stride. Ashley Young equalised and then the much-maligned Marouane Fellaini put them in front by half-time. In the second-half United continued to cruise, with goals from Mata and Smalling at one point bringing us within sight of that dreadful 6-1 score-line. But in the end, the Reds settled for four and in the end Aguero scored again, making the final score a little less embarrassing for City. But by then the damage had been done, and the win put the Reds four points above City. We'd won back our bragging rights and we'd done it in style. It seemed that at last, this United side was going places and we'd soon be back on our perch.

But then we met Chelsea, and our amazing Red Spring came to an end by that most Mourinho-like of score-lines: 1-0. United went into the return match against the Blues (following the 1-1 draw at Old Trafford), resurgent, chasing a seventh successive win. However, Chelsea were on a run of their own. The victory over United put them ten points clear of Arsenal at the top of the league. United – despite our fantastic run – were still a distant third. Despite starting the game well, and enjoying over 70% of the ball – an astonishing statistic for an away side at Stamford Bridge – United never truly threatened the Blues unbeaten home record (they'd now gone a full calendar year without suffering defeat in front of their own fans).

Incidentally, though Louis van Gaal was one of Jose Mourinho's three mentors (see chapter three for more details), the Portuguese has not followed the Dutchman in his dogmatic insistence on possession football. "A near-superhuman ability to absorb pressure has been a feature of all his major trophy wins (his title-winning Real Madrid side won a pivotal late-season game at the Nou Camp with 28% possession; his Inter team famously advanced from the same venue with only 24% possession *en route* to the Treble)," noted Alex Hess for *FourFourTwo.com*.

At Stamford Bridge Eden Hazard – who'd snubbed United for Chelsea – proved the match-winner, with a 38th minute strike, the win moving them to within two victories of the championship. "The reaction of Chelsea's players as referee Mike Dean sounded the final whistle, celebrating wildly in front of their supporters, suggested they believed this was the victory that has pushed them to the brink of glory," wrote Phil McNulty.

United's own players left the field with their heads bowed and shoulders slumped. Still, McNulty was able to accentuate the positives for Reds fans: "This defeat may have ended their recent winning streak but they once again produced compelling evidence that they are now a very different proposition from the side that struggled, even though they were grinding out results, earlier this season.

"United were still able to make the more impressive start and should have taken an early lead. Rooney looked a certain scorer when he raced on to Luke Shaw's cross but placed his finish inches wide, so close that goalkeeper David de Gea joined United's fans in celebrating a goal until they realised after several seconds that the effort was off target."

A point of note. The concession of United's goal stemmed from one of the *Gaal-acticos:* "Falcao, given a rare start, was easily bundled off the ball by John Terry and when Oscar played in Hazard with a clever backheel he applied a cool finish between De Gea's legs. Van Gaal protested furiously to fourth official Craig Pawson that Falcao had been fouled but to no avail."

In truth though, it was the final knockings of the *Gaal-actico* era for Van Gaal. By the end of the season both Di Maria and Falcao were gone. Di Maria's was a sad case. In September and October, he'd had United fans *laughing* he was so good. Quick and full of direct-running, he'd looked tailor-made for the Premier League and for United in particular. He scored great goals too; his chipped finish at Leicester being the stand-out. But therein lay the rub. For it was after the game at Leicester that the caution-to-the-wind approach from Van Gaal ended. He'd shoehorned as many superstars into that team as was humanly possible, and for a while it had looked like wonderful things would come of it. It wasn't just the Di Maria goal, it was Falcao's smashed shot against the crossbar too. And the wonderful attacking flair on display throughout. United twice held two goal leads in the match, though, and twice lost them. It wasn't just that they were dodgy at the back – they were – but also because too many of their players weren't willing (or able) to track back. United wound up losing a match they'd won twice, 5-3. And after that Van Gaal insisted upon solidity and structure over flair and speed. Di Maria was forced to subdue his individual talents for the good of the team. He wasn't the same player. Without him United found a team, but it wasn't as glorious as the one that might have been, and within that brilliant March and April of 2015 Van Gaal felt that his philosophies were being proved right; the team was after all more important than the individual. He was willing to sacrifice players he'd sanctioned the signing of in order to stand by this. This would have consequences for the following season.

It wasn't just Van Gaal's tactical rigidity stymied Di Maria at United. The player was unsettled right from the start. He was truthful enough to admit he'd have preferred a move to Paris Saint Germain instead of United. His family never settled in Manchester, and eventually were put off the city altogether after a break-in at the Di Maria residence. That was the beginning of the end for him. In the end, he got his wish, and his next destination was the French capital.

But if Di Maria's case was a sad one, one in which we were left with a very real sense of *what might have been*, Falcao's was an ironic one: he ended up with Mourinho at Chelsea, loaned out again by parent club Monaco.

United v Chelsea, 2015-16

By the time United met Chelsea in 2015-16 half of the Premier League season was already gone, and so was Jose Mourinho; the Portuguese's defence of the league title having proved even worse than David Moyes defence of Sir Alex Ferguson's last championship. "Chelsea did not defend their title last season so much as prosecute it for fraud," said Paul Doyle in *The Guardian*.

The two sides met during the post-Christmas, pre-New Year lull – on 28th December – and it was a game which wouldn't live long in the memory. Games between Manchester United and Chelsea in recent history have had a lot hanging on them. They've battled it out with championships, FA Cups, even Champions League crowns at stake. And yet this one was different. This one wasn't hotly anticipated. It wasn't built up for weeks in advance by Sky and the tabloids. There were a number of reasons for this: firstly, this *wasn't* the only show in town. No, it wasn't even a sideshow. It was a match between the team who were sixth in the table (United) and the team who were *fourteenth* (Chelsea). Secondly, because Guus Hiddink was in the visitor's dugout rather than Jose Mourinho.

The game lived up to its rather half-hearted billing; the

Reds and the Blues played out a goalless draw in which the two goalkeepers (David De Gea and Thibaut Courtois) were the stars. Afterwards, United striker Wayne Rooney admitted United were enduring "a tough time". They'd expected to kick on from last year's fourth place finish, but three weeks before the Chelsea game they'd lost at Wolfsburg, meaning they were eliminated from the Champions League after the group stages, highly embarrassing for a club with United's standing in the competition. Things were hardly going better in the Premier League. Though they'd topped the embryonic table after the second and seventh round of fixtures, they were now languishing outside the top four. The team looked stodgy, devoid of inspiration, and they couldn't score goals for love nor money. Nearly a fifth of the way through the season, their joint top-scorer was still Own Goal, on one. A glut of goalless first-halves at Old Trafford frustrated fans and players alike (from 5th October United fans went *three months* without witnessing a goal scored by a Red in the first-half; indeed, the only goal of any variety we did see was scored by a Norwich player, during a disastrous 2-1 reverse). They wanted the team to *attack-attack-attack* as United teams of old had. But Van Gaal was stubborn. He wouldn't budge. He seemed more interested in possession statistics than he did in goals scored. After the Chelsea game they'd scored just three goals in their past six matches. Worse, they'd only picked up three points from those games.

The previous season, the Reds had been inconsistent and Chelsea had been a model of consistency, which was why United could have six-match winning streaks and still not come within sniffing distance of the Blues. This season United were perhaps *the* most consistent Premier League club. But they were even further away from the table-toppers. Perhaps that was because Van Gaal found the wrong kind of consistency. The Reds consistently had the best defensive record and kept the ball for the longest time, but they scored a record low number of goals for a United Premier League season. They consistently managed risk to their own goal, but did not take enough risks when faced with the opposition's goal.

After two years lacking an identity after Fergie, Manchester United had found one. But it wasn't the right one, not as far as the fans were concerned. The board too, once Champions League qualification was eventually ruled-out. Van Gaal had managed to instil a winning mentality against the bigger clubs, our traditional rivals, as results in his two seasons as boss bear out. In 2015-16, United's only loss against either Liverpool, Manchester City, Arsenal or Chelsea came at the hands of Arsenal (3-0 at the Emirates Stadium). They beat Liverpool home and away, and won at Manchester City. (In 2014-15 they were similarly successful.) But they also lost away to Sunderland, Bournemouth, and West Brom, and at home to Southampton, and Norwich, who were relegated. Also relegated were Newcastle – whom United took only two points from two matches against. United sides of old would have racked up the goal-difference against this type of team; now we couldn't put them away. If they'd had the guts to convert any of those defeats – particularly the home ones - into wins or even draws, they would have qualified for the Champions League of 2016-17. And maybe Van Gaal would have kept his job. But as it was they couldn't, and he didn't.

But there was a guy who knew how to win home matches – hell, he once went an incredible nine years, 151 games, and four clubs without a home defeat – and *he* was available. Jose Mourinho was that man, and what's more after what went on at Chelsea in 2015-16 he wanted the job even more than he had when he'd been passed over for it the first time, when David Moyes was given the nod instead.

What went wrong for Chelsea and Mourinho in

2015-16, and particularly the Eva Carneiro mess, is covered in detail in another chapter (Chapter Four: "A United manager wouldn't do that." Can Manchester United tolerate the dark side of Jose Mourinho?) But let's just say it started badly – Chelsea lost the season's traditional curtain-raiser, the Community Shield, against Arsenal 1-0; the first time Jose had been defeated by his long-time rival in 14 attempts – and quickly got worse. Manchester City hammered the Blues 3-0 at the Etihad Stadium in the second league match of the season. Chelsea were up to their old tricks again and stealing the Barcelona winger Pedro right from under United's noses, but the £21 million man couldn't paper over the cracks which were already starting to show.

By the end of August, the champions were down in thirteenth place in the table, with just one win from four games, and in early September a Steven Naismith hat-trick condemned Chelsea to their third loss in five; as many as they'd suffered during the entire previous season.

By October, they were hovering just above the relegation zone, with a record of just eight points from a possible 24. And though things did improve slightly during that month, on 24th, Chelsea lost again, this time at West Ham, where Mourinho was sent off. Then Liverpool came from behind to beat the Blues at Stamford Bridge the following week, on Halloween. It seemed the Premier League was all out of treats for Jose.

November was a little brighter for Mourinho and Chelsea, but there wasn't much festive cheer in December: although the Blues progressed to the knock-out stages of the Champions League, domestically, they were in disarray. They lost at home to Bournemouth (which made it eight losses in 15 games), and then at Leicester, 2-1 (nine in 16). Leicester would eventually take Chelsea's title, but for Mourinho the defeat had even more serious ramifications. Two days later, on 17th December, the Portuguese was fired. If Abramovich had waited just over a week longer before he pulled the trigger, he could have aped the owners of Rio Ave.

"When his father, Felix, was sacked as manager of Rio Ave on Christmas Day 1984, months after securing promotion and a cup final, the steel entered a young Jose's soul," wrote Andrew Murray in August 2016's *FourFourTwo* magazine. "No matter how well you do in life, it seemed people forget your glories and focus on the present, without looking to the future."

Mourinho felt he'd built up more than enough Brownie-points during his two spells as Chelsea coach – delivering the Premier League crown to Stamford Bridge after a *fifty year* absence; winning two further titles, an FA Cup and three League Cups – to be given more time, but he wasn't.

His former mentor at Barcelona, Louis van Gaal, made it to the end of the season, but 2015-16 was the end of the road for him, too. Eventually, Mourinho would step into his shoes. Van Gaal's legacy to his former assistant? Some very good young players and the FA Cup. An uneven, unhappy squad. No Champions League football. A club at the cross-roads.

Awaking the sleeping giant

"I feel great," said Jose Mourinho, upon the announcement he would be the next manager of Manchester United. "I think I'm in the right moment of my career because Man. United is one of these clubs where you really need to be prepared for it because it is a giant club. Giant clubs must be for the best managers and I think I'm ready for it."

Manchester United *are* a giant club, but they aren't as giant as they might have been. On a European scale – which is how the club want to be seen – we are light years away from 'rivals' such as Barcelona, Real Madrid and

Bayern Munich. Lack of investment in top, top quality players since the beginning of the Glazer regime and the failure to build upon our Champions League triumph of 2008 have set the Reds as far behind the true giants of the European game – Barcelona, Real Madrid and Bayern Munich – as a club like, say, to pick a name at random from out of a hat, Liverpool were behind United after a few years of the vast, money-spinning, never-ending drama of the Premier League.

United enjoyed a perfect storm at the start of the Premier League era. We'd improved and upgraded Old Trafford after Hillsborough, and the Taylor Report, making use of allocated funds to do so. The increased capacity of the stadium meant we could enjoy twice as much match-day revenue as some of our rivals. Then there was the new TV money, from Sky; and Sky latched upon United, both as entertainers and as a *story*. Here was a club – a sleeping giant - desperate to win the league after 26 years. And they did: the Reds hit the ground running: thanks to the cunning of their Scottish manager Alex Ferguson, the grit of men like Paul Ince, Bryan Robson, Peter Schmeichel, Mark Hughes and Steve Bruce, the wing-wizardry of wingers Lee Sharpe and Ryan Giggs, and above all else, the guile and mystique of the King, Eric Cantona.

The sleeping giant had been awakened. And it was hungry for more.

United made hay while the sun shone, and when guys like Ince, Hughes and Robson left, they were eventually able to introduce a home-grown core to the club which – under the guardianship of Ferguson and Cantona – would continue to sweep all before them. Not since the fabled Busby Babes had the club seen such a rich crop of young talent rise to the fore: in Ryan Giggs, David Beckham, Gary and Phil Neville and Nicky Butt United had half a team already, and all of them had been indoctrinated into the *Manchester United way*. They were immensely talented, yes, but they were also steely-eyed in their determination, and single-minded in their desire to win, and to win again. They'd – all of them - caught a dose of the Fergies.

The emergence of the Class of '92 saved the club millions. Instead of having to replace a key figures in ageing squad, the Reds could simply slot these guys into place, and, the odd stumble aside (that 3-1 opening day defeat to Aston Villa in 1995 which prompted Alan Hansen's infamous quote: "You can't win anything with kids") it worked.

Not only did they save the club millions, they made the club many more millions too. Though the Neville brothers and Nicky Butt weren't exactly oil-paintings, Giggs and Beckham were every marketing man's dream come true (and a fair few teenage girls and boys, too). Beckham in particular became a celebrity, a brand, paving the way for future superstars such as Cristiano Ronaldo.

And it was fantastic to watch the kids doing well, tearing into all before them, half-crazy with the obsession to win. But their emergence informed later decision-making within the club, especially after the Glazer takeover in 2005. Before Munich, Manchester United had not acquired the habit of buying players, but after it, we had to. And in the seventies and eighties, despite the club being a long way from their perch, they still bought star players and smashed record transfer fees (Bryan Robson in 1981, and Mark Hughes in 1988, for example). In the nineties, and noughties, this continued: although we played the kids, we also improved the squad, when needed, by buying in players for specialist roles (Roy Keane, Andy Cole, Jaap Stam, Dwight Yorke, Ruud van Nistelrooy, and Rio Ferdinand to name but a few). Hansen might have been right about the kids. We wouldn't have won everything had we *only* played kids. Remember, that 1995-96 title win was primarily secured off the back of magnificent seasons from seasoned stars Peter Schmeichel and Eric Cantona.

But after the Glazer takeover it all of a sudden became club policy that Manchester United do not buy anyone over the age of 26 (the age when most outfielders are entering their prime). Instead, the Reds were supposed to sign 'ones for the future'. The plan was to make stars rather than buy them. And if we did buy them, bring them in young, so that the Manchester United way – the winning way - can be imprinted upon their very psyche. And in some ways it was an honourable intention and in some ways it worked – Cristiano Ronaldo, for example. But in many ways it didn't, and countless below-par players filled holes in the squad. For an entire decade after Roy Keane left the club, we did not have a midfield to speak of, as we tried to fill the void with various stop-gaps, hopefuls, and no-hopers. And the Glazers laughed all the way to the bank because Ferguson – mostly – continued to get a tune out of lesser players, and continued to win trophies. The board saw they could do things on the cheap and get away with it, because we were still – mostly – top of the tree domestically. We could wing it.

But while this was happening, our *European* rivals were stealing a march on us. Never was this illustrated more painfully than in 2009, a year after United had won the Champions League in Moscow, when we sold our goalscorer that night to Real Madrid for a world-record transfer fee. We'd never before sold our very best player. We didn't think of ourselves as anyone's feeder-club, least of all *them*, Madrid, the "mob" Fergie claimed he wouldn't even sell "a virus". And yet, he went. And the Reds replaced him with Michael Bloody Owen on a free transfer. Meanwhile, Barcelona – who we'd beaten in the semi-final in 2008, remember – were busy augmenting their own wonder-crop of wonder-kids with astute, but expensive, transfers (Ibrahimovic, David Villa, Dani Alves). Real Madrid, along with Ronaldo, brought in (for huge fees) Kaka, Xabi Alonso, and Karim Benzema over this time (amongst many others). Barcelona would win two out of the next three Champions Leagues, and the other was won by Jose Mourinho's Inter.

Manchester United have, belatedly, joined the party, and over the past three years – since Ferguson's retirement and our failure to qualify for the Champions League twice – they have spent big, at last, on genuine stars (though some have not lived up to their billing). Wee Davie Moyes might bemoan the fact he wasn't given the funds his successor was at Old Trafford, but he still managed to break the club's record transfer fee, bringing in Juan Mata for £37.1 million. Van Gaal broke that record again, in acquiring Angel Di Maria for £59.7 million. Indeed, seven of the top ten highest fees paid by the club have come since Sir Alex Ferguson's regime came to an end. And the club have one FA Cup to show for it.

But this gluttonous spending has *had* to be done in order to make up for over a decade's lack of investment: too many players at the club have not proved good enough. Louis van Gaal shipped out a lot of the dead wood, but unfortunately many of the players he brought in – for hefty fees - did not meet requirements either. Indeed, in both of his seasons, he showed less and less faith in his own signings as the seasons progressed, returning instead to a kind of default setting, using the old tried and tested.

Now, United are well behind on the continental stage, and we have fallen behind Manchester City (and Leicester!) domestically. And although Chelsea had a rotten season last year, when taken on balance, their last three years have been much better than ours too. Arsenal also, given their record of Champions League qualification and two FA Cups. Not only that: the influx of new TV money – which remember is shared equally amongst the league members, unlike in Spain and Germany, where Real Madrid, Barcelona, and Bayern Munich get the lion's share – has meant the Reds are being caught up by clubs like

West Ham United and Liverpool.

Old Trafford is no longer the trump card it once was. Other clubs are acquiring large stadiums by hook or by crook: Arsenal's, of course, is already built, and their match-day revenue now outstrips United's; but West Ham too have, like Manchester City, lucked into a new stadium; Spurs and Liverpool have plans in place to build new grounds; Chelsea are looking to extend Stamford Bridge.

And – to some players – United is no longer the draw it once was. The club can't promise Champions League football for the 2016-17 season. For every player who has a little boy inside them screaming to play for the Reds (Robin van Persie), there are three or four others whose agents implore them to chase the cash and to remain on the main stage, and then there are another couple who simply don't want to live in Manchester; who want to live in Paris (Angel Di Maria), Madrid, Barcelona, or at the outside, London. In the close-season before 2016-17, Portuguese bright-young-thing Renato Sanches and cultured German centre-back Mats Hummels both snubbed United in favour of Bayern Munich. The former said: "I wanted Champions League football. Because of that one club was ruled out, and you can envision which club that was." Hummels is a United fan. The one thing he wanted above all else for his seventeenth birthday was to travel over to Manchester for a Champions League game. That was the prestige we had then, and what we are in jeopardy of losing.

There is a danger that if United continue to miss out on Champions League football it will become a vicious circle: the club can't attract the best players because we aren't in the Champions League and we can't qualify for the Champions League because we don't have the best players. There is a danger that if this happens, we might become a sleeping giant once again – up for it in the cups, sure (like we were back in the seventies and eighties, and like Liverpool have been since their own glory days) but unable to compete in the long-term in the marathon-sprint which is the Premier League.

Short-termism

I asked you to swallow a rather bitter pill in that last section, didn't I? But United fans have to accept the current state of play in order that we can make sense of Jose Mourinho's appointment. Although the Portuguese seems to go against everything United stands for, he is perhaps the only appointment we could have made, and the only one who makes sense in today's football climate.

The club has to move with the times. Upon his unveiling, Mourinho himself said: "I think we can look at our club now in two perspectives. One perspective is the past three years and another perspective is the club's history. I think I prefer to forget the past three years. I prefer to focus on the giant club I have in my hands now."

We have to move forward, and quickly. And Jose Mourinho is perhaps football's ultimate fast-mover. When comparing Mourinho with Sir Alex Ferguson, Patrick Barclay noted: "so much of what he (Ferguson) has done has taken so long. There was a twenty-year span between his first European trophy and his fourth. Jose Mourinho won three in seven years."

One of the many sniffy comments directed towards Jose Mourinho is that he is a short-termist coach. A stop-gap, desperate solution. Need a trophy quick to get the fans off the board's back? Call Jose. But remember, if you do go the route one Mourinho way, you'll have to accept that with him there is no such thing as long-term strategy and team-building. It is all about the now. Jose has been about the now ever since his father was sacked on Christmas Day 1984.

But *the whole world* is about the now, these days. We are

all used to getting what we want at the touch of a button. We're spoilt. We have forgotten the concept of all good things coming to those who wait. We're not prepared to wait for the dial-up modem speed of a long-term team-building exercise (blooding young players and the like), not while every day the media are telling us our club is in crisis (always in the tabloids, they show the club badge with a huge crack running down the centre of it).

And Jose Mourinho is the ultimate *now* manager for the *I want it now!* modern football fan who demands instant success and who'll call the radio phone-ins or take to Twitter if he or she doesn't get it.

Jose wins, quickly, and he wins emphatically. "It's one of the more staggering facts of Mourinho's career," observed Alex Hess, "that only one of his eight league titles has been won by a margin of fewer than eight points. Three have been won by a margin of 10 or more." So we can all take to social media and troll our friends.

His appointment was also the obvious one for the board, with Jose Mourinho's own brand augmenting United's, and quickly driving the share price back up, at least in the short-term.

"Those who look at a motley job history and question just how long he'll stay at Old Trafford are almost certainly right to do so," admitted Alex Hess. "But they are also missing the point. Mourinho may be a short-termist appointment but that is the reality of football today, certainly at the level United operate at: the dynasty-building dictator is dead, replaced by the freelance Super Coach."

Mourinho is a name; he is box-office. As a Super Coach, he also makes the club an instantly attractive proposition to the best players around Europe again. "There was a feeling when David Moyes was offered Sir Alex Ferguson's old job that United and their unpopular owners were trying to do things on the cheap, followed by a real concern that, with poor results and a struggling manager, the club was no longer sufficiently attractive to leading players around Europe," wrote Paul Wilson in *The Guardian*. "That impression was dispelled under two years of Van Gaal, even if the results were ultimately unsatisfactory. United sweated the brand and upped their off-field business activity to the extent that they were able to find around £250m for new signings and can apparently do so again. With Mourinho and his agent, Jorge Mendes, on board United will not have to worry about attracting top players and whether he spends big money or not one would imagine the new manager's approach will be less scattergun and more targeted than that of his immediate predecessor."

The earthquake, calmed?

Commentators point to the evidence of Jose Mourinho's CV in order to illustrate their point that surely the Portuguese won't stay at Old Trafford beyond his usual three-year cycle. Even in his second spell at Chelsea, when he was the self-appointed 'Happy One', he still found enough reasons to be miserable by his third season at the helm to make his position untenable. Why will things be any different at United?

Well, maybe they won't. But maybe they will. The difference here is he really wants the job, as I have demonstrated in this chapter. Old Trafford is not simply a staging post on a journey, as you got the impression Porto and Inter Milan were. It is the final destination. After United, surely everywhere else is down, for him. And it's not as though Mourinho has always tried to engineer his own exits. You sense that if Abramovich had not been so trigger-happy during Mourinho's first spell at Chelsea Mourinho might have actually stayed and tried to build a dynasty. Real Madrid was always only going to be a short-stint (and actually he lasted longer there than most other managers), of course, but Real Madrid is always the exception to any rule. Manchester United should be, too. Maybe United are the club to calm his earthquakes.

What's clear is that amongst the playing-staff at Old Trafford, the appointment has been greeted with enthusiasm (you couldn't really say *any* of them looked enthusiastic at almost any time under LVG, other than when Jesse Lingard was behind the camera).

Wayne Rooney said: "He's one of the best managers in the world. It's an exciting time for Manchester United. He knows the Premier League very well and I'm looking forward to it (working with Mourinho)."

David De Gea said: "Talk about Jose Mourinho and you're talking about a winner. Winning is United's, Jose's and my philosophy. We can make a great team and I welcome him. People talk a lot and they know little. I know how all this works, but what I think is disrespectful is when people start making out that it's something I have said. I've got three more years on my contract with United and the desire to win more titles here. When it comes to United, if you don't win everything, it's not good enough. This FA Cup is important for the club, it's important for the fans, and it's an important step towards winning major titles again."

Even Daley Blind, who comes very much from the Louis van Gaal camp, said: "I've met Jose several times but don't know him personally. For example, I played for Ajax against Real Madrid when he was the coach of Madrid, so I saw him then. I think he's a coach who's achieved a lot and I'm very excited to work with someone like him. I'm going do my best and work very hard."

But the final word goes to someone without the United camp now, but a top Red nonetheless; one of the kids who helped United become the giant club they are today. "I think it is perfect," said David Beckham. "Bringing him back to the Premier League needed to happen. It's not the same without him. I can't wait to see him. I only hope I can go to the first game."

2

WHEN MANCHESTER UNITED SIGNED JOSE MOURINHO AS MANAGER, ED WOODWARD DESCRIBED HIM AS: "QUITE SIMPLY THE BEST MANAGER IN THE GAME TODAY". IS MOURINHO THE BEST MANAGER IN THE GAME?

At the very top of European football there is a knot of giant clubs; let's call them Super Clubs. A knot. Imagine the top-knot on Gareth Bale's head and you're halfway there. Bear with me here.

That knot of Super Clubs, then. You can identify most of them by reading a list of those clubs who have contested the Champions League final which brings down the curtain on each season. Mostly, you see the same names. Real Madrid, Barcelona, Juventus, Bayern Munich, Chelsea, Manchester United, Inter and AC Milan, Liverpool. To most of these Super Clubs, the Champions League is the ultimate prize, and they fight tooth and nail to get their hands on that famous trophy.

Competition is fierce. And it is close. The fact that the last Super Club to retain the Champions League (or the European Cup as it was then) was AC Milan back in 1990 bears testimony to that.

Great rivalries exist amongst this elite, then, as the business of carrying off the main prize goes on and on. But at the same time, if you happen to tug at any of the loose threads which make up that knot, you'll find that in the end the relationships between these Super Clubs is closer and more tangled than you might initially expect. You'll find interwoven narrative threads, recurring characters and themes and if you tug sharply enough - so hard that Gareth Bale might say 'ouch' - you'll discover that actually, the main prize isn't so much the main prize at all. Getting to the business-end of the Champions League is great and all, but the *business* is the ultimate end.

There is another way of identifying those clubs tied together in that knot. They are those clubs whose representatives were on the guest list for an exclusive meeting at a top London hotel in March 2016, at which changes to the qualification system for the Champions League was discussed. Reportedly, Barcelona, Real Madrid, Bayern Munich, Paris Saint Germain, Chelsea, Manchester United, Manchester City, Chelsea and Arsenal were there and the possibility of guaranteeing entry to the biggest competition in European football was mooted. That Chelsea, Manchester United and Liverpool were all set to miss out on qualification to the 2016-17 Champions League money-spinning extravaganza was of course, totally coincidental, and that the likes of Barcelona, Real Madrid and Bayern Munich were all set to miss out on the massive TV paydays which potential match-ups against those same

Chelsea, Manchester United and Liverpool sides was also by-the-by.

That March meeting wasn't the first time Europe's Super Clubs have cosied up, nor will it be the last. Leicester City winning the Premier League against all the odds put the wind up these aristocrats. So did Atletico Madrid coming close – again – to toppling their city rivals in the Champions League final. Those paupers – not much more than the superhero's mild mannered alter-ego to look at them - weren't even supposed to be on the same pitch as Bale and his top-knot!

Money is supposed to guarantee a place at the top table and in most cases, the team which pays the highest wages will win the league. Money buys you in to the knot of elite clubs, too: Paris Saint Germain and Manchester City were the only clubs who would not cross-over in an imaginary Venn diagram which showed recent Champions League finalists and those invited to that top London hotel. But that was OK. *They might not have a bonafide history on a European scale, but they are billionaires. They could buy the bloody hotel and fire the doormen if they were denied entry.*

The ideal, for these elite clubs, would be a closed shop. A Super League for Super Clubs. Leicester City's name's not down, so they're not coming in. But for now they'll have to make do by skewing the competition in different ways, and by smaller degrees.

They'll make sure they keep their eyes on the main prize, which is of course, the business of football. They'll secure the best TV rights deals and they'll hoover up the best players and build the best stadiums and they'll hire the best managers. They'll hire proven winners. Personalities who'll get viewers tuning in to the pay-per-view TV coverage. They'll look for a Super Coach.

The Super Coach

Great managers have always been around, but the Super Coach is a relatively recent phenomenon. And just as you'll find those same names cropping up at the end-game of the Champions League tournaments or at the high-table at some swanky London hotel, so you'll find the same names cropping up when it comes to Super Coaches. For there are only a limited number of Super Coaches at any one time, barely enough to go round. And so, every two to three years, we'll have that same managerial merry-go-round. We see the same clubs: Chelsea, Inter, Barcelona, Real Madrid, Bayern Munich, flirting with the same Super Coaches: Jose Mourinho, Carlo Ancelotti, Pep Guardiola. These are the current Super Coaches of choice, but there have been others, too, as we shall see. Horses for courses.

Manchester United used to stand aloof while the rest of Europe's top clubs tossed their (official club motor vehicle partner branded) car keys in a bowl every couple of seasons and waited to see which one of the Super Coaches they'd go home with this time around. The club and its fans used to look upon that same managerial merry-go-round with a mixture of amusement and contempt, safe in the knowledge that Sir Alex Ferguson remained at the helm. Fergie lasted 26 years as manager of Britain's biggest football club, winning 13 Premier League titles and two Champions League titles amongst a total trophy haul of 38. With Fergie in the hot-seat, the club and fans could convince ourselves we were above all that constant chopping and changing; there was no revolving door at Old Trafford. But then Fergie retired, and the board bungled his succession not once but twice and at last United had to reach into the bowl of car keys. Maybe right at the last, club officials felt a little embarrassed at the indignity of it all, but then they looked up; saw Jose Mourinho winking provocatively. And that was that. United had become like every other elite club after all; they'd grabbed a thread from that Super Coach knot and tugged as hard as they could, and in the end, pulled out Jose Mourinho.

As a matter of fact, if you pull at *any* thread in that knot long enough and hard enough, you'll eventually discover Mourinho. For he has been at the heart of so many of the major stories of European football over the past decade and a half that his presence has become ubiquitous. Ed Woodward's claim on unveiling the Portuguese as United's new supremo, its Super Coach was that Mourinho was "quite simply the best manager in the game today" is debatable and this chapter will consider him against his Super Coach competition. But what is clear is that Mourinho is one of a very exclusive club of Super Coaches, whose experience of and influence on football culture has made him pre-eminent.

This chapter will study Mourinho's Super Coach rivals through the prism of European finals over the past decade, particularly the Champions League. We will compare trophies won, examine win percentages, and also consider the longevity of their spells at the European top table. For whilst some Super Coaches have been flash-in-the-pan; good for a couple of stellar seasons before fading (Andre-Villas Boas is one example) others have truly stood the test of time, and proved time and again that we are right to consider them the cream of the crop.

For what has been truly great about Jose Mourinho is his sustained excellence as a club football manager. Since the early noughties he has consistently delivered trophies, broken records, and silenced critics. The Portuguese first came to prominence on a European stage with UEFA Cup win with Porto in Seville in 2003 against Celtic and ever since, he has been a proven winner. That's 13 years at the very pinnacle of a cut-throat business, and whilst men like Alex Ferguson could boast much longer careers, football has irrevocably changed now: it is managed, played and digested as though on fast-forward. A 13-year career at the very top now is the equivalent of a 30 year one a few decades ago: witness the rate of burn-out amongst managers; the number of them now who require sabbaticals prior to taking on the next challenge.

Even in 2003 the landscape of European football was different. Spanish and German teams weren't as pre-eminent as they are today. Indeed, three Italian teams lined up in the semi-finals of the Champions League that year (Inter, AC Milan and Juventus were joined by a galactico-stuffed Real Madrid) and two went on to contend the final, an event which was hosted at Old Trafford. Juventus and AC Milan played out 120 minutes of goalless football before Carlo Ancelotti's Milan beat Marcello Lippi's Juventus on penalties.

Ancelotti has – like Mourinho - stood the test of time, but Marcello Lippi (who won one Champions League, five domestic titles and one domestic cup) went on to manage the Italian national team to World Cup glory in 2006, before a disastrous campaign to defend that trophy in 2010 saw him sacked; since then his only job has been in Japan, where he managed Guangzhou Evergrande.

In 2004, Mourinho went one better than in 2003 and guided FC Porto to a remarkable Champions League triumph. In hindsight what is truly remarkable is the clubs which went deep into that competition. Whereas in the past few years, we've been able to predict with some accuracy that at least two heavyweight Spanish teams (take your pick from Real Madrid, Barcelona, and Atletico Madrid) and a fashionable German side (Bayern Munich or Borussia Dortmund) and maybe a Juventus at the outside will be in the running as the tournament enters its most competitive stages, in the 2004 competition the semi-finals comprised three clubs which might be described as unfashionable. Monaco, Deportivo La Coruna, and Mourinho's FC Porto made the final four, alongside Jose's next club, Chelsea.

Chelsea had just come into their Abramovich money, but were still untested at this level. Monaco surprised them over two legs and it was felt a more pragmatic coach than the Italian Claudio Ranieri was required in order to deliver Abramovich's greatest desire.

Claudio Ranieri though, whatever happened to him?

Ranieri's Chelsea team had defeated Arsenal in an all-English quarter-final (Wayne Bridge settling the tie with an 87th minute winner at Highbury.) And back then Arsene Wenger could quite easily have claimed to be one of the pre-eminent coaches in European football. His stylish, quick, and very European Arsenal team - which included Thierry Henry and Dennis Bergkamp, Patrick Vieira, Freddie Ljungberg and Robert Pires, at the height of their powers – would go on to finish the Premier League season undefeated, becoming only the second team in the history of top division English football to achieve that feat after Preston North End's original 'invincibles' in 1888-89.

Super Coach Contenders – Arsene Wenger

Arsene Wenger is the longest-serving and most-decorated manager in the history of Arsenal Football Club, who are in turn the third most successful English club. Now Sir Alex Ferguson has retired he is the elder statesman of the Premier League, and also its longest-serving manager. And just as Ferguson imprinted his own identity on Manchester United, so Wenger has imprinted his upon Arsenal. Hell, even Arsene's name is only a couple of letters away from Arsenal.

These days it is easy to be critical of Wenger – and many within the media are; as are some of his rivals; as are even the very same fans who once lauded him. Jose Mourinho famously dubbed him a "specialist in failure",

and that gibe was pounced upon by the media and used as a
stick to beat him with. And it wasn't without a kernel of
truth: Wenger's last Premier League title came in 2003-04,
and, two FA Cups aside, he has won nothing worthy of
note for over a decade. 'The Professor' has started to look
tired now. Worn down by the ever-present challenges to his
authority from without the club. He is accused of out-
staying his welcome; tarnishing his legacy.

But what a legacy. Wenger's proudest achievement is
that 2003-04 Premier League title, in which his charges
went the entire league season unbeaten. But he also won
two other titles, both in competition with arguably Sir Alex
Ferguson's greatest United teams and in total six FA Cups.
He also came *this close* to winning two European trophies:
losing on penalties to Galatasaray in the UEFA Cup Final in
2000 and to a resurgent Barcelona, after being ahead for
most of the night, in the Champions League Final in 2006.

But Wenger's legacy exceeds mere trophies won and
unbeaten records. The Frenchman can lay claim to
changing the face of English football in many ways, from
the new training methods and dietary regimes he brought
in, to his extensive scouting networks outwith these shores.

When he first arrived in England, noted Jim White, in
his book *Premier League: A History in 10 Matches:* "It quickly
became apparent the forty-eight-year-old's arrival would
have a profound effect not just on Arsenal, but on the
club's rivals. There had been a few foreign managers in the
Premiership before him, most notably Ruud Gullit at
Chelsea and Osvaldo Ardiles at Spurs, but neither had
translated their playing prowess into an ability to build a
title-winning team. (…) Wenger was the Premiership's first
career coach, its first student of methodology, its first
football professor. Just as the influx of foreign players
attracted by television money had brought new attitudes,
new focus, new professionalism to English football, so he
now brought new systems, new approaches to preparation,

a new appreciation of sports science. Not to mention an encyclopaedic knowledge of dietary supplements."

In the intervening years Wenger has made Arsenal unrecognisable. Under his leadership, the Gunners moved to a new, 60,000 capacity stadium in North London. They now enjoy higher match-day revenues than any other English club. He also changed the entire playing philosophy of the club. No longer did we see "boring, boring Arsenal". No, instead we witnessed a new fluid, flair-filled style from them; a style which led Brian Clough to quip: "Arsenal caress a football the way I dreamed of caressing Marilyn Monroe." This is now their identity.

While some might sniff at his recent record, Wenger has always done things the right way. The problem is that there are no rewards for moving slowly nowadays in elite level football and men like Jose Mourinho are quick enough and smart enough to know this.

We will consider in detail the war of words which ensued between Mourinho and Wenger in another chapter, however for now, let it be said that the two are poles apart as men, and their footballing beliefs are also wildly different. This was demonstrated very well by their opposing takes on a game which didn't even involve a Mourinho team. After Arsenal beat Spurs 5-4 in the north London derby, Wenger purred at the quality of attacking football on display. Mourinho, when asked for his opinions – and he was never backwards in coming forwards in giving his views, even when he wasn't asked – snarled: "5-4 is a joke result (...) It was like a hockey match. For a team to give away four or five goals, the defenders must be a disgrace."

Super Coach Contenders – Rafael Benitez

In 2005, another surprise package won the Champions League trophy: Liverpool. *En route* to the final, they beat Jose Mourinho's new club Chelsea in a fractious semi-final decided by Luis Garcia's 'ghost goal', thereby denying the Portuguese back to back Champions Leagues. The controversial winner at Anfield – which took Rafael Benitez's Liverpool into the final in Istanbul - was the incendiary which fuelled another long-standing rivalry for Jose Mourinho; one which transcended their clubs and crossed borders. However, unlike the enmity with Wenger, it was not based on differing football philosophies. Indeed, the two started out as friends – or at least *not* enemies. They shared a similar footballing credo; the teams were largely set out to play on the counter-attack. Instead it was based on the fact the pair were thrust together so many times in so many crucial matches in such an intensive period of time that the two couldn't help but see the other as the main stumbling block to success. They fell out because the one was always in too close proximity to the other. Eventually this closeness was accentuated to such a degree that it was almost incestuous: after Liverpool Benitez had a habit of taking over clubs Mourinho had already managed.

Rafael Benitez had done well at Valencia prior to taking up the managerial hot-seat at Anfield. He'd won two *La Ligas* and one UEFA Cup in a glorious three-year spell. But in 2005, in guiding the Merseyside club to a surprise win on penalties over Milan in the Champions League final, he'd inducted himself into that select band of European managers who could truly be considered to be *box office*. However, looking back, it is clear to see the Champions League win in Istanbul was the apex of Benitez's career and since then it has been downhill all the way.

Post-2005 Rafa Benitez's career has been a nomadic one. Though he spent six years at Liverpool, he never delivered the consistency of excellence required to mount a credible tilt at the Premier League title. The closest they came was in 2008-09, when they finished runners-up to Sir Alex Ferguson's Manchester United. Though Liverpool did the league double over United (including a 4-1 win at Old Trafford) they couldn't sustain their challenge over 38 matches. A poor run of form over the busy Christmas and new year period coincided with Benitez missing a game (in which the Anfield club dropped points) because he had his kidney stones removed. This was in no way, shape or form Rafa's fault, however what *was* his fault was his demeanour when he returned. It soon became clear he lacked *the stones* to compete with Ferguson when it came to the mind-games: in response to the pressure which Fergie had been slowly and surely ratcheting up on the Liverpool boss, Benitez cracked in an almost Keegan-esque display of emotion. He came across badly; seemed paranoid. His insistence on repeating the word "facts" as though to illustrate the truth of his argument instead having the opposite effect. Ferguson laughed all the way to the title.

After that, he was never the same, and that's a fact. After another year of relative failure at Liverpool the inevitable change came in 2010, when he was relieved of his duties.

Benitez was still trading off 2005 however, and he bagged himself the job at Inter Milan next, but he only lasted six months. He did deliver the FIFA Club World Cup, but again, his team's league form was incredibly inconsistent. And back then, Inter fans were used to consistency, and they were used to winning, too. After all, Benitez took over the job after Jose Mourinho left, the Portuguese having guided them to the most successful season in their history, and an unprecedented treble. Not only was Benitez haunted by Ferguson, he was also haunted by his arch-rival Mourinho.

Following the disappointment of his time at Internazionale, Benitez took a two-year break from the game before again trying to walk in Mourinho's shoes, this time at Chelsea (in 2012-13), where his appointment provoked open revolt amongst the Stamford Bridge faithful. He *did* win the Europa League, becoming only the second manager after Giovanni Trapattoni to have won the UEFA Cup/Europa League with two different teams. But his place was never secure. The Chelsea board refused to give him the title of anything but 'interim manager', and at the end of the season he was gone.

Back to Italy, and to Naples, where again he delivered a cup but not the consistency of league form Napoli president Aurelio De Laurentiis demanded. Indeed, Napoli didn't even qualify for the following season's Champions League, and that was viewed as a failure.

They say to understand a man you must walk a mile in his shoes. Benitez took this idea to ridiculous lengths, as he ploughed his way across three countries and through three clubs, following Mourinho. After Inter and Chelsea came Real Madrid. And yet Rafa still didn't seem to have developed a better understanding of Jose Mourinho: they continued to needle each other from afar and Mourinho continued (mostly) to gain the upper hand. Mainly this was because Benitez generally failed, where Jose hadn't. It was no different in the Spanish capital. Benitez lasted seven months at Real Madrid, but bungled badly (in fielding an ineligible player in the Spanish cup, and seeing Madrid disqualified from the competition; and worse, in overseeing a terrible 4-0 reverse against arch-rivals Barcelona).

But now it seems Benitez has run out of former Mourinho-led clubs who want him, and so he's gone his own way. He's pitched up at Newcastle United, where he has already overseen a relegation (though in truth the damage was already done before the Spaniard took the helm for the Magpies' last ten matches). He is now so far outside the elite, that select band of specialist coaches, that he isn't even managing a top division club any more. His record is good – he has won one Champions League along with two other European trophies; two domestic league titles and a brace of domestic cups, but his stock has been sinking for a while now; he is a long way off his nemesis Jose now.

Super Coach Contenders – Carlo Ancelotti

In that Champions League final of 2005 the man in the opposing dugout to Rafael Benitez was Carlo Ancelotti. Ancelotti is perhaps the only manager operating today who can boast a similar long-term record of success to Mourinho.

Ancelotti is the only manager to have won the Champions League three times and reached four finals. Unfortunately, the one he lost – with Milan – was the one most English fans will remember: when Liverpool came from 3-0 down at half-time to win on penalties in Istanbul. He has also won three domestic league titles and three domestic cup competitions. (He can arguably rival Mourinho in the celebrity stakes, too, given that he had a role in July 2016's *Star Trek Beyond.*)

Ancelotti finally laid to rest the ghosts of 2005 two years later, in Athens, against the same dog had bitten them. A 2-1 victory in the 2007 Champions League final, thanks to a brace from Pippo Inzaghi, gained some measure of revenge. However, despite his domestic and continental successes, Ancelotti only lasted another two years at the helm of the Italian giants before he was the victim of owner Silvio Berlusconi's notoriously itchy trigger-finger. Milan would be left to rue their decision; a solitary *Serie A* trophy has found its way into their San Siro trophy cabinet since the departure of the man they nicknamed *Carletto,* whilst first city rivals Inter and then Juventus have usurped them as Italy's biggest club. *Carletto*'s own personal trophy cabinet in the intervening year by far exceeds that of Milan's.

Ancelotti's final season at Milan came in 2008-09. They finished third in Serie A, behind Juventus, and rivals Inter. Losing out to Inter stung bitterly. Inter's manager? One Jose Mourinho.

Ancelotti's next port of call on the managerial merry-go-round was Chelsea. (Funny how those same names, those same clubs keep cropping up, isn't it? Chelsea's recent history shows Abramovich has collected almost the full deck of European Super Coaches on the hunt for that elusive *je ne sais quoi*, the nirvana of perfect, fluid football and results and trophies – though not, note, Pep Guardiola. Since 1996 they've employed genuine A-List managers such as Mourinho (twice), Luiz Felipe Scolari, Guus Hiddink (twice), Carlo Ancelotti, and Rafa Benitez, with varying degrees of success. They've also employed garlanded former players who were giants on the European stage - Ruud Gullit and Gianluca Vialli – though the Stamford Bridge club don't tend to do this anymore. And they've also gone for the up-and-comers on the European stage, hipster names like Andre Villas-Boas and Avram Grant. Funny too how, amongst this scattergun approach, the manager who did finally deliver the object of Abramovich's desire was the largely unheralded former player, Roberto Di Matteo.

Real Madrid work in a very similar way, discarding used coaches like Panini swaps. *Their* list of recent managers features many of the same names – since 2010; Mourinho, Ancelotti, and Benitez. Ancelotti delivered Madrid's *decima*, their tenth Champions League triumph, but was still sacked. Funnily enough, their eleventh was delivered in May 2016 by another former player. You might have heard of him. He goes by the name of Zinedine Zidane.)

Anyway Chelsea, and Ancelotti. In 2009-10, Ancelotti was given the chance to attain some measure of revenge for his coming off second best to Jose Mourinho in Serie A, where they'd endured a rather tense relationship. In the Champions League Round of 16, Ancelotti's Chelsea were drawn against Mourinho's Internazionale. It also, of course, meant an early return to the San Siro for the Italian boss. However Mourinho again had the better of his counterpart, as the Nerazzuri won both home and away (3-1 on aggregate) to proceed to the next round.

Domestically things went a much better for Ancelotti, as Chelsea won a league and cup double, breaking all kinds of records along the way. In scoring 103 Premier League goals, they became the first team in the Premier League era to top 100 goals in a season (and also the first English top division since Spurs in 1962-63 to do this, if you don't concur with Sky and believe there was no football before the Premier League). On the final day of the season, Chelsea had to better Manchester United's result in order to become champions. They did so emphatically, by beating Wigan Athletic 8-0.

The 2010-11 season was bubbling along nicely enough for Ancelotti and Chelsea (though they were ten points behind Manchester United in the Premier League), but then the owner went behind the back of the Super Coach and signed Liverpool's star striker, Fernando Torres, for a British record £50 million just before the transfer window slammed shut in January. Torres, as we know, failed, and badly. And Abramovich's interference disrupted the squad (just as it did when Roman served up the unwanted Andrei Shevchenko for Mourinho during the Portuguese's first spell at the Stamford Bridge club). Chelsea wound up finishing second to Ferguson's United, and Abramovich wound up sacking Ancelotti. The Italian left with his win percentage at Chelsea the third-highest in Premier League history, behind only Mourinho and Fergie.

Ancelotti moved from one European capital to another, and in this tale of two cities, this aristocrat of the game wound up in Paris, where a revolution had taken place. In 2011 Qatar Sports International bought Paris Saint Germain, in one fell swoop making them by far the richest club in France and one of the top three richest clubs in world football. However, money – and a Super Coach - didn't buy the French team instant happiness. Instead PSG were pipped to the post in *Ligue 1* by unfancied Montpellier. That was the last time such a thing would happen though. Money soon skewed the competition and by the following season a star-studded PSG cruised to the title. They also did well in European competition, reaching the quarter-finals before losing narrowly to Barcelona on away goals.

Money had talked then, but Ancelotti walked. Offski again; this time to another European capital city which was hungry for glory in the capital European competition: Madrid. There, the Italian delivered Real Madrid's fabled and famous tenth Champions League trophy, beating city rivals Atletico 4-1 in the final, after extra-time. In winning the trophy, Ancelotti became only the second manager after Bob Paisley at Liverpool to win the tournament three times. He also became the first coach to win the Champions League twice as a player and three times as a coach.

Amazingly, he was fired a year later. Florentino Perez, the Madrid president said that although Ancelotti had won the hearts of both the board and fans, and would always have a place in Real Madrid's history as the coach that led the whites to the *decima*, "at this club the demands are huge and we need a new impulse in order to win trophies and be at our best."

Swings and roundabouts. Ancelotti, secure in the knowledge that he remained a Super Coach, took the Super Coach's next step *of the day*. He took a leaf out of Guardiola and Klopp's books and took a sabbatical. Whereas

Guardiola went to New York, Ancelotti chose Vancouver. (Klopp probably went walking in the mountains, ear-splitting heavy metal on his iPod and a mad look in his eyes.)

And then Manchester City set in motion 2016's big Super Coach merry-go-round by pinching Guardiola from Bayern Munich and the Bavarians plumped for Ancelotti, and the wheels kept on turning and the same names kept on cropping up.

Eight years ago, the likes of Pep Guardiola would never even have been mentioned in the same breath as Manchester City, and certainly lazer blues fans could never have imagined they would have had the standing in European football to be able to steal the popular and successful coach of a giant club such as Bayern Munich. In 2008, Manchester City were in a state of turmoil. At the time, City were being bankrolled by Thaksin Shinawatra, the former Thai prime minister and a man with a not exactly enviable human rights record. Shinawatra – surely the reason Fit and Proper Persons tests for potential owners were brought in to football - had been forced into exile following a military coup in his country and political manoeuvrings back home meant his assets had been frozen. City had no funds. They were basically up shit creek.

Towards the end of the 2007-08 season, a massive black cloud hung over the club, blocking the blue moon right out. The last match of the season, and their last under the stewardship of the Swede, Sven-Goran Eriksson, came at the Riverside Stadium, Middlesbrough. City lost 8-1. Ten days later, their giant neighbours Manchester United won their third Champions League crown. They'd also won the Premier League title, and in Cristiano Ronaldo and Wayne Rooney, boasted two of the best young players in Europe. Back then, over summer, City fans were in despair. The club was in very real danger of going bust. It was inconceivable they could poach the Super Coach of Germany's biggest club.

But then, on transfer deadline day, Monday 1st September 2008, the Emirati businessman Khaldoon Al Mubarak changed everything. In amongst the rolling info-dump on the Sky Sports News tickertape – which advised us that Manchester United had signed the sulky and silky Bulgarian Dimitar Berbatov from Tottenham Hotspur for £30.75 million, that Everton had broken their club record transfer fee to take the 20-year-old Marouane Fellaini from Standard Liege for £15 million, and that such luminaries as Flora, Riera, and Gulacsi had arrived at Liverpool (no, me neither) – was the bombshell. Thaksin Shinawatra had agreed to sell his stake in Manchester City to Al Mubarak.

Good times ahead for City fans. Stop. Major investment promised. Stop.

Then again, City fans knew from the harsh lessons of history – Franny Lee's loo-roll bank-rolled takeover - to take such promises with a punch of salt; and after all, investment had been promised under Shinawatra too…

But then, as the Sky Sports News countdown clock ticked down towards doom (well, actually the closing of the transfer window – or, as they would have it, the transfer window *slamming shut*) came the first indication that the Emiratis would make good on their promises. For Manchester City had signed *Robinho*. That Robinho. The Brazilian international. The one from Real Madrid. The one Chelsea had been after. For £32.5 million. A British record transfer fee. City fans must have been pinching themselves. And the best was yet to come. And yes, they could forgive and forget what the slightly confused-looking Brazilian said was unveiled as their new *galactico*. He thought he'd joined United.

An easy mistake-a to make-a, of course. United fans used to crow: "City, Manchester City: nobody knows their name". And it was true. Go to any world city, climb into a cab, engage the driver in the usual cab-patter, and soon the talk would invariably circle around to football. They only knew United. Referred to them as 'Manchester', as though Manchester was a one-club city. And for many years it had been. But now it wasn't. Now, everything had changed.

City, like Chelsea under Abramovich at the beginning, had a rather scattergun approach to team-building. They simply bought anyone that moved and worried about how they'd fit them into the team later. Mostly they bought from Arsenal. Eventually, they threw enough at the project that some of it stuck, and under the manger Roberto Mancini in 2011, they finally obliged United fans to tear down that 35-years banner in the Stretford End by actually going and winning a trophy; beating Stoke 1–0 in a mostly forgettable FA Cup Final at Wembley.

More domestic success quickly followed: under Mancini and his successor Manuel Pellegrini they captured the Premier League title, in 2011-12 and 2013-14. They won the League Cup in 2013-14 and 2015-16. But they couldn't crack the Champions League. A semi-final in 2015-16 - in which they surrendered meekly to eventual winners Real Madrid - was the best they got.

And so they, at last, turned to someone who had the knowhow to take them one step further towards their holy grail. They looked to a Super Coach.

They looked to Pep Guardiola.

Super Coach Contenders – Pep Guardiola

The 2008 Champions League Final in Moscow was a match-up between the team Jose built – Chelsea: then managed by Avram Grant - and the team that Mourinho would eventually go on to manage – Manchester United, who had Sir Alex Ferguson at the helm. The final was unique: the only time two English sides have faced-off on the biggest stage. Sky had always marketed the Premier League as *the best league in the world* and for the first time, everyone believed it. But in the end, that final proved the exception, not the rule. Though United and Chelsea would both individually reach finals in the following eight seasons, teams from the German and Spanish league began to take precedence. There was at least one Spanish team in five of the next eight finals (including two all-*La Liga* affairs), and four German sides reached the final (including one all-*Bundesliga* match-up). Despite the fact the final was twice played at the home of the English national game, Wembley, there was only one winner: Chelsea, who ironically won their first Champions League crown when they were perhaps at their lowest ebb, against German giants Bayern Munich, in their own backyard. Chelsea made history in more ways than one that night. Not only were they the first London club to win the Champions League – Nottingham, Birmingham, Manchester and Liverpool had all bagged the trophy well before the capital – but it was a very rare occasion in which an English team beat their German counterparts at their own game: on penalties.

But back in 2008, English (and even Scottish) teams were dominant in continental competition. Three-quarters of the semi-finalists in the Champions League were from the Premier League: Chelsea beat Liverpool (at last) to win through to Moscow, and United beat Barcelona in the other clash. (And Glasgow Rangers contested the UEFA Cup Final, which they lost 2-0 to Zenit St. Petersburg at the (then) City of Manchester Stadium.)

United's semi-final against Barcelona was the first time the teams had been paired since the group stages of the competition in 1998-99, when the Reds had gone on to win it, in miraculous fashion, at Camp Nou. Perhaps it was an omen. But if it was, it wouldn't last into forthcoming seasons. United and Barcelona would meet again on an number of occasions, and at crucial times, in the competition, and Barcelona would get the upper-hand over them every time. Generally by quite a heavy margin.

But in 2008 it was different. In 2008 United won, narrowly. It might have been different had Cristiano Ronaldo not skied a penalty at Camp Nou in the first-leg, denying United a vital away-goal, and making the second-leg an extremely tactical, chess-like game. The Reds won the second-leg thanks to a scorcher from Scholes.

In 2008 it was different because then, Barcelona were managed by Frank Rijkaard. The Dutchman was a great manager in his own right. He'd won back-to-back *La Liga* championships in 2004-05 and 2005-06, the second as part of a fantastic double: Barcelona also won the Champions League that year, defeating Arsenal in the final in Paris. At the time, it was only Barcelona's second Champions League title. But losing to United in the semi-finals in 2008 meant the Catalan giants had gone two years without a major trophy under his tenure, and that was simply unacceptable. He departed at the end of the season.

His replacement changed everything. But at first he seemed like a surprising choice. Most fans, and even some within the Barcelona hierarchy wanted a box-office name: Michael Laudrup's name was mentioned in dispatches; so too Jose Mourinho's. Both were interviewed. But neither was selected. In the end the guy they chose seemed to come straight out of left-field, or, more specifically, from the training fields at Barcelona's *La Masia* facility, where he'd been coaching a bunch of youngsters in Barcelona's B team.

To be fair to Josep 'Pep' Guardiola, he wasn't exactly an unknown. He'd been a celebrated former player for the club. Long-serving too: over eleven years he'd played over 250 games for Barcelona, after coming up through the ranks. But he had very little managerial pedigree, and he was most definitely not a Super Coach.

However, when he stepped down at the end of the 2011-12 season as the most decorated coach in Barcelona's history, having won a record 14 trophies in just four years, he most definitely *was*.

Pep worked fast. In his very first season in charge, Barcelona became the first Spanish club to win the treble. The final part of that treble was the Champions League trophy, which Barcelona secured by beating the holders, Alex Ferguson's Manchester United, in the final in Rome by two goals to nil, thereby gaining revenge for the semi-final defeat in 2008. In doing so Guardiola became the youngest manager to win the Champions League.

But it wasn't just the substance or the statistics with Pep's Barcelona; above all else it was the *style*. We'd seen possession football before, but nothing like this. This, ladies and gentlemen, was *tiki-taka;* a hypnotic "*death-by-a-thousand-passes*" *chic*, perfected by Barcelona's midfield trio of Xavi, Iniesta and Busquets and augmented by the young Lionel Messi up front. Their opponents simply couldn't get the ball off them. It was mesmeric. Pass-pass-pass. It was as though they'd re-invented football.

Rome was Manchester United's first, bitter taste of defeat in a European Cup Final. To be fair, they'd faced a Barcelona side who were in the midst of announcing themselves as arguably the world's greatest ever club side.

Kevin McCarra's match report in *The Guardian* made for painful reading: "The holders were relieved of the European Cup and must take what comfort there is in the appreciation that there is no shame in being outclassed. They could barely *engage* with Pep Guardiola's side, let alone menace them."

The only comfort for the Reds was that: "This could have been a rout to rank with Milan's drubbing of Barcelona in the 1994 final."

McCarra concluded that United's "standards are high but here they met opponents who produced celestial football."

Most of the rest of the British press-pack seemed to be falling over themselves to come up with puns. In a piece entitled "That's another fine Messi", the *Daily Mail* shouted: "Humbled! Tiny Messi, all 5ft 6in of him, soars over dismal United... just call it the Head of God." *The Daily Star* ran with "Lionel Flair is perfect 10". They waxed lyrical about Messi's performance, hailing him as a "genius with magic in his boots". *The Daily Express* went route-one with their headline – "Fergie in a right Messi" - but *The Daily Mirror*'s "Thrown to the Lionels" at least showed *some* creativity. The prize for the most puntastic piece however went as usual to *The Sun*, who led with the excellent "Catalan v Matalan". *The Sun* claimed that United were played off the park by "a Barcelona team superior in every department".

The Catalans had left United trailing in their wake. But in truth, Barcelona did the same to pretty much everyone they faced around this time. They played football from another planet. They were "celestial".

In 2009-10, Barcelona retained their La Liga title (and in some style, too: they bagged a whopping 99 points, which was then the biggest points total ever attained in any of Europe's major leagues) but couldn't repeat the trick in the Champions League. Talk about the curse of the holders. And a curse was right: in the semi-finals Guardiola first locked horns with Jose Mourinho, as Barca met Internazionale. Jose drew first-blood, countering Barcelona's possession game with some insanely stubborn resistance; their tactics were akin to guerrilla warfare. Somehow the Italians won through, and went on to win the trophy. But defeat left a sour taste in Guardiola's mouth; particularly the way Mourinho celebrated it, out on the

Camp Nou turf. It was the beginning of another Mourinho rivalry; perhaps the biggest of them all.

And in 2010-11, that rivalry was turned up to eleven. For Mourinho had pitched up at Barcelona's arch-rivals Real Madrid. Mourinho's presence immediately jeopardised Guardiola's monopoly on trophies: Madrid beat Barcelona in the Copa del Rey final; an extra-time strike from Cristiano Ronaldo subjecting Guardiola to his first cup final defeat. But Guardiola's revenge was best served cold, and on an even bigger stage. Barcelona were icy-cool to dispatch Real Madrid 2–0 at the Bernabeu in the Champions League semi-final first-leg, and in the return at Camp Nou, they mostly froze out Mourinho's Real to secure safe passage to the final – Guardiola's second in three years. Their second against Manchester United, too: fresh off the back of retaining their *La Liga* title, Barcelona beat the Reds 3-1 at Wembley.

The *El Classico* rivalry, and particularly the enmity between Jose and Pep, had grown increasingly bitter over the season as the two giants duked it out for titles. And in 2011-12, this took its toll. At the end of an even more fraught season – in which Mourinho snatched the *La Liga* title away from Pep - Guardiola stood down, citing tiredness.

After a sabbatical he was back, and re-energised, ready to take over at Bayern Munich for the 2013-14 season. He took over a club in rude health. The previous season, under Jupp Heynckes, the Bavarian giants had won everything they'd competed for, becoming the first German club to win the treble. They'd won the Champions League by beating fellow *Bundesliga* side Borussia Dortmund at Wembley. That had been their third appearance in the past four finals.

It would take some feat for Guardiola to match the glory of 2012-13, but he almost managed it. Their journey to retaining the *Bundesliga* was virtually a procession; in the end, they won it by 19 points over runners-up Dortmund (and they were 26 points ahead of third-placed Schalke). They lost only two games all season and their goal difference was a whopping +71. The Champions League Final against Dortmund the previous season had been close, and Dortmund had been running them neck-and-neck for the past few years in Germany. But this was the year Bayern took a giant leap ahead of them domestically. In the following seasons this gap has grown wider and wider. It doesn't help that Bayern have acquired a habit of making off with Dortmund's very best players. In 2013-14, it was Mario Gotze; a year later, Robert Lewandowski; and before 2016-17, Mats Hummels. Indeed, Jose Mourinho compared the German league in recent years to the Scottish league (without Rangers), and he snidely observed that a "kit-man" could win it, if he happened to be boss of Bayern.

But though Bayern found it easy domestically in Guardiola's first season, in Europe they suffered the relative failure of losing in the semi-finals. What was worse was the manner of the defeat: a Cristiano Ronaldo- and Gareth Bale-inspired Real Madrid smashed them 5-0 on aggregate, making a mockery of Guardiola's possession game with their swift, incisive breaks.

The thrashing led Guardiola to reassess over the summer; he decided he couldn't afford to be as much of a purist any more. He brought in a big striker – Lewandowski. Admittedly the Pole possessed a good touch for a big man, but he was a plan-B all the same. His Barcelona team made it a point of principle never even to consider one. During his first season, he'd brought in a number of small, neat players in the Barcelona mould – he'd even brought in one of his old charges in Thiago, stealing him from under Manchester United's noses. But now he was proving he was changing with the times.

In 2014-15, Bayern retained the *Bundesliga,* this time winning the title by ten points over Wolfsburg (a gap which was skewed slightly as the Munich side took their foot off the gas after the league was won, and proceded to lose three out of their last four matches). But in Europe, they yet again fell at the final hurdle against Spanish opposition. This time it was Pep's former club Barcelona who did the damage, particularly in a disastrous first-leg at Camp Nou, in which the Catalans ran out 3-0 winners and Bayern failed to muster a single shot on target. They did better in a pulsating second-leg, but they'd left themselves too much to do, and a 3-2 victory was not nearly enough.

In 2015-16, it was the same old story. They won the league by ten points, and with a +63 goal difference, losing just two games *en route* to the title, but again they lost out in continental competition, and again it was at the semi-final stage, and again it was against Spanish opposition – the third season on the bounce. This time it was Diego Simeone's Atletico Madrid did the damage, with an away-goals win.

Super Coach Contenders – Diego Simeone and Unai Emery

Every year *FourFourTwo* magazine compiles a list of Top 50 managers in world football. Over the past few years, top-spot has been dominated by Pep Guardiola and Jose Mourinho as much as the *Ballon D'Or* has been dominated by Cristiano Ronaldo and Lionel Messi. It has swung back and forth between them on numerous occasions. One year Pep; one year Jose. You could rest assured it would be *one of them.*

That all changed when the new list was published in August 2016. For the first time in what felt like an age – for longer than Bryan Adams was in pole-position in the

UK charts with *Everything I Do* - there was a new number one: Diego Simeone. (Incidentally, they had Pep Guardiola in second, Luis Enrique in third, and Jose Mourinho in fourth: maybe not surprising given his horror-show at Chelsea in 2015-16).

The Argentine's feats at Atletico Madrid – that Champions League semi-final victory over Pep's Bayern Munich took them to their second final in just three years – have been astonishing. "He is to Atletico Madrid what Steve Jobs was for Apple," said *FourFourTwo*. And they'd be right. He revolutionised a slightly downtrodden institution, encouraging them to think differently about themselves and to claw back market-share against behemoth opposition.

Diego Simeone has won two European trophies and two domestic titles; he has also reached two Champions League finals, however this by no means tells the whole story. His achievements are amplified as he made them as manager of Atletico Madrid, breaking the Barcelona-Real Madrid axis. To win *La Liga* in the 2013–14 season, Atletico had to amass a club record 90 points but more than that they had to overcome perhaps the two biggest and best teams – including two of the best players - the world has ever seen. Although Atletico are a big club in their own right, they are not super-giants like Barcelona and Real, and it is no major exaggeration to claim the title win as the equivalent, maybe, of Partick Thistle triumphing over Celtic and Rangers to win a Scottish Premier League. To put it into some kind of perspective for English readers, the event was almost as shocking as Leicester City winning the Premier League. And though Leicester may well prove to be one-season-wonders, Simeone's Atletico have proved anything but.

Simeone has been so good, you almost forget he was the clown responsible for getting David Beckham sent off in the World Cup in 1998, bringing on the vilification of a nation. We forget, of course, but we don't forgive.

Simeone once described his own playing-style as "holding a knife between his teeth". He manages, we have seen, in a very similar manner. It seems certain he will move on from Atletico sooner or later – likely the managerial merry-go-round next season will throw up a Super Club or two - and his true test will come once this happens.

Unai Emery is another up-and-comer. Like Mourinho, Emery started – as a manager on the European stage - with the UEFA Cup (now Europa League). Unlike Mourinho, Emery never finished with the UEFA Cup. He won the trophy in his first full season at Sevilla, defeating Benfica in Turin in 2014, and then followed that up by winning it again, this time besting the Ukrainian side Dnipro Dnipropetrovsk in Warsaw. He completed his hat-trick in May 2016, in Basel, when a double from Coke provided the fizz in a comeback-win against Jurgen Klopp's Liverpool. Three weeks later, Emery announced he was leaving Sevilla and at the end of June he was unveiled as the new manager of Paris Saint Germain.

This will be his big test. In Spain, he could be forgiven for 'only' winning the Europa League, for concentrating all his efforts on it, because unlike Simeone, he decided there was no point trying to compete in *La Liga* against the Barcelona-Real Madrid axis. He was a conscientious objector, and it worked. But in the French capital, he will need to win, and win well, to satisfy the Qatari owners.

Paris Saint Germain, like Manchester City and Chelsea, are another team which wants to buy its way into the ranks of the Super Clubs. A European trophy – preferably the Champions League – would be a useful passport into the exclusive club. Therefore they have employed an up-and-coming Super Coach with the know-how win one.

PSG's domestic campaign is merely a sideshow: in 2015-16, Laurent Blanc helped them win their fourth consecutive Ligue 1 title. The title was secured with a 9-0 win at Troyes in *early March*. When the season ended and the dust settled, the league table showed PSG had won the league by *31* points over runners-up, Lyon, who actually finished closer on points to relegated Reims than they did PSG. Their goal difference was *+83*. And yet Blanc was sacked off the back of losing out in the Champions League.

Super Coach Contenders – Jose Mourinho

We've studied most of his rivals, and maybe saved the best till last. It is now time to consider the record of Jose Mourinho. These are the bald facts: in terms of trophies won, Jose stands head and shoulders ahead of most of his competition. He has won two Champions Leagues and one UEFA Cup; eight domestic titles and seven domestic cups.

It is the job of this book to *interpret* and analyse these facts and to build a case – or otherwise – for Mourinho. What is certain is the Portuguese built up an enviable personal trophy cabinet very quickly, and he *continued* to build it, across clubs and countries, meeting each challenge with the same hunger and drive as he did the last. When he wins, like Fergie, he is already thinking of the next one. Which is often why he looks so bored at presentation ceremonies, or else absents himself from them altogether in order to call his family. Sometimes he doesn't even bother with the medals; preferring to toss them into the crowd instead.

And he has consistently delivered that *next* title. He is the closest thing to a guarantee in this game: just look at his personal records across clubs: all those home wins. Just look at how consistently he breaks records and breaks new ground: he wins trophies in multiple – doubles and trebles; he delivers new records in terms of goals scored and points won. Also, clean sheets.

Sure he has had his blips. He has been sacked by Madrid and Chelsea (twice), but as Sir Alex Ferguson puts it in *Leading*, "Every football manager has been sacked. I was sacked – albeit not for football reasons – and Jose Mourinho, Arsene Wenger and Carlo Ancelotti have all been sacked. The only football manager who has not been sacked is the one who is two minutes into his first job."

His time at Madrid is often considered a failure, but that is mainly because of the negative headlines he generated in terms of his mind-games and a few ugly incidents on the touchline. But as Paul Wilson noted in *The Guardian*, "even successful managers find it tough going (at the Bernabeu) – 29 managers in the past 30 years tells its own story – and of that number only Leo Beenhakker, Vicente del Bosque and Mourinho managed to stick it out for three seasons."

At Porto, he won the Champions League against all the odds, beating clubs with ten-times bigger budgets along the way. And although he is often accused of spending his way to success, at Porto, his was a squad largely comprising rejects from other clubs; men whose desire to prove people wrong matched his own. And even *at* Chelsea, where he spent a Czar's ransom on players, even his rivals had to admit it wasn't simply a case of Mourinho buying the title. "The success that Jose Mourinho achieved in his first season at Chelsea in 2004-05, when he won the Premier League and League Cup, was mainly due to his stubbornness, the determined manner he scratched out victories and draws and the fact that he had the players believing he was the Messiah," wrote Alex Ferguson in *Leading*. "It also did not hurt that he spent £100 million during his first season at the club. However, he is a great leader and spectacular manager who has achieved major triumphs in four different countries. It's hard to think of anyone else who has done that."

His achievements with an ageing squad at Internazionale were also exceptional.

"Jose Mourinho might lay claim to being the greatest manager in the world," wrote Chris Anderson and David Sally in their book, *The Numbers Game*. "The Portuguese is just one of three men to win the European Cup with two different clubs, and the only man to do so in the competition's Champions League era. He is one of only four coaches to win league titles in four different countries, and he is the only man on both lists. Whether it was at FC Porto in his homeland, at Chelsea, at Internazionale, at Real Madrid or back at Stamford Bridge, like him or loathe him, Mourinho has a golden touch."

Golden touch sure; but is he the very best? Guardiola, Simeone, and Ancelotti might have something to say about that.

Well, the best way to settle any argument is by referring to facts. Rafael Benitez might concur. And history books show Mourinho has won the most trophies. Even in terms of win percentages, in a much longer career, Mourinho fares well against his direct rivals for the crown of best coach in world football. Discounting Diego Simeone for a moment, both because his record is skewed on account of having to compete against two superpowers throughout his career, and because he hasn't translated his success *across* different clubs, which is a defining factor in identifying a Super Coach, the following are the win percentages of the three managers I believe are the best around.

Carlo Ancelotti – his career record is 58.25% (his record fluctuates from a fantastic 74.8% at Real Madrid, to Reggiana, where it limped in at 41.45%).

Jose Mourinho – his career record is 66% (which takes into account the highs – Real Madrid, where he had a 71.9% win record and Porto, where it stood at 71.7% – and the lows - Uniao de Leiria - where it stood at 45%).

Pep Guardiola meanwhile has no Reggianas or Uniao de Leirias dragging down his own record. He has only ever managed *the best*, the Superclubs Barcelona and Bayern Munich. Therefore his career record win percentage is 72.89% (72.47% at Barcelona and a whopping 75.16% at Bayern).

There is of course another way of settling the debate as to who is the best Super Coach in the world, and that is simply settling back and watching the drama of the 2016-17 Premier League season unfold. For it is in the Premier League this year that the highest concentration of Super Coaches *ever* will be found, duking it out for top-spot, for a vital place in the top-four, and Champions League qualification.

This, my friends, will be the Year of the Manager.

Super Coach Contenders – Battlefield Premier League (2016-17 Season)

It is fair to say that the highest concentration of *galactico* coaches will be in England's Premier League in 2016-17. Indeed, one of the major reasons why the forthcoming Premier League season has been billed as potentially one of the most exciting ever, is because of the Super Coaches who will be present.

Why are they all here? Well, for one, the new TV deal kicks in, meaning these guys will have a lot of money with which to back up their convictions. Because of that new TV deal, every single Premier League club - not just your Manchester Uniteds, your Chelseas, your Manchester Citys, your Arsenals or your Liverpools, but your West Broms and your Hull Citys - will be in the top forty richest clubs in the world. They all have money to burn.

They're here because they are running out of options on the continent: and there are only a finite number of clubs to go round. In Spain, Barcelona and Real Madrid are trying a different route. They are both employing 'figurehead' ex-players in the role of head honcho (at Barcelona, Luis Enrique; at Real Madrid, Zinedine Zidane). In Italy, Massimiliano Allegri is doing fine, in charge of Juventus, thank you very much, having won back-to-back doubles in his two seasons at the helm. Beyond that, Inter and AC Milan are no longer the forces they once were domestically, let alone on a European scale. In France, PSG have already bagged a new manager in Unai Emery. In Germany, Bayern Munich have brought in Ancelotti, perhaps the only true Super Coach who hasn't joined the Premier League circus.

So who is here?

At Manchester City: Pep Guardiola. Despite Manchester City's petro-dollars, Guardiola is the first absolutely A-list manager the Eastlands club have signed up.

At Arsenal: Arsene Wenger.

At Liverpool, the infectiously enthusiastic heavy metal football Jurgen Klopp. Klopp's achievements at Dortmund amplified by the fact he achieved them *against* Bayern Munich, who kept stealing his best players. At Dortmund he achieved back-to-back Bundesliga titles and a cup (as part of the German club's first ever domestic double). He narrowly lost out to Bayern in the 2012-13 Champions League final at Wembley, thanks to a last-minute goal from Arjen Robben. (Dortmund's preparation for the final was hampered by the announcement that Bayern were set to steal *another* one of their players; this time Mario Gotze). Klopp also lost the Europa League Final with Liverpool in May 2016, when Seville overwhelmed them.

At Chelsea: Antonio Conte, fresh from the European Championships in France where he was in charge of possibly the worst Italian squad ever to perform at a major finals, but squeezed every ounce of juice out of them to come within a whisker of the semi-finals. Conte is the proud owner of a fantastic wig (surely that's a wig!) and also a good record as a manager. A highly decorated (and far less hirsute) player whose most successful spell came at Juventus, he won three Serie A titles as manager of the same club, as well as two cups.

And at Manchester United, Jose Mourinho. Mourinho is seen by many as the spark which might set the tinderbox alight; sending the Premier League spiralling into a frenzy of mind-games and not-to-subtle digs at rivals. Mourinho thrives on conflict, and conflict drives narrative, and Jose Mourinho's sometimes amusing, sometimes inspiring, sometimes combative, sometimes curmudgeonly presence at the top table of English football has been missed, particularly by Sky. Whether he has it in him to drag this Manchester United team to the top of the tree over the next season or two is uncertain. We don't even know whether he is the best manager in Europe, despite all the arguments for and against within this chapter. But what we do know is he is the European manager *most suited to* - and experienced in - the Premier League, with all its hurly-burly.

3

"FOOTBALL IS A HUMAN SCIENCE AND NOT A SPORTS SCIENCE." WHAT IS THE MANAGEMENT STYLE OF JOSE MOURINHO?

Jose Mourinho's managerial career has taken him to Super Clubs ranging from the glorious Blue Whale of Real Madrid, through the venerable whoppers, Internazionale, Porto and Manchester United, to the *nouveaux riche* sharks, Chelsea. But during his playing career, he trawled through some of the genuine minnows of the game: from the government department-sounding Comercio e Industria, where he finished his 'career', through Sesimbra to Belenenses these were mostly bottom-feeding clubs from the mostly semi-professional Portuguese lower leagues.

The closest he came to a big club was Rio Ave, where Mourinho began his playing career (thanks, largely to the fact his Dad was manager there at the time). And from then on, it was all downhill.

Based in northern Portugal, Rio Ave are traditionally a yoyo club though in recent years they have been on the up, competing in the UEFA Europa League in 2014-15. But they are still minnows: the capacity of their home ground, the Estadio do Rio Ave, is just over 12,000, and traditionally it only sells out for the visits of Portugal's big three: Benfica, Porto and Sporting Lisbon. Even *with* a full-house, the whole place holds less than the East Stand at Old Trafford, Jose Mourinho's new home.

I contacted the press office at Rio Ave in order to try and get a steer on the early Mourinho. Were there any signs then that the young Jose might become one of the best coaches in world football? Were they proud of him? But their response was short and to the point. Honest too: they *could* have painted him as some kind of prodigal son, but they didn't. They simply stated the facts (which I could have gleaned simply by checking Wikipedia): though Mourinho had been on the books at Rio Ave between 1980 and 1982, his position listed as a central-midfielder, he had only played a handful of games (16) and there was now nobody at the club who'd been present during that period to remember him even if he had made more of an impression.

People might have forgotten about Jose Mourinho the player, then, but they don't forget about Jose Mourinho the coach. Jose the coach is not a minnow. He is not run-of-the-mill and he does not truck with run-of-the-mill clubs. He leads, and others follow. In many ways Mourinho has become the template for a modern, professional, specialist coach.

In their excellent book, *The Numbers Game*, Chris Anderson and David Sally wrote: "Many of the foremost managers of the current era – Mourinho, Wenger, Benitez – were either mediocre players or didn't play at all. Successful players are more likely to hark back to the methods that made their careers glorious, rather than adapting and innovating, as managers at all clubs must, since there is no permanently winning formula."

Managers are different beasts these days thanks to Jose and his ilk. Their approach to the job is holistic and it is done in a scientific way. They employ sports scientists and nutritionists. Psychologists. Statisticians. They lead, mostly, by treating managing and coaching as a profession and not just as an extension to a playing career; an alternative to punditry or perhaps buying a pub. They don't rely on being able to yell loudly to impress their authority on their playing staff; they don't show up their staff by being consistently the best player during the Friday five-a-sides in training. They don't rely on the old boys' network as much, (though some work a little too closely to agents for comfort) and instead rely upon new technology and communications networks to know everything they need to know. They bring their laptops to job interviews and they wow the owners of Super Clubs with all-singing, all-dancing Powerpoint presentations.

Some of this is, of course, hokum. And if *all* modern coaching was about was being able to create a few slides on Powerpoint then guys like Mourinho, Benitez and Wenger would have been quickly forgotten about; their names permanently struck off the short-lists which come about every year when the managerial merry-go-round starts up again. Mourinho might have described Arsene Wenger as a "specialist in failure", but what these guys are is specialist coaches, *career* coaches. And the proof of the pudding is in the eating. They have been successful. And players, who might once have been suspicious of being led by a man like Mourinho who'd never played the game at the highest level, who called Rio Ave the highlight of his playing career – *he doesn't understand the pressures, he doesn't know what it's like* - began to trust their own careers to guys like him. They saw that the coaching methods of men like Mourinho and Wenger brought success and trophies, and maybe even more important than that, through properly thought-out eating plans and specialist training programmes, extended careers (which meant they could get paid for longer).

The Secret Footballer, whose noteworthy columns in *The Guardian* seemed to sum up the general feelings of elite level footballers plying their trade in England, wrote: "The rise of managers such as Arsene Wenger, Jose Mourinho, Andre Villas-Boas and Brendan Rodgers has (…) won over the players who once believed that the only manager worth signing for was the one who had a few medals tucked away from his playing days."

And whilst we might disagree with him on Brendan Rodgers, and, to a lesser extent Andre Villas-Boas, the Mourinho-lite figure who turned out to taste nothing like the real thing, players have generally accepted that the specialist, career coach is here to stay. They've bought in to the fact they *need* specialist coaches and not just guys who can still strut their stuff in the Friday five-a-sides.

An overnight sensation twenty years in the making

When Jose Mourinho first announced himself to the football world early in the millennium, many commentators asked where on earth he'd come from, where he'd been hiding, and whether he was simply going to prove a flashy, touchline-skipping flash-in-the-pan; a millennium bug who we'd have all forgotten about by 2010. But Jose wasn't a flash-in-the-pan.

In Harry Harris' exhaustive biography of Mourinho, *Jose: Return of the King*, he quoted Andy Roxburgh, UEFA's technical director. "'He's an overnight sensation who is twenty years in the making,' says Roxburgh (…) Roxburgh has been acquainted with Mourinho all that time. It was through Roxburgh that

Mourinho acquired his first coaching badge, when he attended a Scottish Football Association course in Largs."

If coaching is a trade, Mourinho learnt it from the ground up. Right from the off he knew his limitations as a football player. He was under no illusions as to his own qualities and he knew he was more skilled in observing the game and making judgements about it than he was out on the field. Encouraged by his father, Jose Manuel Mourinho Felix, who had been capped by the Portuguese national team (in 1972, as a goalkeeper), and who then went on to coach Rio Ave to three second division titles and a cup win, Jose spent a lot of time in and around the training pitch, acquiring knowledge and developing a philosophy about the game. Even when Jose Mourinho was still registered as a player, he was helping his father organise training sessions and studying the tactical side of the game. He augmented his practical experience with a formal qualification: he studied sports science at the Technical University of Lisbon and also attended coaching courses in Britain.

Eventually Mourinho was realistic enough to knock playing the game on the head. But while his dreams of making it as a player had been shattered, he found he could dream bigger as a coach. He sought to redefine the role of coach in football by mixing coaching theory with motivational and psychological techniques. It was a grand ambition, and one which might not have come to fruition were it not for a few happy circumstances.

By the late 1980s the young Jose Mourinho had still not made the impact on the game which he'd hoped he might. His career to date was a peripatetic one: he gained valuable experience working with a number of youth teams, he worked as a scout for his father, and he also worked as a PE teacher in Lisbon. And it was in the Portuguese capital that Mourinho experienced his lucky break in the early 1990s, when he encountered the man who would become his second mentor. When Jose met Sir Bobby Robson,

Robson was manager of Sporting Lisbon. The Geordie required an interpreter and Jose jumped at the chance. His skills as a linguist were just another string to his bow. Robson came to trust the young Portuguese implicitly, and came to respect his views on football, too. When Robson moved to Porto in 1993, he took Mourinho with him. Same again when Robson got the job at Barcelona. His role as one of Robson's inner-circle saw him get involved more and more with the football side of things, but Barcelona fans would still, sneeringly, refer to him as the interpreter, or the translator.

Robson eventually moved on from Barcelona, but this time Mourinho didn't follow his mentor. He'd become an important part of the Barcelona back-room team and when Robson's replacement came in, he was kept on. Robson's replacement was the bullish Dutchman, Louis van Gaal. Van Gaal had himself worked as a PE teacher, and though he'd enjoyed a more distinguished playing career than Jose had, he was still no Johan Cruyff. Van Gaal saw something of himself in Mourinho, and took him under his wing, becoming Mourinho's third and final mentor. He offered the Portuguese the benefit of his insight and he helped Mourinho gain more practical experience: he allowed Jose to lead training sessions and even put him in charge of the first team in minor cup matches. He charged Jose with compiling detailed scouting reports on Barcelona's forthcoming opponents and these would then be presented to the players. This was a role in which Mourinho would later employ Andre Villas-Boas at Porto and Chelsea, before Villas-Boas too made the step-up to become a coach in his own right.

Mourinho's was a holistic education. He was involved in almost every aspect of the club and he was always learning. Van Gaal eventually trusted him enough to make him his assistant manager. For the outsider looking in, it looked like some promotion for the young Portuguese interpreter, but behind the scenes they'd seen his drive and attention to detail first-hand and they knew this was an upwardly-mobile young man and one whose knowledge of football was, despite his poor playing career, first rate.

What Mourinho had really lacked as a player was pace, but now his career was going places fast. Although he'd only recently been appointed assistant manager he was desperate for a chance to land the top job. But to get there, he first took a sideways-step - maybe even a step down. In 2000, he left Barcelona to become assistant manager again, this time at Benfica, under Jupp Heynckes. Proud as their history was, and though they'd at this time won more European Cups than Barcelona, Benfica didn't sit at the same European top table as the Catalan giants any more: indeed, in the early years of the millennium the Eagles were in serious financial trouble. Some of the players weren't being paid; the former Liverpool and Arsenal midfielder Michael Thomas amongst them. They hadn't won the league in seven years, which was almost unheard of given their standing in Portuguese football, and indeed, they seemed to be dropping further and further behind traditional rivals Porto and Sporting.

Van Gaal begged Mourinho not to go: "No, don't go. Tell Benfica if they want a first-team coach you will go; if they want an assistant you will stay."

But as it turned out, Mourinho didn't have to wait long until his ambitions to be *the* number one were satisfied. Just four weeks into the Primera Liga season, Heynckes left the Lisbon club by mutual agreement. He'd incurred the wrath of Benfica fans by releasing their favourite, and the club's captain Joao Pinto. Pinto then went and spoiled things even more by signing for Benfica's rivals Sporting. Though Heynckes had tried to argue that Benfica were in financial disarray and had to cut their cloth accordingly – and that included getting Pinto's hefty salary off the books – the German coach had also brought in a number of new players on big wages of their own, including the famously 'committed' Pierre van Hooijdonk. And then, in the opening game of the season, they meekly lost a 'Classico' against Porto 2-0. They then lost their first European tie of the season. Heynckes quit, however, following a win. But it had nearly been a defeat, and a shocking one: lowly Estrela da Amadora had almost pulled off a famous win at the Stadium of Light, and would have done, if not for two late, late goals by Van Hooijdonk. Before those goals though, the atmosphere in the stadium had turned decidedly poisonous. On the terraces, there was open revolt against the Heynckes regime; his every appearance on the touchline marked with whistles and cat-calls. In a post-match interview, the German snapped: "I can't take this club anymore. If they want me gone, I'll leave tomorrow."

His 37-year-old assistant, Jose Mourinho stepped up to the plate.

Mourinho didn't exactly encounter a dream start in his dream job. His first game as manager ended in defeat, 1-0 at Boavista, and in his first home game as a manager, his new charges threw away the lead in the last minute against Braga, drawing 2-2. By the end of his first month, Benfica sat in seventh place in the table. It was early doors, but they were already a full nine points behind leaders Porto. That would take some clawing back.

Benfica's problems on the road continued into the next month, with a chastening 3-0 defeat at Maritimo, but that was the moment Mourinho took them on an upward curve. By December they were back on track. A 3-0 derby triumph over Sporting was a major highlight. After it, Mourinho for the first time used the media to send a message, testing the Benfica President, Vilarinho's loyalty. In a post-match interview, he called upon Benfica to extend his contract as well as that of his assistant as a 'demonstration of faith'. "We thought that the only way to end speculation and the constant threat of being sacked in the event of a bad result...was renewing our contracts for another season, he said."

However President Vilarinho called his bluff and Mourinho's proposal was not met. Mourinho and his assistant called a further press conference and this time they announced they would be leaving Benfica. "He (President Vilarinho) thought it was better not to accept our request. We understood that decision showed a lack of trust in our work, and that we should offer our resignation..."

Mourinho parted ways with Benfica on 5th December 2000. He'd been manager of the club for just nine matches. In England, Mourinho has often been compared with Brian Clough, and this abrupt departure almost reached Clough-at-Leeds-United levels, though not quite – Clough only managed Leeds for six games.

It was a disaster for Mourinho. For the soon-to-be 38-year-old, it was debatable whether he'd ever get the chance to manage a top club again. Of course we now know what we know, and Mourinho's spell at Benfica has proved merely a blip. The Portuguese has moved on to bigger and better things. And in fact it is Vilarinho for whom the parting of the ways has proved a disaster in the longer-term. In an interview much later, having watched Mourinho carry off a bevy of beautiful trophies year after year, the Benfica President rued his poor judgement and expressed his frustration at losing Mourinho: "Put me back then and I would do exactly the opposite: I would extend his contract. Only later I realised that one's personality and pride cannot be put before the interest of the institution we serve."

The institution Mourinho next served was unfashionable Uniao de Leiria. It had taken him six months to land a new job but this time he hit the ground running. At Leiria, Mourinho truly seemed to imprint his personality on the club, something he hadn't quite managed to do at the bigger Benfica. He made the team prickly; tough to beat. They went at teams quickly, on the counter. And in Derlei, the Brazilian striker who would later follow him to Porto (and score twice against Celtic as Porto secured the UEFA Cup in 2003) he found an outstanding finisher. In the winter months, Leiria consistently tabled higher than Porto, and the day before Mourinho's 39th birthday, they won again, this time to leapfrog Jose's former club Benfica, into third. It was some statement.

And in the end it turned out to be a parting-shot. Before the end of the month, Mourinho was head-hunted by one of the bigger Portuguese clubs his upstart Leiria were embarrassing: Porto. He replaced Octavio Machado in the hot-seat and immediately set about turning Porto into *Mourinho's* Porto. They would lose just two matches between then and the end of the season, and this run was good enough to ensure a third-place finish for the club. He promised next year would be better. He promised next year they would be champions.

And they were. This time they lost only two games in the entire season, and they finished 11 points clear of his former club Benfica. Revenge was sweet.

Mourinho's success in 2002-03 with Porto was based on everything he'd learned over twenty years in the game, watching and waiting for his opportunity. It was based on making the side firstly compact; tough to break down. It was based on inspiring the players into wanting to run through brick walls for him. As we shall discuss in another chapter, he brought in many players who had been rejected or left to rot in the reserves by other clubs (notably Maniche, from Benfica): these were players who, like him, bore a grudge, and were perfectly willing therefore, to buy into Mourinho's siege mentality. It was based on hard bloody graft.

When the players returned to training before the 2002-03 season, they realised just how hard that graft would be, as Mourinho applied the lessons he'd learned as a sports scientist and PE teacher to make his players fitter than any at their competitors. Not only that, but Mourinho also "put detailed reports of the team training on the club website," said Wikipedia.

"The reports were filled with formal vocabulary, as, for instance, he referred to a 20 km jog as an extended aerobic exercise. While they attracted some scorn for the pretentiousness, others praised the innovation and the application of a more scientific approach to the training methods practised in Portugal.

"One of the key aspects in Mourinho-era Porto was (…) the pressuring play, which started at the offensive line, dubbed '*pressao alta*' ('high pressure'). The physical and combative abilities of the teams' defenders and midfielders allowed Porto to apply pressure from the offensive lines and forced opponents either to concede the ball or try longer, uncertain passes."

The human science

Jose Mourinho made players like Maniche feel wanted again, and that made players like Maniche play out of their skin for him because they were grateful. A simple psychological trick, sure; but one which Mourinho *knew* would work based on his psychological insight and his experiences of the culture of dressing-rooms. (Claudio Ranieri last year pulled off something similar when leading his unfancied team of 'rejects' to the unlikeliest of Premier League titles.)

Mourinho, as Mike Carson wrote in *The Manager* has a "profound understanding of people. 'I have to say we are speaking about human beings and human sciences. So is football a sports science? I think it is probably a human science and not a sports science.'"

He makes his players feel that they are all in it together. He treats them respectfully, as equals. And this works both ways: there is no imbalance even in the most talented, *galactico*-strewn dressing-room, despite Mourinho's never having really *made it* as a footballer.

"One senses there is no question of his feeling less talented or somehow awed by genius," wrote Carson. "Logically, why would a man of his track record and ability have a problem striking a healthy balanced relationship with talented footballers? And nor does he see himself as in any way superior. They are professionals together: his role is to lead; theirs to play."

They are professionals together, and each side trusts the other to do the job to the best of their ability. The issue of trust: it goes right to the heart of what makes a good manager. As the Secret Footballer would have it: "The best managers gain the absolute trust of their players, put you on your toes whenever they set foot in the room, and have a playing philosophy that is greeted with enthusiasm and carried on to the pitch with spirit and belief. Above all, though, a manager must have the respect of everybody at the club."

Respect and trust then, but not at the expense of friendship and camaraderie. Carson noted: "It is a commonly held belief in many cultures that friendship precludes effective leadership. But closeness to the players has been a defining characteristic for Mourinho. 'Of course, many people say we can't be friends with the players. I say exactly the opposite. If you are *not* friends with the players you do not reach the maximum potential of that group. You have to be friends with them, but they have to understand that between friends the answer is never the answer they are expecting, or the answer they want to hear.'

"The friendship approach involves regarding the players as peer colleagues – people who do a job every bit as important as yours. Mourinho gives an example of a symbolic action that betrays very clearly the value a manager really attaches to his players': the manager does not turn left into business class, upon boarding a plane, leaving his charges to turn right, into coach. They travel together. "'If I go in business it's because they go.'"

The Secret Footballer gave us further insight into how these 'symbolic actions' work. This is one story which did the rounds on the Premier League grapevine: "A friend who played for Chelsea under Mourinho told me that on a pre-season tour of America, the squad had been booked to do a photo shoot for their sponsor, Samsung. Upon hearing that Samsung hadn't provided any riders for the players, Mourinho promptly instructed his team to get back on the bus. After a lot of panicking, presumably by Samsung's PR department, it was agreed that a box packed full of electrical products would be waiting for each player upon their return to England. I have no idea whether that story is true but that's what this particular player told me and he has no reason to lie. I like the cut of Mourinho's jib anyway, and if a manager did that for me, setting aside the freebies for a moment, I would instantly feel that we were all in it together and that he had my back. I would want to play for that man and do well for him."

"The 'Mourinho Method'," wrote Harry Harris, "is based on being up close and personal with the players, forging relationships, which often linger beyond their time together at a club. (…) His former players reveal that constant attention: persistently calling their mobiles, sending texts, wanting to know how they slept, making sure they are happy, whether they are eating correctly. Even the girlfriends and wives are under the Mourinho spell as important conduits for his mission to know the ins and outs of his players, so they, too, are made to feel part of his 'team'. Mourinho's mission is to motivate his players to give their all."

Indeed, Mourinho's close contact with his players is cradle-to-grave. Not only does he stay in touch with most of them after their day-to-day working relationship has ended – those text messages; Mourinho must have very dextrous thumbs – he also makes contact with the incumbent players at a new club before he has *officially* started work in order to assure them they will still be loved as long as they play for him.

"Before Mourinho starts a new job," wrote Harris, "he sends an open letter to the players. The first time he did it was at FC Porto in January 2002. Back then it was written on old-fashioned paper but times move on." Now the message comes via email, on phone or tablet. But "the basic instructions have not significantly altered in more than a decade of management. An outline of his belief that football is a collective; that all the individual's personal ambitions be put aside for the team mission to flourish. He promises to be fair but reminds the players that every decision he takes will be in the best interest of the club and the team. If they fully commit to his way of working, he'll devote himself totally to improving them and he prides himself on leaving a club with the players much improved than when he joined them."

But securing freebies and the best seats on the plane for his players; regular texts, emails and phone calls of reassurance and encouragement are only the start of Mourinho's psychological approach. Carson wrote: "The blend of individual and team motivation and behaviours is at the heart of what Mourinho does best."

Mourinho: "focuses on personal motivation and passion, reasoning that a motivated side is a stable side: 'To lead a side you must motivate it, and to motivate you must be yourself motivated. I motivate people with my own motivation. If you are fully motivated, if you show them that, if you make them feel that you have that, they will do well.'"

Mourinho motivates by setting an example, but he also does so through confrontation. "When Mourinho arrived in England in 2004," wrote Carson, "everything came together in one huge wave of opportunity: 'Chelsea was a moment in my career where the expectations were in the right moment for myself, and I think they were in the right moment for that group of players, and I think we met each other in the right moment in our careers. I was coming from Porto – European champion and so on – but English culture demands more. It demands you are successful here. Not there, here! This is the country of football. OK, you won the Champions League. You can have it. But come in and do it here now.'" Same with the players. "'The guys desperately needed to make the jump from potential to real, and I think they needed the kind of leader I was. I called it confrontational leadership: confrontation not just inside, but also outside. We make a confrontation between us and the others – this sports confrontation of which one is the best, which one is going to win…'"

His motivation techniques varied from player to player, and was particularly successful with Frank Lampard, who was outstanding under Mourinho at Chelsea. Mike Carson wrote: "'I don't remember exactly the words, but I remember saying clearly to Frank Lampard, 'You are one of the best players in the world, but nobody knows.' In one of the seasons Frank was a finalist in what is now the Ballon d'Or, and I think he didn't win because he was not a European champion. Between 2004 and 2007 he became for sure one of the best players in the world. So we motivate people also with individual challenges, and for him that was a challenge we put there and he understood and he was ready for it. It was a brilliant phase. I learned so much from them and I think they learned a lot with me too. If Frank's 2012 Champions League had come before, he would have been voted the best. Chelsea were stronger in 2004 and 2008 – but that is the magic of football.'"

Later, at Inter, Mourinho faced a different set of challenges: "When Mourinho arrived at Inter from Chelsea, he inherited a fascinating situation that could have spiralled downwards," said Carson. "'When I arrived at Inter I had I think 14 players who were more than 32 years old. I had a team with 75 per cent of the guys in the last years of their careers, and with a history of frustration in European competition. This wasn't just about not winning the Champions League (…) it was a story of last 16 and out. At the same time I had a team that was dominant in Italian football, so a team that had three or four consecutive titles in Italian football but nothing else.'

"'My job was to try and create a team that was able to win the Champions League, but they had to understand that to make a team strong enough to win the Champions League (…) you have to be very strong in the other 47 matches. So the best way to motivate a team to win the Champions League was to keep winning domestic competitions.'"

Zlatan Ibrahimovic worked under Mourinho at Inter in 2008-09 before being transferred to Barcelona. In his autobiography *I Am Zlatan Ibrahimovic* he wrote of Mourinho's motivational techniques: "He worked us twice as hard as the rest to get us ready. Lives and breathes football 24/7. I've never met a manager with that kind of knowledge about opposing sides. It was everything, right down to the third-choice goalkeeper's shoe size. He builds us up before matches. It was like theatre, a psychological game."

Like theatre. And Mourinho even made use of props. " 'Go out there like hungry lions, like warriors,'" observed Zlatan. " 'In the first battle you'll be like this - ' – he pounded his fist against his open hand. 'And in the second battle - ' he gave the flip chart a kick and sent it flying across the room. The adrenaline pumped inside us and we went out like rabid animals. (…) I felt increasingly that this guy gives everything for the team, so I want to give everything for him."

Of course, Zlatan would be Mourinho's second signing when the Portuguese was awarded the manager's position at Manchester United. Over Mourinho had kept in constant touch with the Swedish striker, always reassuring him, making sure he was happy even though the two were no longer together. That paid off when Zlatan turned his back on the potential easy ride of a swansong season or two in America, or China, and instead headed to Manchester, for a challenging new chapter of his career.

However, there are signs that during Mourinho's last two postings – Real Madrid and Chelsea – the players have been maybe a little less than enamoured with his methods. Certainly in both cases the Portuguese was accused of the cardinal sin of losing the dressing-room. And whilst this wasn't a direct consequence of his text-pesting ways – no, at Madrid, the prime cause of this was his desire to set the players up against their Barcelona counterparts, creating rivalries and friction, something which was eventually seen by those same players as detrimental to the national team; and at Chelsea Mourinho's main fault as far as the players were concerned was his shameful treatment of the popular Eva Carneiro – but it didn't exactly help. This was a new generation of players, and Mourinho was further away from them in age than he had been with the boys at Porto, Chelsea, and Inter. The new generation had different drivers, new ways of communicating, new goals. Perhaps they were no longer overly keen on being molly-coddled by their bosses. Perhaps the Mourinho Method was starting to become old hat.

If you are not in your late teens and early twenties, for a moment imagine that you are, and then read the following from Harry Harris's *Return of the King* on Jose's time at Madrid: "Several of his players cared more about their public appearance than about winning trophies, according to Mourinho, who, after three years in charge at the Santiago Bernabeu, was not impressed by their attitude: 'Lots of times at Real Madrid, the players would be queueing in front of the mirror before the game while the referee waited for them in the tunnel, but that's how society is now. Young people care a lot about this: they are twenty-something and I am fifty-one and if I want to work with kids I have to understand their world. How can I stop my players on the bus doing, er, what do you call?... Twitters and these things? (…)So I have to adapt to the moment. I'm a manager since 2000 so I'm in my second generation of players. What I feel is that, before, players were trying to make money during their career, be rich at the end of their career. But in this moment, the people who surround them try to make them rich before they start their career. (…) So we are working hard to give the best orientation to young players, to follow examples of guys from the past – the Lampards, the Terrys – who were always fanatical for victories."

Though he at least recognises times have moved on, there is something faintly embarrassing about Mourinho's statement. His reference to 'Twitters' makes him sound like some kind of old fuddy-duddy: your daft great uncle who pretends he doesn't know what all the fuss is about and gets the names of all the new technologies wrong on purpose. I mean, what will Mourinho make of Jesse Lingard, for example? Mourinho will be managing the Warrington-born youngster at United next season, trying to find out what motivates him; makes him tick. Possibly the most famous thing Lingard has done at United is scoring the winner in the 2016 FA Cup Final. Second, third and fourth on that list are all extra-curricular: they occur outwith his playing remit. This is Lingard of the social media *meme*, the dab-dance (his ridiculous goal celebration). This is Lingard who, when the United team-bus was attacked by West Ham fans before the final match at the Boleyn

Ground, and along with the rest of the squad was made to lie on the floor for his own safety, instead seemed more concerned with making a video of himself smirking and laughing and yelling out, for some reason, the word: *squaaaaaaadddd*. This in a United squad who, as a whole, chose to ignore Louis van Gaal's regular email bulletins prior to and after matches, analysing their performances and suggesting where they could improve. According to one mole in the United squad Van Gaal got wise to the players ignoring his missives and had the United IT staff monitor how long the emails were open in order that he could be sure they'd been read and digested; so the players simply decided they would all leave their emails open *so it would look as though they'd been read.*

The Mourinho Method – as well as the methods of his former mentor Van Gaal might have worked on the first-generation players (Zlatan Ibrahimovic is one example) but it remains to be seen whether they will be embraced by the new young starlets.

What is clear is that once the cracks start to show, things only get worse for Mourinho and his dressing-rooms. Here are two examples from his time at Madrid which illustrate the attitudes of players. This, from Harry Harris: "Newspapers reported an alleged falling-out between Mourinho and two of the *galacticos*: Iker Casillas and Sergio Ramos, globally revered goalkeeper and defender, respectively. After a defeat to Barcelona, stories appeared that Ramos had sniped at Mourinho: 'Because you've never been a player, you don't know that that sometimes happens.' It was suggested that Mourinho and Ronaldo barely spoke to each other at the end of his time in Spain.'"

And this from Andrew Murray's article in August 2016's *FourFourTwo* magazine: "Mourinho demands unswerving loyalty from his players. If he doesn't feel it, paranoia sets in. At Real Madrid, he became convinced that there was a mole in the dressing room who was leaking both team line-ups and tactics to the press. (…) Mourinho believed the mole to be goalkeeper Iker Casillas, whose wife Sara Carbonero is a high-profile TV presenter. By the end of Mourinho's three year Real Madrid spell, his relationship with Spain's World Cup-winning captain had irrevocably broken down."

They all hate us, we don't care

Jose Mourinho's other major motivational tool is of course the siege mentality he inspires within his clubs. Almost literally, he creates a fortress. This from Andrew Murray in August 2016's *FourFourTwo* magazine: "Part of Mourinho's methodology is to create a mystique around his club, the theory – learned under Professor Manuel Sergio while at university in Lisbon in the mid-1980s – being that the less the opposition knows, then the better your chances of winning. 'He changed a lot of things at Inter,' says former Nerazzuri left-back Maxwell, 'especially at our training ground. He wanted more privacy for us to work.'"

From behind the crenelated walls of this fortress, Mourinho sends out sling-shots; sees if he can hit anything. He goes out of his way to set up antagonisms, enemies, nemeses from outwith the club, be they the press, a rival team, or a football association.

Apart from Real Madrid who are *the* establishment club in Spain - by royal approval - Mourinho has always worked at clubs at which he can play up their 'outsider' status in order to bring about a siege mentality amongst his players and staff. That's not to say he didn't try to play the 'outsider' card at Real Madrid too, with his paranoid rantings about the authorities wanting Barcelona rather than them to win. Just that at other clubs it at least sounded half-feasible. At Porto, domestically, his fight was with Benfica, traditionally the bigger club; the *capital* club, and not outpost second city Oporto, and in Europe it was with those teams who usually won. At Chelsea, he conveniently forgot the uplift of Abramovich's money and made it about challenging the historical powerhouses of the game, in particular Liverpool and Arsenal, but also United too. At Inter, he didn't have to look far: AC shared the same stadium. At United, he won't have far to look either, with Pep Guardiola rocking-up at City.

Ah, the beef with Guardiola (and Barcelona). As we've stated in earlier chapters, Mourinho has had many bitter rivals – Wenger and Benitez, to name but two – but by far his biggest rivalry is with Pep Guardiola (and Barcelona). The enmity goes back to 2008, when Frank Rijkaard was sacked. According to Sid Lowe in his book *Fear and Loathing in La Liga*, Mourinho's agent, Jorge Mendes, "badgered Beguiristain to interview him" and the Portuguese gave "a hugely impressive presentation explaining how he would turn the team around while also promising to play the Barca way."

Mourinho was steeped in the culture and history of the club. He had worked at Barcelona before – not just as translator, but as assistant manager to both Bobby Robson and Louis van Gaal. And now he had a highly successful track record as a bonafide number one at both Porto and Chelsea.

"He (Mourinho) had," wrote Lowe, "friends at the club. When he left in 2000, he promised to come back whenever he could and publicly declared himself a *cule* (a true Barca fanatic); this was the chance to prove it."

But, "if Mourinho was a *cule*, Guardiola was *the cule* (…) More than a player, Guardiola was a legend, a kind of ideologue: the metronome that kept the Dream Team ticking over."

"Ballboy, youth-teamer, Catalan and captain, Guardiola enjoyed enormous goodwill but he was only thirty-seven and hadn't coached a top-flight side," wrote

Lowe. "He was about to win the league with Barcelona B in his first season as coach, but it was Barcelona B. The first team needed authority, guarantees. Many thought this wasn't the time for half-measures; this was the time for Mourinho, not for a novice."

And yet, eventually they chose Pep over Jose. Mourinho was devastated (just as he was when Fergie chose Moyes as his successor at Manchester United rather than the Portuguese). But not for long. After that, he was simply very, very motivated to prove them wrong. And not just wrong. He wanted to rub their fucking noses in it.

And he did, with Internazionale, when an outstanding defensive display saw them beat holders Barcelona at Camp Nou in order to progress to the Champions League Final in 2010. Inter won the final, too, at Real Madrid's Bernabeu stadium, against Bayern Munich, and Mourinho won himself a contract at Real Madrid. There were conditions. Mourinho wanted more power than Madrid had granted to any coach in their history. They agreed. They didn't have a choice.

As Sid Lowe noted: "Power was ceded on one condition: that he won. Madrid had become desperate. This was a Faustian pact: (Madrid president Florentino) Perez had his concerns and was far from convinced that this was a good idea but he had gone four successive seasons without winning anything and the run could not continue, so he signed the only man who would definitely bring silverware – one season guidebook describing Mourinho as (...) a veritable guarantee of success."

United fans: does that sound familiar?

Anyway, at Madrid, Mourinho set about trying to plot Barcelona's downfall from close quarters. It wasn't just the fact he felt Barcelona had overlooked him for the job now that motivated him, it was the way the media fawned over the fabled Barcelona style. That really got to Jose, for whom winning was always the most important thing; the headline news. He hated the duality which had been set up: his Real Madrid as *the dark side,* and Pep's Barcelona as *the light.*

"There is, broadly speaking, a philosophical tension within football," wrote Chris Anderson and David Sally in *The Numbers Game.* "There are those who prefer to see the ball swept about the pitch in beautiful patterns, the game played by Barcelona and Arsenal and Spain, inflicting upon their opponents a death by a thousand cuts. And there are those, Jose Mourinho and Sam Allardyce and the rest, who prefer to see attacks carried out quickly, efficiently and devastatingly. The former is often associated with beauty and the latter with ruthlessness; but such terms are subjective judgements, distractions designed to make randomness easier to handle."

Anderson and Sally noted: "Jose Mourinho (…) would sacrifice glory to avoid the ignominy of defeat." His are the "teams who do not seem to want the ball, who are happy to spend most of their lives in the dark. There are the counter-attacking units of Jose Mourinho and Portugal, or the frenetic, swarming teams of Zdenek Zeman and Antonio Conte and Jurgen Klopp's Borussia Dortmund. It is possible, as in the latter cases, to be attractive without dominating possession. There is true beauty in the dark. And there is ugliness, too, the charge often levelled at teams like the Wimbledon of the 1980s, Graham Taylor's Watford or, more recently, Tony Pulis's Stoke. These are the *wilful* have nots: the sides who have made a virtue, an art form, out of not having the ball."

Mourinho's "go-to system is the 'low-block', where the back four retreats to the edge of the penalty box, the midfield only pressing around 60 yards from goal," wrote Andrew Murray. "Mourinho subscribes to the view that football is all about making the fewest errors and that 'whoever has the ball is more likely to make a mistake.'"

His teams rarely muck it up defensively, and Mourinho couldn't understand why others couldn't appreciate the true beauty of his 'dark' victory over Barcelona with Inter Milan and he began to think that the authorities, referees, and the media were punishing his teams whilst letting Barcelona off the hook because they were from *the light side*. His hatred poisoned the atmosphere and infected his players. El Classico games became battlegrounds, and if anything Jose and his men *played up* to their dark-side image just to piss everyone off.

Sometimes it worked; sometimes it didn't. And in the end, the Portuguese came over sounding like a broken record. After Barcelona beat Real Madrid to Champions League final in 2011, on a night on which both he and his captain Pepe received their marching orders, "he bemoaned the power that his rivals wielded in European football, effectively accusing UEFA of fixing it for Barcelona to reach the final. 'One day,' he said (…), 'I would like Josep Guardiola to win this competition properly.' Mourinho said he felt 'disgusted' to be working in football (…). It was an extraordinarily bitter, almost comical rant." (Sid Lowe)

And his players were getting sick of it; especially given the fact that half of the team they were instructed to hate, hate, hate, were their international comrades in the Spain team. Behind Mourinho's back, Barcelona and Real Madrid's Spanish players called a truce. Mourinho continued to wage war.

"Problems arise," wrote Andrew Murray in August 2016's *FourFourTwo* magazine, "when the players start to tire of the constant mental demands Jose places on them to overcome a perceived foe, from other teams or managers, to journalists or referees."

"'Mourinho tries to take the maximum from his players,' former Chelsea left-back Filipe Luis told *FFT*. 'I think that's one of the reasons he loses the dressing room sometimes. He asks so much of his players that some can't handle it for too long.'"

Mourinho has left both of his past two clubs under a cloud, leaving disgruntled dressing-rooms behind him. And if another way to understand and grade the Super Coaches – Mourinho, Guardiola and Ancelotti - is through evaluating the state of the teams they leave behind for their successors, you might instantly jump to the conclusion that the Portuguese does not fare nearly as well as Guardiola, who imprints a style upon the club which can be carried forward, and Ancelotti, who generally leaves every club still very well-liked. And it is true to some extent: Jose Mourinho tends to leave teams in an immediate pickle. (Mind you, with hindsight, so did Sir Alex Ferguson, and he was the best manager in Premier League history, bar none.) But Real Madrid haven't been too badly damaged by him, have they? With a team not totally different to the one he used, they have won two out of the last three European Cups. Chelsea too might have a season out of the Champions League limelight in 2016-17, due to Mourinho's terrible start to the season, but Antonio Conte has inherited a team which is most of the way there; certainly there aren't many critics who would dare predict that they would finish outside the top four again in 2017.

The dark side

Jose Mourinho's teams might be maligned for their 'negative' football; for choosing to sacrifice possession of the ball in order to keep their shape – that low-block – and lie in wait for a chance to perform a rope-a-dope counter-attack. And it is true; for a while, Mourinho's style has seemed a little outdated, especially when contrasted to Barcelona's seeming re-invention of the game.

But if the unlikely winners of the European Championships and Premier League (as well as the runners-up in the Champions League) in 2016 have taught us anything it is that the possession game has been found-out. Teams know how to play against it now. Possession-football is now the style which is becoming outmoded. After all, there is no permanently winning formula in football. It is a game which constantly updates itself.

"After a decade where Barcelona and Spain have introduced tiki-taka to the football world, the counter-attack is certainly back in vogue," wrote Andrew Murray. "Leicester, Portugal, and Atletico Madrid. After winning the Premier League title with Chelsea in May 2015, Mourinho said: "If you don't play counter-attack it's because you're stupid. Because counter-attack is a fantastic item of football. It's ammunition you have and use when you find your opponent unbalanced."

In his review of the European Championships in France for *The Guardian*, Barney Ronay wrote: "There were various trends on the pitch. Possession football continued its journey from winning style to outmoded combine harvester. Spain, Germany, Switzerland, England, Belgium, Hungary, Russia and Ukraine were all in the top 10 for pass completion rates. Between them they won 11 matches out of 33. Four of the quarter-finalists were among the 10 teams with the lowest percentage of possession overall. Want to win? Stay away from that ball."

Last season United fans could see for ourselves that our approach was all wrong, and yet Van Gaal, nothing if not stubborn, insisted on engaging in this "sterile domination, the endless recycling of possession, sweeping mandalas painted on the pitch to no end or purpose. Bayern Munich, under Louis van Gaal, were accused of the same thing. Possession for possession's sake, circulation football, an addiction to the light."

The same will surely not be said of *Mourinho's* Manchester United. And that is not necessarily a bad thing: remember, some of our most glorious performances in recent history have been counter-attacking displays – rapier-like breaks which rely upon the pace and power of our forwards. I'm thinking of the glory days of that Ronaldo-Rooney partnership, or even Rooney and Nani, against Arsenal.

And Mourinho's teams aren't *all* dark-side, just like Darth Vader isn't when Luke Skywalker removes his helmet at the end of *Return of the Jedi*. As Danny Higginbotham said in *FourFourTwo* magazine, with Mourinho, it's a balance "of substance *and* style. When Chelsea won the league in 2014-15, they'd scored as many goals as Manchester City by January, playing some great football. And in the second half of that season, they ground out results, maintaining a lead that they had established through style. Football is a results business, he delivers both."

Not Arrogant, Just Better

In previous sections, I have described Jose Mourinho as motivated. I also quoted Mike Carson, who wrote that "a man of his track record and ability" has no problem "striking a healthy balanced relationship" with talented individuals. Indeed, his ego is more than a match for theirs. This is another way of approaching one of the key complaints about Mourinho's managerial style; that he is arrogant; that he takes too much of the glory for himself; that his own antics overshadow the actions of the players. To some extent this is true: when Mourinho's teams win, Mourinho wins, but when they lose, Mourinho does not often lose. They are not necessarily always in it together, and often, despite his throwing winner's medals into the crowd or not wholly joining in on post-match celebrations, his victories have been self-serving, have moved him on to bigger and better clubs and jobs.

As noted by Nick Miller in *The Guardian's 'The Fiver*' on 9th August 2016: "when he (Mourinho) talks about the titles that the teams he's managed have won, he talks in the first person: "I am European champion" or "I won the league in four countries", but curiously enough he rarely says: "I was 16th in the league after I lost nine from 16 games last season and I got sacked."

But there is more to it than that.

He *needs* to be arrogant in order for his methods to work, for in essence, the teams he sends out, the club he represents, soon come to take on his persona, his identity – for good and bad. As Alex Hess noted in his piece on Jose Mourinho in *FourFourTwo*'s 50 Best Football Managers in the World 2016: "Just as it was his singular personality that drove Chelsea to a dominant league title a year earlier, so his temperament seemed to be the cause and catalyst of last year's mad tailspin. When Roman Abramovich finally sent him packing in December, Stamford Bridge reduced to scorched earth, it seemed less an act of ruthlessness and more one of festive goodwill."

He stands for his clubs, in both senses of the word. Harry Harris quoted Gary Neville on Sky Sports after Chelsea beat Manchester City in a (yet another) title showdown two years ago: "Mourinho's master class of tactics was universally applauded. Sky Sports expert Gary Neville praised the way Mourinho set up his team to nullify the threat of the title favourites and said that even his demeanour on the touchline had an impact on the result. 'He doesn't mind us praising him, does Jose Mourinho. He loves the attention of big matches. You saw him tonight and he was like the conductor of the orchestra. He walks out at the start of the match and sits on the bench before his team have even come out. He comes alive on big-match days and that's what the best managers do.'"

Arrogance is a vital function of Jose Mourinho's identity and it permeates the clubs he manages and becomes *their* identity too. And as the Secret Footballer noted: "The most successful clubs are the ones that have a clear identity, a direction from which they rarely stray. We call it 'a philosophy.'"

Mind you, maybe you've heard that word – philosophy - too many times from Louis van Gaal.

But don't forget, Jose Mourinho is arrogant with *just cause*. He is a special one, even if you don't like him. His medals haul speaks to that.

And, as Alex Hess observed: "Mourinho doesn't just bring trophies, he brings an aura of swaggering supremacy that spreads through an entire club. He doesn't just win leagues, he flicks Vs at everyone else on the way. And that, more than youthful exuberance or buccaneering wing-play, is the United Way."

At United we like them arrogant don't forget; with their collars turned up and their chests puffed out. Remember that old banner: *Not Arrogant, Just Better…* It would be nice to see it back, wouldn't it?

4

"A UNITED MANAGER WOULDN'T DO THAT." SIR BOBBY CHARLTON CAN MANCHESTER UNITED TOLERATE THE DARK SIDE OF JOSE MOURINHO?

When he first arrived at Chelsea in 2004 Jose Mourinho wanted things done by the book. Literally. He took it upon himself to issue each and every one of his new playing staff with an all-new staff handbook; a code of conduct which outlined the penalties and fines which would be levied if the players stepped out of line. Lateness, partying, drinking, smoking, and even snubbing the press were now no-nos.

It was all set down in black and white, so there was no confusion. And you might say some of the rules were draconian, even rather condescending to professional athletes. But given the make-up of Chelsea's squad and what they'd already been 'up to', it was actually a pretty prescient move on the part of the new Blues supremo. (In 2001, a motley crew containing John Terry – whose career rap-sheet would also include sleeping with his team-mate's wife, assault and affray, and, more seriously, racism; Eidur Gudjohnsen – drink-driving; Frank Lampard – being a public schoolboy; and Jody Morris – numerous night-club brawls from London to Leeds – had made up the infamous Chelsea Four, who spent the day after the 9/11 attacks on the World Trade Centre getting pissed in a Heathrow Airport bar and openly insulting the grieving Americans who were also *in situ*, waiting for flights back home.)

As Mourinho's biographer Harry Harris understood: "At a time when the image of footballers off the field is under scrutiny, Mourinho has devised a clause to cover behaviour away from the club." Mourinho wanted every base covered.

One of the most unusual clauses regarded snacking. Players were expected to forgo even the tastiest morsels from the club's official snacking partners in order that they were lean, mean, fighting machines where it counted – on the pitch.

One of the most common-or-garden clauses regarded behaviour in and amongst other club officials and staff. Harry Harris noted: "The rulebook says, 'Player misconduct towards technical staff, medical staff, kit staff and press staff will not be tolerated.'"

Let's just let that one percolate; breathe a moment, like the good bottle of Portuguese red Jose might offer to, say, Sir Alex Ferguson during a civilised post-match debrief between two opposing, but friendly, managers.

Bad employee of the month

And move on to an entirely unrelated subject. Eleven years later, on 8th August 2015, Jose Mourinho's Chelsea opened the defence of their Premier League crown with a home tie against Swansea City. During that eleven years Mourinho had been away, in Italy, and in Spain, but he was back at his spiritual 'home' now, and was commencing his third season at the helm. He was, as he'd told us all, 'the Happy One'.

Only, he wasn't, not any more. Jose wasn't happy with Chelsea's close-season transfer business. He felt the club was resting on its laurels, allowing their rivals – principally the two Manchester clubs – to catch up with them. Frankly, he had a cob-on the size of Chelsea's fancy Cobham training facility.

A nice easy season-opener should have changed all that. Chelsea had battered Swansea the previous year with striker Diego Costa bagging a hat-trick. A repeat performance would do nicely, thank you very much. Only, it didn't quite work out like that. Despite the fact that Oscar's free-kick gave Chelsea the lead, Swansea – the Premier League's self-styled nice-guys – soon clawed themselves back into the game. Debutant Andre Ayew netted the equaliser within six minutes of Oscar's strike; a subtle reminder Mourinho had no debutants of his own to field in the starting line-up that day.

But Swansea's parity was even more brief than Chelsea's lead had been. Within 90 seconds Federico Fernandez put through his own net and Blue was the colour all over again.

And that would have been that for the old Chelsea - Mourinho's 2004-05, or 2005-06 vintages; even for his Blues side which had cruised to the championship the previous year. They would have clung on to win. But not now. Mourinho's 2015-16 vintage were showing signs of a rare fragility; a rare uncertainty at the back. Swansea were threatening and the Blues just couldn't kill off the game.

Seven minutes into the second half came the defining moment of the match, or what we *thought* was the defining moment of the match; the moment *Mourinho* told us was the defining one: Chelsea 'keeper Thibaut Courtois saw red for hauling down Swansea striker Bafetimi Gomis, who was through on goal. And finally Mourinho could call upon a new signing, but not one of the calibre he wanted, and not in the circumstances he wanted. Asmir Begovic had been bought from Stoke City to provide competition for Courtois; to keep the young Belgian on his toes. It was thought he'd get the occasional run-out in the early rounds of the League Cup. That type of thing. And yet here he was, stepping into the breach in the first Premier League game of the season. He was unable to stop Gomis's penalty. Swansea were level, and Chelsea would have to find a winner with only ten men on the field.

In the manager's technical area on the touchline, Mourinho was apoplectic; flapping his arms around in disgust. He spent the remaining half-hour pacing back and forth within the white lines of the technical area like a caged tiger, bristling with rage. He knew the TV cameras would be trained on him they always were; almost to the point of ignoring what was going on on the pitch. The real drama here was not whether Swansea, who'd be playing with an extra man for over 30 minutes, managed to make the most of their advantage or whether Chelsea could claw themselves back into the lead: it was the rumbling volcano of Mourinho. Would he erupt?

"The phenomenal box-office appeal of the Premier League resides not merely in the quality of its football but in the guarantee of drama," wrote Richard Williams in *The Guardian*. "The technical area, its boundary marked out by a white line not less than a yard from the playing surface, symbolises a significant change in football over the past quarter-century. Taking over from the old dugout, it provides the stage for the figures who really dominate the narrative of this never-ending soap opera. Television directors began to train cameras on the dugouts, primed to capture a moment of high drama or low comedy, from

Ferguson tapping his watch to Wenger having trouble with his zip."

There'd been high drama in the Stamford Bridge technical area before. A year earlier, in October 2014 during a London derby between Chelsea and Arsenal, a decade of gibes and insults finally got to Arsene Wenger and – infamously – he encroached into Mourinho's technical area and gave the Portuguese a shove. Not a right-hook, not a WWE-style body-slam: a shove. Think Paolo Di Canio on Paul Alcock (not that Mourinho stumbled to the ground in instalments as the referee had). But the media had bigged it up like it was the rumble in the jungle.

Afterwards Wenger characterised the incident as "animated". "No problem," Mourinho retorted, adding: "A football pitch is a football pitch."

"But the point is that the technical area is not a football pitch, or part of it," wrote Richard Williams. "The pitch is where the game takes place, and it belongs to 22 players. The existence of a secondary stage only a yard away from the action invites managers to act as an extra member of their team, becoming more directly involved. Only a few years ago the idea of a top-tier manager getting involved in a physical confrontation with a rival manager or opposing players would have been unthinkable. But the insatiable appetite for drama and the invitation to make use of those few square yards of grass combine to offer too great a temptation to human nature's baser instincts."

Now all eyes were on Jose. Would he provide the audience with a moment even more definitive, even more dramatic than Courtois's sending-off? Would he give in to his temper, and to his "baser instincts"? Would he maybe make like Nigel Pearson, the Leicester City manager, who scuffled on the touchline with a Crystal Palace player, or like Alan Pardew, who when in charge at Newcastle, head-butted the Hull City man David Meyler?

"As long as the technical area remains a vital element of the £5bn soap opera there will be no change," wrote Williams. "And so, having virtually eliminated hooliganism from spectator areas, English football can expect to see more of it on the touchline."

On the field of play, Gomis scored again, but his strike was disallowed on a marginal offside call. Mourinho fumed. Then the Ecuadorian Jefferson Montero roasted Ivanovic (as he had all afternoon) and it took an excellent save from the substitute goalie Begovic to keep the scores level. Mourinho shook his head and waved his Chelsea players forward. They'd escaped that scare. Now they could go on and win it, ten men or no.

The Blues martialled their reserves. Began to go at Swansea, who wobbled. They might have had a man advantage but it had taken a supreme effort for them to get back into the game and they were visibly tiring now. Chelsea pushed them farther and farther back and it seemed less and less likely that the Swans would pull off another opening day shock at one of the Premier League's big boys (the previous campaign had started with the Welsh side humbling Manchester United 2-1 at Old Trafford, in Louis van Gaal's first league game in charge of the club).

The Chelsea of last season would have killed them off. But this wasn't the Chelsea of last season. Hazard tried to beat his man, and succeeded, but then stumbled. Passes were slightly over-hit, and possession lost. Swansea wasted time. Chelsea couldn't get any proper rhythm going; any momentum. Mourinho raged at every stoppage, every lost moment.

Then, with vital seconds ticking away, Hazard went down, apparently injured. The referee Michael Oliver waved Chelsea's medical staff onto the pitch – twice. Mourinho, who as the Belgian's manager probably knew better than most about Hazard's tendency to feign injury, tried to wave the medical staff back. Ignore Hazard! He'll soon be on his feet again! There's nothing wrong with him! We need to keep attacking; keep going at Swansea: we can't afford another delay.

But on they went, regardless, to treat the player. And finally Mourinho exploded. As the medical staff returned to the bench, he gave them both barrels. He screamed at them. But that was nothing out of the ordinary; he'd been yelling at the fourth official all afternoon. It was only later that we learned the full story and suddenly *this* was the defining moment, not just of the match, but of Mourinho's entire second spell at the Stamford Bridge club.

The game finished 2-2 and most of the immediate post-match analysis concentrated on the penalty and the sending-off. Mourinho was interviewed and sneered: "They (Swansea) didn't have chances against 11. The team was playing very, very well in the first half. In the second, in one minute, it was a penalty, red card and the goal - 2-2. If you have 10 men and are winning you can defend well and try to find a strategy but to play with 10 men and try to win the game is more difficult. I would say we were the best team with 11 players and with 10 we fought hard, some fighting at the limit of their condition."

But soon, the story of what had happened on the touchline, as Mourinho railed at his own medical staff, took centre stage. If the fact Mourinho's heated exchange with the medical staff on the touchline was in clear contravention of his own rules (check the rulebook Jose: you had it written) was bad enough, his supposed justification of it – that his medical staff did not "understand football" - was unacceptable, sexist, and immoral.

You see, although two of the club's medical team had been summoned onto the field by referee Michael Oliver, only one of them felt the full-force of Mourinho's anger. And whilst head physiotherapist Jon Fearn was largely left alone, the club doctor Eva Carneiro was left to face the brunt of it. It was alleged Jose called her a 'daughter of a whore' in Portuguese during that exchange on the touchline, and that would later form the basis of her complaint against Mourinho and the club. But it was the flippant sexism of his remark about Carneiro's not understanding football which was truly insidious.

He went further: as the *Manchester Evening News* reported even *two days after* the initial incident, "on August 10, Mourinho allegedly told Steve Atkins, head of communications and PR at Chelsea, that he did not want Dr Carneiro on the bench the next match, adding: 'She works in academy team or ladies team not with me'."

The whole sorry affair opened a can of worms. It went all the way to an employment tribunal; Carneiro alleging Mourinho sexually discriminated against her. A case was also brought against Chelsea FC.

The *Manchester Evening News* reported the written opening remarks of Mary O'Rourke QC, for Dr Carneiro, who submitted: "Not understanding the game is a common allegation put to women in the football world."

Mourinho might be Portuguese and he might have sworn at Carneiro in Portuguese, but mostly the language he used in addressing the club doctor was one of international, institutionalised, *accepted* sexism. As a male, in the overwhelmingly male-dominated arena of elite level football, he spoke from a position of power, and his words were cheap; lazy. They were bullying. (Carneiro had a hard enough job of it anyway; "Dr Carneiro claims she experienced a number of issues, including a lack of action by Chelsea following sexually explicit chanting at various away games - in particular at Manchester United and West Ham - and a lack of female changing facilities.")

Mourinho is an intelligent, well-educated man. He has a daughter; he should have known better. Mourinho is a human being. He should have known better.

"Ms O'Rourke said: 'This is a tale of two employees, one good (Dr Carneiro) and one bad (Mourinho). The bad employee forces the good employee out of the job of her dreams and the employer does nothing to stop it. The bad employee berates, sexually harassed and demoted the good employee for carrying out her professional duties, namely her health and safety duties as the first team doctor, pitchside.'"

Chelsea and Mourinho denied all of it. "The respondents claim Dr Carneiro was 'preoccupied with developing her profile' and associating herself with the first team in a way discouraged by the club for backroom employees."

Basically, they tried to smear her name and reputation. They might not have used the same explicit language as Mourinho had used on the touchline, but read between the lines and you get the gist: Carneiro is not the daughter of a whore but she is a publicity whore; she *might* be a different kind of whore, too.

As a character assassination it was brutal. Surely between them Chelsea and Mourinho had made it impossible to work in football again. And, unbelievably, it wasn't even the first time Mourinho had hounded a doctor out of the club. In 2005, during his first season at Stamford Bridge, shortly after Arjen Robben failed to recover from what was thought to be a short-term injury in time to participate in the
League Cup final and a last-16 Champions League tie with Barcelona. "Robben's injury," wrote Mourinho's biographer Harry Harris, "is linked with the surprise announcement that doctor Neil Frazer has quit after five years at Stamford Bridge. Frazer allegedly left following a string of clashes with Mourinho, who wanted Robben fit for the Carling Cup final."

Later Mourinho appointed "the doctor who guided Kelly Holmes to her double Olympic success to help

Chelsea win gold this season: Dr Bryan English from UK Athletics. English played a key role in getting Holmes fit to win both the 800m and 1500m in Athens and his record of getting athletes back to fitness quickly is the reason Mourinho has got him on board."

Eva Carneiro also came to Chelsea from an athletics background. The Gibraltar-born sports medicine specialist had been a rock at the Olympic Medical Institute, helping prepare British athletes for the 2008 games in Beijing. And then, in 2009 she was brought in to Chelsea's medical team by Andre Villas-Boas. In 2011 she was promoted to club doctor for first-team affairs and was a regular sight in the Chelsea dug-out, where, unfortunately, she was subjected to sexist chants by opposition fans. It was hardly an ideal working environment, but she stuck with it, much like the official Sian Massey-Ellis does, because it was her "dream job".

But after the Mourinho incident on 8th August, it became a nightmare. It dragged on and on. She was finally hounded into quitting her position over a month later, on 22nd September 2015. Away from fortress Stamford Bridge, where there was vitriol aplenty, public opinion was very much on her side, and reaching fever pitch in its condemnation of both Mourinho and Chelsea. Nevertheless, the out-of-touch FA saw fit to clear Mourinho of making discriminatory comments towards Carneiro at a hearing on 30th September.

Campaign group Women in Football said they were "appalled" at the decision. FA chairman Greg Dyke, and Heather Rabatts, the head of the FA's own inclusion advisory board, were highly critical.

Then, in October, the obvious happened: lawyers acting on behalf of Carneiro served notice of a claim of constructive dismissal against Chelsea Football Club. The hearing was scheduled for June 2016. Sam Wallace, the *Daily Telegraph's* chief football writer, "contrasted the speed with which Chelsea resolved issues with players and managers with the 'disgrace' of its seven-month delay over the proper treatment of Carneiro."

Of course, conspiracy theorists might posit the idea that Carneiro's day in court was timed specifically so that it would fall in the close-season, and not interfere with the important business of the Premier League. And some might take that one step further and suggest that maybe, just maybe, it was timed specifically for then in order that it could get swept tidily away under the carpet before the new season began; a new season which would see Mourinho at the helm of a new club; the biggest in English football: Manchester United FC. But that is all supposition. Just as Chelsea's claims Carneiro consorted too closely with the Blues' players is all supposition.

In the end the trial was over quickly; settled on confidential terms on the second day of the hearing. Chelsea did what they should have done ten months earlier and issued an unreserved apology for distress caused to Carneiro and her family. They said: "We wish to place on record that in running onto the pitch Dr Carneiro was following both the rules of the game and fulfilling her responsibility to the players as a doctor, putting their safety first."

Though the terms were confidential, experts thought the final settlement would have seen Carneiro receive around £5 million (legal documents submitted to her employment tribunal revealed she had previously rejected an offer by the club of £1.2 million to settle the claim). And of course the cynics and the bullies of the football community nodded sagely and said *ah yes, we knew she was always in it for the money.* Some in the media followed suit. *The Daily Mail*, true to type, reported that "Chelsea's former doctor Eva Carneiro was all smiles as she left her home in Surrey today just 24 hours after securing a rumoured £5million pay-off from the club over sexism allegations."

They were quick to talk-up her cushty new life, talking up her opulent home, car, and dental work: "The 42-year-old was spotted being driven away from her sprawling property in Oxshott, Surrey, in a white BMW and waved subtly to the camera before breaking out in a huge, gleaming smile." But rather less forthcoming with the salient information as to how she'd been forced into the uncomfortable situation in the first place. They wanted to talk about the material rather than the moral. They wanted to speak of her "huge pay-off". They wanted the sensationalism of the story: "The terms of the settlement will remain secret but yesterday the tribunal heard Chelsea offered £1.2 million to silence Ms Carneiro, who they said made 'scandalous' claims about working for manager Jose Mourinho. But she rejected the money – more than four times her annual salary – and the offer of her 'dream job' back."

Of course Carneiro had a nice car and a big house; she was a professional, in a good job. For the *Mail* to point to those things as somehow indication she was money-grabbing is disingenuous. As is their hint – the inverted commas are the clue - that it can't have been much of a dream job in the first place if she refused the chance to go back to it. *What, turn down Jose Mourinho? Turn down a working environment in which you are ritually and habitually subjected to abuse?* Surely not.

But your crusading *Mail* was there to ask the crucial questions after the (shady) deal had been "done in a back corridor of the court" outside the men's room: "when asked 'Why no apology from you Jose?' by *MailOnline* outside the court today he refused to comment and grinned as he was rushed away in a waiting car."

Mourinho had been due to give two days of evidence in front of the Croydon Court, starting that day.

Of course he was grinning now that he didn't have to. During that two day grilling, the Portuguese had been due to face "an embarrassing dossier of witness statements and documents - including texts and emails - being made public." Those "scandalous" claims about him again.

But it was the scandalous claims about Carneiro which *were* heard and reported widely. Ian Herbert of *The Independent* wrote: "Chelsea's barrister would have asked us to believe she was an individual 'hungry for fame.' That she had the temerity to sit behind Mourinho at matches to feature in the TV feed; asked a first team player to drench her in an ice bucket challenge; signed autographs, posed for photographs and asked for a substantial pay rise if she was to return to work having claimed she had been constructively dismissed.

"Well, a half-decent barrister would have cut much of that to ribbons. Such as the farce of suggesting that Carneiro purposefully selected a seat on the bench to seek the limelight rather than being within incidental camera range. The desperation of suggesting that to seek the involvement of a player in a charity initiative was in some way malign.

"Carneiro was nominated for that challenge by a player, Didier Drogba, and her lawyers may also have been ready to tell the court that she used the publicity generated by the opportunity to promote Macmillan Cancer.

"Since Chelsea are a club who have done much to put behind them their image as a less-than-pleasant outfit, what staggers most is that they were willing to humiliate Carneiro in their defence of a manager with whom they have long since parted company. But would it not have been beyond those at the top of Stamford Bridge to have pursued a case based around the particulars of Mourinho's alleged insult of Carneiro, and whether he was professionally entitled to demote her? What had Chelsea to lose by limiting themselves to a case around the salient facts? Losing in court and paying out a fraction of its colossal turnover?

"The real cost," argued Herbert, is not the £5 million which the *Mail* so latched on to, it will be the "young women who may follow Chelsea and Leeds looking at the way the clubs treat women and deciding to take their support elsewhere."

Manchester United had just made Jose Mourinho their new manager in the week the case was heard. For a Manchester United fan, it made for very uncomfortable viewing. The case drew a great many parallels with the Patrice Evra-Luis Suarez racism row. There was the club, in this case Chelsea, in that Liverpool, going on to blithely support their employee who'd so obviously done wrong: remember Kenny Dalglish ordering the Liverpool players to wear those embarrassing Suarez tees as they warmed up before a subsequent fixture? Remember how the lawyers tried to split hairs in the case, calling in the language experts in order to try and prove that what Suarez had spat into Evra's face, whilst also digging his fingernails into the United man's back, was not *wholly* racist, only a bit racist, or maybe just nasty... Or maybe even a term of fucking endearment.

As with the Evra-Suarez case, much of the case turned on the fine line of whether Mourinho screamed into a professional doctor's face "daughter of a whore" or "son of a bitch", which, it was claimed, would not be sexist. Academic experts in Portuguese swearing were called in to the London South Employment Tribunal in Croydon in order to give their views. I am an expert in English swearing but I have no academic qualifications in swearing to back that up. I do know, however, what is wrong and right – most people do. And just like Luis Suarez, Mourinho, and Chelsea, were wrong. Whichever way you cut it.

During the trial, the Chelsea barristers tried to impugn Carneiro by inferring she got too 'pally' with the playing staff. Well, that playing staff - who still counted amongst them one of the infamous Chelsea four as well as numerous other 'bad-boys' such as Diego Costa in their ranks – also seemed to know the difference between right and wrong. Whether they were standing up to be counted against the ingrained, institutionalised sexism within the game or whether they were simply standing *with* a person they felt was a member of the team, no matter that she wasn't playing-staff or even a male it's unclear. But what is clear is that after Mourinho broke his own rules and verbally attacked Eva Carneiro, the Chelsea players wouldn't have it. The precious bond, the us-against-them mentality which Mourinho fosters in his sides, was broken. They wouldn't win for him anymore. Chelsea endured one of the worst title defences in living memory: only Leeds United's in the first season of the Premier League, and Manchester United's under David Moyes could compare.

Jose Mourinho lost the dressing room, and eventually, his job.

That was the price he had to pay.

Ahem. Here endeth the sermon.

"Wherever the line is, Mourinho will either cross it, or jump up and down on it until it finally buckles of its own free will."

"The unseemly episode involving former Chelsea doctor Eva Carneiro," wrote Andrew Murray in August 2016's *FourFourTwo* magazine (not *that* Andrew Murray; the Scot might be outspoken on a number of issues which are not strictly tennis-related, but he didn't choose to wade in on the Mourinho question), "smacked of a diversionary tactic, intended to distract from an uninspiring 2-2 draw at home to Swansea, but blew up into a court case for constructive dismissal because Mourinho was too stubborn to apologise for criticising an employee for doing their job.'"

Such diversionary tactics are not new in football management. Sir Alex Ferguson, after all, was a past-master at drawing media and fan attention away from a poor performance from his team by creating a storm elsewhere. He'd question the fitness of the referee or he'd go on the offensive regarding a perceived slight from an opponent. Once he stooped as low as kicking a boot into the face of one of his own players. But he never tried anything as despicable as Jose Mourinho did with Eva Carneiro. His treatment of a club employee went much too far and even his own players – men who'd been willing to do or die for him in the past – deserted him during the aftermath.

It was the worst example of his belligerent behaviour making unwanted headlines, but it wasn't the only time he'd gone too far as we shall see. Over the years, Jose Mourinho has become infamous for a series of misdemeanours which have been at best questionable and at worst they have dragged the name of the club he manages through the mud. We're not just talking "Mourinho and Arsene Wenger's frequent attempts to out-pantomime each other via the medium of handshakes." (*FourFourTwo's* Andrew Murray). We're talking the kind of nonsense which Scott Patterson, writing for the *Republik of Mancunia* fanzine, characterised as "embarrassing, cringeworthy, and unacceptable. When looking at this behaviour (…) even the most biased United fan would struggle to claim Mourinho doesn't have huge flaws to his personality." This kind of low-rent behaviour prompted the honourable Sir Bobby Charlton - when asked whether Jose Mourinho was ever a serious candidate to take over from Sir Alex Ferguson at the first time of asking - to say: "A United manager wouldn't do that. Mourinho is a really good coach but that's as far as I would go really. He pontificates too much for my liking."

In that instance, Charlton was referring to a technical-area-skirmish during a *Classico* game between Real Madrid and Barcelona in which Mourinho was captured on camera sneaking up behind the Barcelona assistant manager, Tito Vilanova, and then attempting to gouge out his eye. Mourinho was perhaps thinking his actions would be hidden by the melee around him – players and staff from both dugouts were involved in a vigorous game of push-and-shove - or perhaps he wasn't thinking at all. Perhaps it was all in the heat of the moment. Later though, when the red mist had seeped away, Mourinho could have at least apologised; taken some of the poison out of the atmosphere which surrounded the biggest fixture in Spain. But he chose not to.

"When Mourinho was asked about the incident after the game," wrote Sid Lowe in *Fear and Loathing in La Liga,* "he claimed not to know 'this Pito Vilanova or whatever his name is'. He knew very well, of course; just as he knew that *Pito* is Spanish for cock. He had quite literally added insult to injury."

The eye-gouge incident took place in a Spanish Super Cup match in the 2011-12 season. At the end of that year, the visibly worn-out Barcelona manager Pep Guardiola quit, having surrendered the *La Liga* title to their great rivals Real Madrid. During the close-season Tito Vilanova was promoted to become Barcelona's manager and Guardiola's replacement. But in December 2012, Barcelona announced Vilanova was suffering from cancer. Despite chemotherapy and radiotherapy treatment, the cancer was aggressive, and in July 2013, Vilanova was forced to resign. He died in April 2014, at just 45-years-old.

At the time of the eye-gouge Mourinho claimed not to know who Vilanova was, and certainly the Portuguese couldn't have known Vilanova would become seriously ill, and eventually perish. But still, in hindsight the assault has been framed as something even more diabolical than it was: it has developed into Mourinho, sneakily, but quite deliberately, *picking on the sick bloke.* And that smacks of something very unsavoury indeed. It smacks of bullying.

And just as the Chelsea players would later have had enough of Mourinho's antics that they effectively downed-tools after the Eva Carneiro incident, so the Real Madrid players drew the line at the despicable behaviour of their boss in the technical-area in *El Classico.* Such cringeworthy episodes were harming the Spanish national team, where the vast majority of players were provided by either Real Madrid or Barcelona – they'd conquered all before them by winning the European Championships in 2008 and 2012, and the World Cup in 2010, but the persistent bickering – and worse – was threatening to put their bid to retain *both* of the major international competitions – thereby becoming the first national side to do so – in jeopardy. *FourFourTwo* magazine noted that the players from the rival factions reached out to each other, and, behind Mourinho's back engaged in peace talks. "Casillas spoke with Barca captain Xavi and the duo vowed to curb bad behaviour *in El Classico* for the good of both clubs and Spain. Jose then saw this as an act of betrayal and fell out with his no.1."

Peace talks were a foreign concept to Mourinho, and his Method; you can't motivate through antagonism if the players are lovey-dovey with their biggest rivals.

But it wasn't just rival clubs Mourinho raged against. It was anyone and everyone. Over the years the target of his ire and spite has ranged from the French FA (in August 2006, "Mourinho claimed Claude Makelele was being treated like a 'slave' by the French federation. France's head coach Raymond Domenech called the terminology 'staggering and insulting.'" *FourFourTwo* magazine), to the South Central Ambulance Service (in October 2006 Mourinho "claimed that Petr Cech had to wait half an hour for an ambulance at Reading, but those claims were rejected by NHS chiefs, who said it was seven minutes.") And from the Italian media (in March 2009 he "accused journalists of 'intellectual prostitution' after they echoed Luciano Spalleti's view that Inter's Mario Balotelli dived in a draw with Roma - *FourFourTwo* magazine) to his own players (in the 2015-16 season at Chelsea, Mourinho claimed there were "three rats" in the dressing-room).

He fought with barbed diction, but also with his poking-fingers, and with his fists too. As Andrew Murray wrote in August 2016's *FourFourTwo* magazine: "Wherever the line is, Mourinho will either cross it, or jump up and down on it until it finally buckles of its own free will.

"'Mourinho is a superstar at using the media to his advantage,' *Corriere dello Sport* journalist Andrea Ramazzotti, who covered Mourinho's Inter from 2008 until 2010, tells *FFT*. 'After Zlatan Ibrahimovic was sold to Barcelona in 2009 he became more tense. He needed to create a strong bond in the team so he looked for a common enemy for the team to attack: the journalists. 'It began one day, talking about a lack of trust. By the end of the season, he'd stopped attending the press conferences and the Nerazzuri had won everything.' Nothing particularly untoward here. not until Mourinho and Ramazzotti got into a fight by the Inter team bus in December 2009 following a 1-1 draw with Atalanta. 'A lot of water has gone under the bridge since that little episode,' smiles Ramazzotti. 'All I can say is that those were very unique days. I wasn't in the mood for jokes or to be messed around.'"

For Mourinho, football is a war-zone and *everyone* else is the enemy.

The enemy of football

Jose Mourinho is adept at using the media to propagate his propaganda and to bolster his siege mentality. He has his players champing at the bit to 'get back at' those who have wronged them. They become his warriors and they fight tooth and nail. And often they fall foul of the authorities.

In "Mourinho's first season (...) Chelsea faced 12 separate disciplinary charges," wrote Harry Harris. They were fined by pretty much every authority they could be fined by – from the FA to UEFA - for, variously, having "a brawl (...) against Blackburn", accusing Manchester United of cheating, and finally, for lying.

The charge of lying was perhaps the most damaging to Mourinho and Chelsea. Mourinho had tried to use a lie to motivate his players for a 2005 Champions League last-16 clash with Barcelona, but it was a lie which spiralled out of all control. He could have backed down from it at any point, just as he could have diffused the other ugly incidents in his career – the Eva Carneiro scandal and the Tito Vilanova mess. But, petulantly, he stuck to his guns, and that would have terrible consequences.

This time the victim wasn't a member of his own medical team or one of his rival's back-room staff, but it *was* again someone who wasn't Mourinho's *own size*. He picked on the match-day referee: one Anders Frisk. After a tense first-leg at Camp Nou on 23rd February 2005 in which Chelsea lost 2-1 and had Didier Drogba dismissed for two bookable offences, Mourinho accused the Swedish referee of fraternising too closely with the Barcelona manager Frank Rijkaard. He claimed to have witnessed Frisk 'inviting' the Barca manager into his dressing-room at half-time – an act which is expressly forbidden by UEFA. Basically, Mourinho called into question the honesty of the referee and accused him of favouring the home team, the 'precious' Barcelona. His evidence: the sending-off of Drogba and *that* half-time old pals act between Frisk and Rijkaard. The only problem: Mourinho completely fabricated the half-time meet-up. It never happened.

But the dirt had been dished and Chelsea fans were enraged. Within two weeks, as Harry Harris noted: "referee Anders Frisk announced that worries over his own and his family's safety had prompted him to quit refereeing. (…) Frisk, ironically a big Chelsea fan, said he had received death threats since the match."

That wasn't the end of it, not by a long chalk.

Although the Chelsea players, fired-up by Mourinho's comments, won a pulsating return leg 4-2 at Stamford Bridge, UEFA and Mourinho had effectively declared war on each other.

UEFA Comms chief William Gaillard "issued a detailed and highly damaging set of charges, which included 'basically using lies as a pre-match tactic'. He accused Chelsea of 'trying to qualify for the next round by putting pressure on referees and officials.'" (Harry Harris)

Mourinho sneered.

Then, "Mourinho was blamed by Volker Roth, chairman of UEFA's Referees Committee, for the incidents that led to Frisk's retirement," wrote Harry Harris. "'People like Mourinho are the enemy of football. It's the coaches who whip up the masses and make them threaten people to death.'"

"But Mourinho insisted he was not to blame. 'Mr Roth, he has only two ways out – he apologises or he will be sued. I regret that Frisk has decided to leave football. If as some people say his decision is associated with the criticism of his exhibition in the match against Barcelona, I find it odd. Every day, everywhere, there are criticisms like these from coaches, directors and players. (…) A referee with the experience of Mr Frisk would not take such a drastic decision because of criticism of his performance… If there are other motives I do not know them and I would like them to be known.'"

Probity's own Sepp Blatter, the FIFA president, waded into the row. He called on "football professionals to show greater respect to officials. 'I am appalled by the verbal attacks directed at referees and it is often such extreme behaviour that sparks off trouble among supporters.'"

"Mourinho," wrote Harris, "was finally charged with bringing the game into disrepute by UEFA. Assistant manager Steve Clarke and security officer Les Miles were also in the dock for 'wrong and unfounded statements' after the tie in Barcelona. A statement was issued by UEFA: 'These charges relate to making false declarations... By further disseminating these wrong and unfounded statements, Chelsea allowed their technical staff to create a poisoned and negative ambience amongst the teams and to put pressure on the refereeing officials.'"

Eventually Mourinho was "handed a two-match touchline ban and a 20,000 Swiss francs (£8900) fine (...) Significantly UEFA withdrew its key allegation that the club manufactured a conspiracy that 'created a poisoned and negative ambience.'"

And yet Mourinho *still* wouldn't let it lie. He was unhappy he had not received the full support of the club and pissed off the club didn't launch an appeal. For a while it seemed like he might just flounce out of the club. He didn't, but it brought about the first signs of tension between him and Abramovich, and later, the fall-out from the Frisk Affair caused the Russian to bring in a succession of Directors of Football to try and keep Mourinho on a tighter leash.

Just as with Eva Carneiro and Tito Vilanova the entire episode left a bad taste in the mouth, but in this case at least, it led to a moment of high-comedy. Chelsea met Bayern Munich in the next round of the Champions League and Mourinho was banned from the touchline. "Two newspapers," wrote Harry Harris, "related how Mourinho hid in a laundry basket used for transporting the club's kit to get round the UEFA ban imposed on him. (...)

Mourinho arrived early at the ground and watched the game on a TV in the dressing room where he delivered the pre-match and half-time talks. Ten minutes before the end of the game which Chelsea won 4-2, the manager clambered into one of the laundry baskets. He was then wheeled away to Stamford Bridge leisure club where he spent the rest of the evening" making like he'd been there all along...

Conclusion

It is clear that the appointment of Jose Mourinho as manager of Manchester United represents a massive risk to the reputation of the club. After the 2011 Tito Vilanova incident, Sir Bobby Charlton – a vital touchstone to the unique history of the club still present within the hierarchy – said – in so many words – that United wouldn't touch the Portuguese – and all his attendant histrionics, and his pontifications – with a barge-pole. But at the time, United had just set the English record for most championships won by sealing their 19th Premier League (or First Division) title. And though they lost in the Champions League Final to Barcelona, it was their third final in four years. They looked in a very healthy position. Sir Alex Ferguson was at the helm and he knew all about the fabled United way, having spent so long at the helm.

Even when Fergie finally retired, three years ago in 2013, United were not prepared to risk everything in order to bring in Mourinho – a guaranteed winner – as a ready-made replacement. Instead, they entrusted England's biggest football club to the 'safe pair of hands' of David Moyes. The Glaswegian failed miserably - as did Louis van Gaal, to a lesser extent – and now United have not even qualified for the Champions League for two out of the past three seasons.

It is a very different Manchester United which Mourinho joins now. The board clearly analysed the risk to the club's reputation and set that against the risk to the club's business and marketing strategy were the current (relative) malaise to continue, and decided – cynically – that the risk to the club's reputation would be less costly in pounds and pence (and dollars; and yen) even if Mourinho did go off the deep-end again.

There is no doubt that Jose Mourinho has a well-defined dark side. But United have taken the decision to take him on, warts and all. It was convenient that the Eva Carneiro mess *went away* before the Portuguese got his feet under the table-proper: certainly before the Premier League season started. It will be *inconvenient* if anything as shameful, or as scandalous happens during Mourinho's time at Old Trafford. But for the board, for whom money talks louder than anything else in this world, it will be even more costly should we continue to spend so long off our 'perch' at the top of the tree in English football. More than that, we are also losing out in terms of continental success.

That is why the club has taken such a decision at this time. We are all going to have to hold our noses, climb inside our own dirty-linen baskets, and hope that we come out the other side with our reputation intact – and some success.

5

"THE CULT OF CELEBRITY MEANS MANAGERS ARE NOW ARGUABLY MORE IMPORTANT THAN PLAYING-STAFF," SAID PAUL WILSON IN *THE GUARDIAN*. WHAT IS THE ROLE OF THE MODERN DAY PREMIER LEAGUE MANAGER AND HOW HAS THIS CHANGED OVER THE YEARS?

They kept us waiting, right at the last, didn't they?

The worst-kept secret in world football (since the last worst-kept secret in world football) was that the *galactico* Super Coach Jose Mourinho was going to be joining Manchester United as manager at the end of the 2015-16 season. By all accounts United had cast a wary eye across the city to the noisy neighbours, who like a loose-lipped teenager who'd just pulled the hot new girl in town but still, like, had a girlfriend, yeah, and it would hurt her if she just, like, found out on the internet, yeah, so Loose-Lips had to, you know, force himself not to brag, not to reveal his secret until he'd properly, like, talked to his girlfriend and landed her in Dumpsville in the proper way... Loose Lips was all kinds of definite he wasn't going to reveal his secret, nosireebob, right up to the moment he shouted out that very same secret over pretty much every social media platform. *LOOK WHO I JUST BAGGED! READ IT AND WEEP, SUCKERS. LOLZ.*

City couldn't wait to blab that Pep Guardiola would be joining them at the end of the season. Unfortunately, in doing so, they undermined the position of their incumbent manager/ squeeze Manuel Pellegrini, with a third of the season still to play: City might have challenged Leicester for the Premier League title but instead they surrendered, meekly, just as they did in the Champions League at the semi-final stage. Who's to say what the lazer blues might have achieved if they hadn't fallen over themselves to brag?

United wouldn't countenance doing the same, no matter that they allegedly paid Mourinho a retainer in order that he didn't negotiate with any other club while the Reds completed their secondary business of finishing off the season. It was too important that nothing get in the way of the Reds qualifying for the following year's Champions League competition.

There were accountants to answer to, dontchaknow.

As it happened United didn't make it into the Champions League. Old Loose-Lips City pipped them to it on that farcical last day of the season on goal difference, when – you really couldn't make it up - a training device left behind after an emergency training exercise sparked a bomb-scare and a mass evacuation which eventually meant

United's game was postponed into meaninglessness. But they did win the FA Cup.

It wasn't enough. Even as Louis van Gaal faced the media at his celebratory press conference after the cup final win, every pressman-hack worth his salt knew what the Dutchman didn't. Before the many coaches containing the massed ranks of United fans who'd been at Wembley drew up at Old Trafford again that Saturday night, everybody in the world knew. Knew he was gone. Knew who was going to be stepping into his size-twelves. Clear the decks, dead man walking. In the end, United landed Van Gaal in Dumpsville in about as ham-fisted a way as City did with Pellegrini, only with a little less bragging.

It was expected Van Gaal would attend Carrington on the Monday morning after the cup final to collect his P45 and that Mourinho would sign on the dotted line on the Tuesday. But it didn't quite happen like that. First, Van Gaal was at Carrington for far longer than really necessary, prompting some to wonder whether some kind of hostage situation had not ensued. Maybe Van Gaal had come on like a lover scorned; maybe he had Ed Woodward bound and gagged in his office... And trust me, after that sublimely ridiculous end to United's league season in which our team coach had been attacked by West Ham fans and then that bomb scare, it wasn't outside the realms of possibility.

But in the end, he left. Maybe the Iron Tulip simply had a lot of clipboards to pack away in his box when he cleared out his desk. Maybe that's what took him so long.

So now the coast was clear. And surely all the negotiations had already been sorted. All Mourinho needed to do was put pen to paper on Tuesday and – bosh! – here he was, the new supremo at Old Trafford.

But it didn't go like that. Mourinho didn't sign on Tuesday and he didn't sign on Wednesday. By Thursday 26th May, 17 years after the most glorious moment of

Manchester United's history and that famous night in Barcelona, Mourinho *still* hadn't signed. All we knew was that negotiations were taking place.

That was a cause for concern, actually. For the man in charge of negotiations on the United side of the table was The Equaliser, that google-eyed puppet of the Glazer regime who was capable of dragging United down to the level of also-rans. His name was Ed Woodward and his *ing*lorious history since replacing David Gill as Chief Exec at United had seen him negotiating with imposters in Spain when attempting to sign Ander Herrera, amongst other bungles. So now we were starting to wonder whether Mourinho was even present at all. What if Woodward was simply holed up in an office talking to a guy who *looked like* Mourinho? What if he was about to offer the role of Old Trafford boss to the window-cleaner, or the guy who stocked the vending-machines with crisps provided by United's official global potato-snacks partners?

At last the reason for the hold-up was revealed. Image rights. *The Guardian* reported: "Jose Mourinho's impending appointment as Manchester United manager has been held up by the Portuguese's former club Chelsea owning the trademark to his name (…) It is understood Chelsea bought the rights to Mourinho's name and image in 2005, a year into the first of his two tenures at Stamford Bridge. European Union Intellectual Property Office records show that Chelsea Football Club Limited owns the trademark for five classes of goods until 31 March, 2025."

Official documents listed those goods Chelsea could officially put his name to. That list included, as was widely reported, "after-shave, potpourris and even napkin rings." But it also contained the following (amongst many, many more items): polish for nails and boots, talcum powders, eyebrow cosmetics, vases and cigar holders, attache cases, car muffs, vests, berets, walking sticks, braces, and chequebook covers.

One is tempted to wonder whether those imposters Ed Woodward tried to negotiate the transfer of Ander Herrera with were carrying official Jose Mourinho attache cases.

But seriously, this contretemps goes to the very heart of what is wrong with the business of elite-level football today. Ed Woodward held back from cracking United's (branded) chequebook, at least until the image rights were sorted, but secretly, he must have been rubbing his hands in anticipation. For here was a list of items which went beyond even the exhaustive realms of tat the United megastore sells. And beyond that, perhaps there were new official partnering opportunities. Why, the Reds didn't have an official global walking-stick provider-partner, did they? Hell no. And surely our lack of an official global car muff partner was a bigger oversight than even forgetting to sign Marouane Fellaini before the 20th August deadline in his contract, meaning his value went up by £4 million...

Ed Woodward achieved his exalted position within the Old Trafford hierarchy due to his commercial acumen and his ability to attract global partners. He'd signed up, variously, an official office digital transformation partner, an official leisure headwear partner, an official global noodle partner. He'd allowed United to cosy up with companies from across the world called (randomly) Gloops (the official social gaming partner in Japan), Cho-a-pharm (the official pharmaceutical partner for Korea and Vietnam) Ottogi (the official ready meal partner for Korea), Chi (the official soft drinks partners in Nigeria) and Krungsri (the official financial services affinity partner in Thailand). You might need to look up the official global spirits partner just to get over reading all of that...

In his book *Commonsense Direct & Digital Marketing,* Drayton Bird has this to say about branding: "Your brand, and its image – or personality – result from what you are, what you do, far more than what you *say* about what you are and what you do."

There is a sense that in diluting United's brand in this way, by consistently promoting tat rather than on-the-field prowess and results, the club's very personality is changing. And all for a set of napkin-rings.

Talcum Powders, Eyebrow Cosmetics, Vases and Cigar Holders, Attache Cases...

Indeed the very fact United plumped for Mourinho in the first place says a great deal about where we are today. Mourinho is box-office in the fact that he sells things. He doesn't necessarily put bums on seats, not in the ground, but he sells subscriptions to TV sports packages around the world. He sells polish for nails and boots, talcum powders, eyebrow cosmetics, vases and cigar holders, attache cases, car muffs, vests, berets, walking sticks, braces, and chequebook covers.

"The cult of celebrity means managers are now arguably more important than playing-staff," wrote Paul Wilson in *The Guardian*. "Managerial rethinks never used to be such seismic events and perhaps it is regrettable that the personalities on the sidelines now tend to overshadow the contributions of those on the pitch, but Jose Mourinho colliding with Manchester United was never going to take place quietly or off-camera."

Of course it wasn't. United had the share price to think about. Over in the US, CNBC reported that the Reds had consciously appointed the "firebrand manager" in order to "help push the share price of Manchester United up the league table" (not a mention of the *real* league table). Even in the week before United's twelfth FA Cup final triumph, as the rumour-mill had begun to grind out the Mourinho name with increasing regularity "shares of Wall

Street-listed Manchester United rallied more than 1 percent." (This after falling three percent earlier in 2016 when qualification for the following season's Champions League began to look in doubt.) And when the markets opened on Friday, following the announcement that the rumours had been true and the Portuguese was the new top man at Old Trafford, the Gordon Gekkos of this world must have been rubbing their hands with glee as shares "rose 1.24 percent in the first hour of trade".

"Sports agent and former market strategist, Michael Jarman, said the self-styled 'special one' would help investors buy in to the story of Manchester United," said CNBC. "Manchester United need to ensure Champions League (qualification) and Mourinho's record tends to suggest he basically guarantees clubs that financial prize."

Red Devils fans might take issue with Jarman's version of the 'story of Manchester United'. For his story is one without the romance, without the euphoria, without the characters and protagonists (Matt Busby, George Best, Bobby Charlton, Denis Law, Bryan Robson, Ryan Giggs, Eric Cantona, and Alex Ferguson to name but a few), and without the phoenix from the flames comeback after the tragedy of Munich which lies at the very heart of the club. Winning trophies also lies at the very heart of the club, but Jarman seems to suggest that this is no longer the ultimate motivation of the Old Trafford club. No, his narrative of United makes them sound an awful lot like Arsenal, a team who gave up on winning elite level trophies (other than the FA Cup) a decade ago. Jarman's is an utterly unromantic view: fourth place is enough, as long as it gives the Reds a boost in the share price league table.

Still, Jose Mourinho was as big news for the markets as it was for the fans. He is box-office; a superstar at least as famous as the very best of his players. The big name that the markets, and supposedly the fans, crave. Real Madrid's business model over the past twenty years has been to sign up genuine world football superstars, often breaking the bank to do so. The names drip off your tongue: Luis Figo, (the original, Brazilian) Ronaldo, David Beckham, Zinedine Zidane, Kaka, Cristiano Ronaldo. These guys were the *galacticos*. But, as Sid Lowe noted in his book *Fear and Loathing in La Liga,* when Madrid president Florentino Perez announced the Portuguese as their new manager in 2010, he said: "'This year's *galactico* is Jose Mourinho.'"

The Madrid club weren't renowned for bigging-up their coaches. The whole *galactico* concept seemed to be: if we throw enough world class players onto the pitch then surely the results will come, and it *doesn't matter* who the coach is. But for Mourinho, they changed. And even if the fans didn't immediately *buy it,* the Spanish media did. They were suitably impressed by the celebrity scale of the signing. "*El Pais* called him 'the Michael Jackson of coaches.'" (Mind you; "within a couple of years, on the pages of the same newspaper he was called a psychopath.")

It is clear: Jose is A-list. A smooth criminal.

Before United's cup final win against Crystal Palace, the Reds teamed up with global film distribution partner 20th Century Fox (who are owned by that lovable Aussie rogue Rupert Murdoch, who once tried to buy the club) in order to promote the release of the new *X-Men* film and also, as a seeming afterthought, United's appearance in the final. In it, a fantastically wooden Wayne Rooney (who might have been a cardboard cut-out with a hidden tape recorder, or perhaps a Mr. Potato Head whose batteries were running low) joined forces with Magneto and his superhero chums to spout cringeworthy nonsense along the lines of "anything for the team". (This was the same Wayne Rooney who'd shown his loyalty to the club by demanding a transfer at least twice; once with the intention of joining Mourinho at Chelsea.)

If they re-made the ad now that the image rights problem has been sorted and Mourinho has signed-up, there is no doubt Jose would have gotten the plum role instead of Wayne Rooney and there is also no doubt that he'd have given a good showing. He'd have been smooth, sophisticated.

The Portuguese is handsome, even dashing; well-groomed and well turned-out; charismatic but with and air of the mysterious; honest but with a twinkle in his eye. A real operator.

He was made for the cameras and he knows it.

"Asked in January 2006 who would play him in a film of his life, Mourinho went for the modest choice of the Hollywood actor George Clooney. 'If they made a film of my life, I think they should get George Clooney to play me,' he said. 'He's a fantastic actor and my wife thinks he would be ideal.'

Actually, he wouldn't. Mourinho would be the very best at playing Mourinho; after all he's had years of practice.

He's an excellent actor and an outstanding manipulator. Over the years he has perfected a 'Mourinho' persona. It is often as though with everything he says he's using imaginary speech-marks, bracketing it off as a Mourinho-ism. He is highly quotable; always there with a soundbite, and sometimes with a sound bigger than a bite: a sound *maul* perhaps… Hell, he is so media-friendly (most of the time) that he even came up with his own sobriquet. "Please don't call me arrogant," he said at his first press conference as Chelsea manager in 2004, "but I'm European champion and I think I'm a special one."

There have been many other Mourinho-isms. And just like Sir Alex Ferguson - who should have trademarked the phrase 'squeaky bum-time' such is the regularity of its use – they have entered general footballing parlance. Given how much the football world is now governed by marketing, Mourinho probably *has* patented phrases such as 'parked the bus' (which he debuted as early as Monday 20th September 2004, following Chelsea's 0-0 draw at home to Spurs, when he said: "They may as well have put the team bus in front of the goal.")

And Mourinho-isms are catching. Back in 2014 when his transitional Chelsea team found itself in a title race alongside Manchester City, Arsenal and Liverpool, he described his Blues as the "little horse that needs milk" in amongst the much bigger horses. His animal metaphor soon caught-on amongst his rival managers and they would be a constant theme as the season ran into 'squeaky bum-time'. Manuel Pellegrini snapped that Chelsea were a "rich little horse" as the pressure started to tell on Manchester City; Brendan Rodgers – the manager who is his own number one inspiration – took it to bizarre new levels by describing Liverpool as a Chihuahua.

Mourinho has proved himself king of the analogy, particularly ones involving eggs. This was Mourinho's take on Roman Abramovich's unwillingness to loosen the purse-strings in the wake of an injury crisis at Chelsea: "Omelettes, eggs. No eggs, no omelettes. And it depends on the quality of the eggs in the supermarket. They are class one, two or three and some are more expensive than others and some give you better omelettes. When the class one eggs are not available you have a problem."

And this was his take on the young Chelsea team he was nurturing during his second-spell at the club. The players were: "Beautiful, young eggs. Eggs that need a mum or, in this case, a dad to take care of them, to keep them warm during the winter, to bring the blanket and work and improve them. One day the moment will arrive when the weather changes, the sun rises, you break the eggs and the eggs are ready to go for life at the top level."

The media lapped it up.

Especially in the UK. As David Hytner noted in *The Guardian*: "It is probably fair to say at this point that

Mourinho has found his professional fit in England, his spiritual home from home. Unlike in Spain or Italy, say, there is a media preoccupation with personality and all of the attendant trimmings. Mourinho recognises the buttons and he knows how to press them."

And sure, there were some inside the media bubble who resisted the Mourinho persona, or poked fun at it – Harry Enfield and Paul Whitehouse parodied him with their character, the extremely self-obsessed Jose Arrogantio in their show *Harry & Paul* – and *without* the media bubble there were some who disliked him immensely, particularly those who supported opposing teams who'd experienced what it was to lose against him (Celtic and Manchester United), but at first many enjoyed being taken along for the ride by Mourinho.

He was different. His was a different kind of story.

Aside from his arrogance and quotability, what immediately set Jose apart from his new contemporaries was his *look*.

"That spring (of 2005)," wrote Jim White, "all eyes were on Mourinho. Many of them female. 'This intelligent, witty, charismatic and exceptionally good-looking young pipsqueak' is how Marina Hyde described him in *The Guardian*. (…) As noted by fashion editors as he as by sportswriters he had the results to back up the looks. This was no empty vessel, no mere coat-hanger: this was the future of football. 'The suit is pure stealth wealth, the shirt is a baby blue and button-down with elegant preppiness, even the socks have a certain minimalist luxe,' panted Polly Vernon in *The Observer Sports Monthly*."

Furthermore, The Idle Man fashion blog devoted an entire article to giving us Brits the lowdown on how we could dress *just like* this stylish European. Hmmm. Suit you sir, as another Paul Whitehouse character might say. "Just as the fashion scene changes and adapts, so does Jose," wrote The Idle Man. "Before he burst onto the scene (…)

football managers had always had two very generic looks, either the track suit manager or the manager who wore the massive over coat, similar to Ron Atkinson. Now we've got a new style. Following Jose's arrival on the world stage, more and more managers are going for his simplistic, straight forward style."

"Taking inspirations from wherever he manages, Mourinho's outfits are often consisting of unmistakable suits, the majority from Italian brands such as Armani and Hugo Boss. Mourinho's favourite suit of choice, or so it appears, is the modern looking navy blue, matched with a dark blue shirt underneath and ever darker tie. This look could be used for any smart casual event, no matter what the occasion, as the colour is just enough to draw attention, however isn't over the top. 'The Special One's' outfit isn't complete there however: under the skinny fit blazer, Jose is all about slipping a knitted jumper underneath. Grey is the most versatile colour to test out the trend with, as it goes just as well under navy and black, or serves as a blank canvas for a patterned suit if you are brave enough."

"From his time in Italy, Jose seems to have been inspired by the finest Italian scarves on cold days, however similar to the rest of his look, they are never bright and colourful, always plain colours that could go with any outfit."

Again, the media lapped it up. Here was a guy named 'Rockstar of the Year' by the Spanish *Rolling Stone* magazine in December 2011. You can't imagine, say, Sam Allardyce or Steve Bruce winning similar acclaim. (One imagines the closest Allardyce gets to rock-stardom is when he rocks-out to Chris Rea in his Mondeo on his way home from training.)

Even Mourinho's *dogs* get press attention. (Indeed the only football-dogs who've received as much coverage since Pickles stumbled upon the Jules Rimet trophy discarded on a London street has been Roy Keane's tireless

Triggs.) In 2007, Jose was arrested by Metropolitan Police for physically preventing animal welfare officers taking his mutts down to the doggy-dog pound (he didn't have the right quarantine paperwork for them and inoculations weren't up to date). In the end – heartbreakingly - Mourinho had to say goodbye to the dogs and they were returned to Portugal. He had to say hello to a police caution. But then again *like* Keane before him and like Eric Cantona too, the media love a bonafide, Pedigree Chum badboy, don't they?

We'll discuss Cantona later. But as it happens Roy Keane was only halfway sold on his fellow dog-lover Mourinho's appointment as Manchester United boss. Though Keane acknowledged Jose was the "right man to lead Manchester United", he was rather grudging in his praise. He said the Portuguese was United's only "option when (the Reds) didn't qualify for the Champions League." And although Keane admired Mou's "fantastic CV", Roy didn't have much time for Mourinho personally. "He's not my kind of cuppa tea. I find him really irritating when I've coached against him, but that's just a personal thing."

Keano's snarling remarks notwithstanding there is no doubt the Portuguese has thrived on the attention which has been showered on him on these shores. At the same time there is no doubt that until fairly recently the media have given him a rather softer ride than have done some of his rivals and contemporaries. This is because he has always thrown them a bone; allowed them to fill their column inches and feed the beast. Mourinho has been savvy enough to know that by keeping the narrative going at all times; by generating stories for them; by making sure there was always something to say on that yellow ticker-tape which scrolls along the bottom of the screen on Sky Sports News; he will keep media and fans alike onside.

Feeding the beast isn't a job the occasional dog-sitter can manage – to reach for a Mourinho-esque animal analogy. The beast requires constant attention. You can't just leave it in the kennels and hope everything will be OK: it must be walked, pampered; fed, fed, fed. In Jim White's excellent book *Premier League,* he quotes (the seemingly permanently surprised-by-how-big-things-are) Steve Coppell, after his Reading team's promotion to the top division from the Championship.

"In the Championship, matches last basically a day. In terms of the media interest, the noise that surrounds them, it's over in twenty-four hours. In the Premier League they last a week. You have three days' build-up, the match day itself, then three days of post-mortem. The interest is that much bigger."

Mourinho is one of a very select band that can keep the media interested for that long, over and over again.

The only thing worse than being talked about is not being talked about: The ubiquity of football, and of Jose Mourinho

Over the past century "economic and cultural changes have produced a remarkable shift in the place of football in British society," said the author David Goldblatt in his outstanding book, *The Game of Our Lives.* "Once merely popular, even widespread, now football is ubiquitous and its status in both popular and elite cultures greatly elevated. (...) The sheer volume of newsprint and digital space occupied by football is the most obvious marker of the game's ubiquity. From just a few pages a day in the 1970s, even in the most football-heavy papers, Britain's tabloids and broadsheets started devoting many times that kind of space to football. Football's presence on the internet grew even faster as websites, podcasts and blogs proliferated."

Football is ubiquitous, and Jose Mourinho is pretty much the *most* ubiquitous personality in football today. He is everywhere. Everyone is talking about him. He is almost like the bad-boy everyone loves in a soap-opera: a latter-day Dirty Den for generation Y. His story is the one which keeps everyone hooked.

"Both soap operas and professional football are significant components of Britain's popular culture, but they are sharply separated by gender," wrote Goldblatt. "*Coronation Street* and *Eastenders*, the old form of the genre, have the same kind of narrative and romantic connection to working-class urban Britain that football has acquired. The shows, like football, find themselves referenced and debated in a variety of other media, their stars endlessly featured in other contexts and their storylines taken as a sustained real-time commentary upon contemporary events. Football now manages all these and on a scale equivalent to the entire genre of soap opera. Moreover, beyond the emotionally disturbed, the soaps do not evoke collective ecstasy or carnival, nor do they provide the bedrock of collective identities. The Church, the theatre, festivals and soap operas – football has acquired a place in British culture that exceeds them all, for it is the equal of each in their own domains of ritual, performance, ecstasy and national narrative."

In his book *Premier League: A History in 10 Matches*, Jim White agreed. "According to David Miliband, who after serving as foreign secretary in the last labour government secured a promotion on leaving office to become the vice-chairman of Sunderland (…), the Premier League is this country's major cultural export. Everywhere he went in an official capacity during his days at the Foreign Office he saw evidence of its growing prominence. (…) 'It's our Hollywood.' (he said.)"

Jim White concurred. Towards the end of the 1990s: "Jose Angel Sanchez, director of marketing at Real Madrid, United's rivals for the position of the world's richest football club, had reflected about the Premiership:

English football was now in the business of selling media content. These were the moving pictures it peddled. This was now the sporting equivalent of Universal Studios. And the Theatre of Dreams was an entertainment brand as powerful as Disneyland."

Mourinho The Anti-Hero

Every good story needs a good bad guy…

And if the Premier League is Hollywood, Mourinho is *more* than a Dirty Den figure, he's Darth Vader. After all, Disney bought the rights to the *Star Wars* franchise, didn't they? And if Old Trafford is Disneyland that makes Mourinho… Yeah, you got it.

Over the years he's grown into the role of the archetypal anti-hero. According to Peter Jonason, Gregory Webster, David Schmitt, Norman Li and Laura Crysel (in *The Review of General Psychology*) the anti-hero is defined as one lacking in "conventional heroic qualities such as idealism, courage, or morality". Instead, these individuals "often possess dark personality traits such as disagreeableness, dishonesty, and aggressiveness."

This is known as "The Dark Triad" of personality (something which itself sounds like a Hollywood movie: perhaps the latest instalment of the *Batman* franchise, or maybe the new *X-Men* flick – hey, perhaps there'll be a role for Rooney?). It "is composed of narcissism, psychopathy, and Machiavellianism." Three traits which would figure pretty high up the list were you to ask pretty much any football fan to describe Jose Mourinho (once you got past the words of a four-letter variety).

"Despite the common belief that these traits are undesirable, the media is awash with characters that embody the Dark Triad. Characters like Gregory House, M.D., Batman (a.k.a. the Dark Knight), and James Bond all embody these traits and are some of the most popular media franchises today. As entertaining as these characters are, they provide us with a window into the dark side of human nature."

Well, you know what they say, don't you? The Devil always has the best lines. He's more entertaining than the goody two-shoes hero. More interesting, too.
Conflict drives narrative and Jose Mourinho's devilish; sometimes amusing, sometimes inspiring, sometimes combative, sometimes curmudgeonly presence at the top table of European football has provoked and generated a great deal of conflict and *reams* of stories. He is able to get under the skin of his rivals just as Sir Alex Ferguson did. His 'mind games' are carefully choreographed; tailored to draw even the most mild-mannered of his colleagues out of their comfort zones (Wenger), and sometimes into war zones. He tosses grenades aplenty and then sits back, waits to see what blows up.

He is the tubthumping villain who against all the odds keeps getting back up at the end of a movie. The one who we've *seen* the heroine kill. We heave a sigh of relief: he's surely dead... Only, when the camera pans back to where his body lay, it's gone... Cue great heart-lurching *jump* as he enters, stage-left.

Mourinho acknowledged this aspect of his character himself after an FA Cup final victory over Manchester United, which stopped Ferguson's team from winning another Double, and also 'brought Mourinho back from the dead' after a season of extreme turmoil. "I learned," he said, somehow managing to maintain a straight face, "that it is very difficult to kill me. Very, very difficult."

We know this now, but when Mourinho first arrived upon these shores we didn't quite now how to pigeon-hole him yet. So the Portuguese wrote his own script, developed his own character, and said *here, this is what I am.*

Jose Mourinho was different. Exotic. I'll say this quietly - for it might almost be blasphemous to say it, especially amongst Manchester United fans - but the impact of Mourinho upon the Premier League was similar to that of Eric Cantona twelve years previously. King Eric in many ways paved the way for Prince Jose and their narratives – spun out endlessly by Sky and in the tabloids - do bear some comparison.

The Cantona Comparison

Jose Mourinho was born in Setubal, traditionally the home of Portugal's fishing industry and renowned for its sardines. The Mourinho family were for some time pretty well-off. As Harry Harris noted in his book *Jose: Return of the King*: "Mourinho's uncle Mario Ledo owned a sardine cannery and grew rich under dictator Antonio de Oliveira Salazar's regime." But when "Salazar was later ousted (…) the canning factories were confiscated." Still, though the fishing industry declined during Jose's lifetime there were still plenty of seagulls and trawlers about when he was a boy and sardines remained on the specials board.

Eric Cantona knows something about seagulls, trawlers and sardines.

Plug the words 'Cantona', 'seagulls' and 'trawler' into the Google search engine and within two seconds nearly 30,000 hits have been generated. Mind you, if you plug the words 'Cantona' and 'kick' into Google you get well over ten times that number. And barely a one of those hits refers to Eric's kicking a football. No: they all refer to his kung-fu style kick rendered onto the chest of one Matthew Simmons, a Crystal Palace supporter. It was *the* defining image of the Premier League era.

Despite the fact Sky were marketing the Premier League as "a whole new ball game" there weren't a great many differences between the last First Division season in 1991-92 and the first Premier League season in 1992-93. Once you got past the razzmatazz – the cheerleaders and the fireworks – it was the same old dog. Squads were largely made up of British players. Some of the fare served up was poor: the long-ball remained a respected tactic.

But Eric Cantona was different. In Jim White's *Premier League,* he wrote: "For the middle-class arriviste watching from the stands or more likely from the armchair, he (Cantona) was manna from heaven, proof that the game was worth watching. He was the poster boy of the new Carling Premiership. Nike cunningly played up to the image of lofty intellectualism."

Cantona's launching himself into the crowd was absurd. It was memorable. It was, as radio-host Danny Baker said on his *606* show, railing against those who saw it as a sign of the moral decay of the country, incredibly funny. The story grew arms and legs. Developed "a life of its own, a runaway story that brooked no attempt to control it. For the media, Cantona was, as Ferguson once put it, like Christmas every day, a gift to write about. Loathed or loved, admired or reviled, he made people buy papers and brought listeners to the radio. More to the point he sold television subscriptions."

"Rupert Murdoch's newspaper executives saw in the Cantona kick the perfect vehicle to promote the product being sold by his television division," wrote White. "They were not the game's moral defenders, they were pushing subscriptions to his satellite channel, so why worry if the image of player slugging it out with fan was not exactly wholesome? Especially when they had such brilliant pictures. That it showed the game's dark side made the incident so much more potent. This gave the Carling Premiership edge, spice, vibrancy. Sales of subscriptions the next week were the highest so far in Sky's short history. This was marketing gold dust."

Customers would not take on a subscription to Sky for the promise of, say, matches between West Bromwich Albion and Norwich City, but they would to get closer to the action, to the story of big players and big managers navigating the path between triumph and disaster. The bigger picture of football – as Sky would have it - is that it is larger than a single match; it is a series; a soap-opera; a franchise; it is mythical in scale. "Notoriety," said Jim White of Cantona, "only reinforced the myth."

The Cantona myth provided subscribers with a window into the darker side of human nature and, if you're like Danny Baker and like me, a real laugh too. But if it was all beginning to sound like a shaggy-dog story (hopefully this time with the proper quarantine paperwork), then it was left to Eric to supply the punchline. After he was sentenced to 120 hours of community service, a press conference was called and Jim White noted: "As they prepared to come in and speak, Cantona asked (Maurice) Watkins (his lawyer) a couple of questions about English vocabulary. 'What do you call the big boat that catches fish?' he said. And: 'what is the English for the big seabird?' Even as he told him, Watkins wondered what on Earth he was on about."

Cantona: "had something to say all right. He poured himself a glass of water, leaned back in his seat and uttered the words he had prepared (…) – words that were to become among the most notorious in footballing history; 'When seagulls follow the trawler it is because they hope sardines will be thrown into the sea.' And with that, he got up and left the room. It seemed a pretty straightforward comment about the parasitic nature of press reporting (…) but that did not stop many from being diverted by its cryptic phrasing and heavy French-accented delivery into absurdist levels of textual analysis. (…) It wasn't, however, the words he used that really signalled Cantona's intent in that press conference. It was the fact that in mid-sentence he was obliged to take a drink of water to stop himself cracking up laughing."

Incidentally, just like Roy Keane, Cantona damned Mourinho with faint praise when he was announced as the next Manchester United manager in 2016. In an interview with *The Guardian* he said: "I love Jose Mourinho, but in terms of the type of football he plays I don't think he is Manchester United. I love his personality, I love the passion he has for the game, his humour. He is very intelligent, he demands 100% of his players. And of course he wins things. But I don't think it's the type of football that the fans of Manchester United will love, even if they win. He can win with Manchester United. But do they expect that type of football, even if they win? I don't think so."

(Pep Guardiola was Cantona's chosen one. For "he is the spiritual son of Johan Cruyff. I would have loved to have seen Guardiola in Manchester United. He is the only one to change Manchester. He is in Manchester, but at the wrong one.")

The Premier League, then, packaged Eric Cantona and Jose Mourinho both in the role of anti-hero. And to be fair to them Cantona had form, even before the incident at Selhurst Park. His kung-fu kick was extreme, but it was not exceptional. The Frenchman's career was dogged by controversy and explosions of bad behaviour. He was to all intents and purposes exiled from French football after a catalogue of sin and misdemeanour both on and off the pitch. He threw a ball at a referee and a pair of boots into the face of a teammate. At a disciplinary hearing in front of the French Football Federation, he called each member of the committee a sack of shit. Despite his obvious quality he was drummed out of numerous clubs, deemed more trouble than he was worth. In England, he was mostly much calmer until that infamous kung-fu kick, though he did receive his marching orders four times in his first two seasons at

Manchester United, accumulating red cards quicker than even Roy Keane would.

But what characterised Eric's indiscretions was the sheer unpremeditated nature of them. His actions were violent explosions; the red mist descended and that was that.

We have considered Mourinho's darker side more fully in an earlier chapter, but what is clear is this: Mourinho's own rap-sheet is just as lengthy as Cantona's but the crimes are different. They are not the instinctive *reactions* acts Eric's were. Cantona reacted to perceived injustices and he did so full of rage. Jose Mourinho's actions often seem to be born out of malice. They are carefully coordinated so as to have the maximum effect. Though some have been as funny as Cantona's – take Jose's hiding in a linen basket in order to bypass a UEFA dressing-room ban for example – many have seemed simply spiteful. The petulant actions of a spoilt child.

What is also clear is Cantona stood aloof from many of his contemporaries at the beginning of the Premier League era. He was different. He said funny stuff about seagulls and trawlers. Jose Mourinho also stood out from his contemporaries in terms of the Premier League managers when he took up the role of Chelsea boss at the start of the 2004-05 season. Back then there were only five managers from outside the UK and Ireland (they were Arsene Wenger at Arsenal, Rafael Benitez at Liverpool, Alain Perrin at Portsmouth, Martin Jol at Spurs, and of course, Jose Mourinho at Chelsea.) And though Wenger had rather paved the way for foreign coaches with his early success at Arsenal, Wenger was more the quiet, professorial type. He wasn't arrogant like Mourinho. He didn't even dress like him. (You can't imagine Jose wearing one of those terrible long slug-like, sleeping-bag-style manager's coats Wenger opts for during the winter months of the Premier League season, can you?)

Not only did Mourinho look different to 2004's Premier League managers – and 2004 was a real beauty parade all right; David O' Leary, Sam Allardyce, Iain Dowie, David Moyes, and Harry Redknapp might all have scared small children into believing in the Bogeyman – he sounded different.

Mourinho was something else.

But just as Cantona did, Jose set the trend. Just as Cantona preceded the great influx of foreign players into England's top division, so Mourinho heralded the charge of the foreign managers. By the close of 2015-16 season, there were only six from the UK and Ireland managing in the top flight.

And after Mourinho, most Premier League clubs want managers whose profile is like Jose's. Managers who can enrich the drama. Managers who are, like the players, marketable.

Despite the fact that the very idea appals the traditional football fan, football at an elite level is cashing-in on its exalted status. "The idea that football is a business, that money shapes the game is not new, but over the last twenty years these notions have become almost the defining feature of the game in Britain," wrote Goldblatt. "Clubs refer to themselves as brands, and accountancy firms publish earnest reports on the business of football. The financial pages (...) publish rich-lists. The conversations that roll around the grounds, internet fan forums and radio phone-ins turn on greed and excess, implausible salaries, record transfer fees and the corrosive impact of cash."

It is maximising revenue streams; making hay while the sun shines; wringing just about everything out of the (branded) dirty flannel (just as we have seen in the commercial activity of Manchester United, and its Chief Exec, Ed Woodward). "Football," noted Goldblatt, "makes money in three ways: across the Premier League as a whole, half of that £2.3 billion (the Premier League's annual turnover) is money from television and other media rights, a quarter comes from match-day income (tickets, pies and banquets) and a quarter from other commercial activities including sponsorship, naming rights, property deals and selling tat."

We're back, I'm afraid, to those napkin rings and chequebook covers. Mourinho's face on a new line of United talcum powders might help shift a few extra units so let's get him on board and worry about the rest of it later.

Jose Mourinho has consciously placed himself at the centre of the story of the Premier League and also the Champions League over the past ten to twelve years. People buy into the persona he has created for himself. As such he can command his own commercial endorsement and sponsorship packages, as well as a higher salary. (CNBC's David Reid suggested that although Mourinho's "personal sponsorship deal with Jaguar may (...) be ended early, should Manchester United deem it to be in conflict with the club-wide Chevrolet sponsorship," this blow would be softened somewhat by his salary at Old Trafford: "tabloid newspaper reports claim the Portuguese manager will pocket £10 million each season.")

At the same time, the Premier League uses Mourinho's face as well as his story as one of its unique selling points. You don't get *him* anywhere else, so watch this league rather than any other.

And it has worked. "The capacity of the Premiership to attract subscribers rather than just one-off viewers, and the clear preference of many international audiences for English football over other European leagues, has made Premiership rights the jewel in the crown in dozens of sports television markets," wrote Goldblatt.

The never-ending story: Media fire and WWE-style showdowns

What the marketing bods at the Premier League have done very well is exploit the *stories*, the *narratives* at the heart of elite-level football.

Over the years, as Goldblatt wrote, "media coverage of football has increasingly framed matches and seasons as psychological and emotional duels, most especially the coverage of Ferguson and Wenger's rivalry during the years between Arsenal's first Premiership title in 1998 and the arrival of Jose Mourinho at Chelsea in 2004. Both Ferguson and Wenger had long experience operating within this kind of framework and often fed the media fire, but the whole circus took a step up with the arrival of the Portuguese. Even in such exalted company the capacity of the 'Special One' to capture, shape and manipulate the sporting spectacle, the post-match press conference and the daily torrent of football coverage in mainstream media was unprecedented. The 2005 League Cup final is not remembered for its outcome, but for Mourinho's shushing of the Liverpool crowd after Chelsea's injury-time equaliser."

The tone was set by the "sibling rivalry" between Fergie and Wenger. As Jim
White noted: "As Arsenal began to gain ascendancy (over Fergie's United) it became a media commonplace that Wenger was the modernist, the quick-witted reformer, the quantum opposite of Ferguson. His professional demeanour was contrasted with the Scot's barrack-room bluster. Wenger was the new broom, while Fergie was the old school."

And, at the start of 1998-99, when Arsenal ran out easy 3-0 winners in the season's traditional curtain-raiser, the Charity (now Community) Shield. "The headline in the *Evening Standard* had changed somewhat in tone from the days (when it led with) Arsene Who? (upon the Frenchman's appointment as Arsenal manager). It now read: 'Wenger 3 Fergie 0'."

Fergie would soon set about getting his own back, and the media revelled in it, just as they did when Jose Mourinho arrived on these shores. And over recent years the Premier League has come to be sold as a series of WWE-style showdowns between the managerial heavyweights of the day. We've had Wenger v Fergie, Fergie v Benitez, Wenger v Mourinho, Mourinho v Benitez. And next year we'll have Mourinho v Guardiola, which is arguably the biggest of the lot.

Such showdowns are made for TV. Indeed, for the first time you can get *closer to the action* with TV. If football is all about what's happening on the touchline – the antagonisms between the managers – then the 'fan' has a better view from his or her armchair than he does from the stand, where his or her sight-lines may be blocked by a stray flag or scarf, or even a pie. With TV, we can achieve eye-bleeding close-ups, and slow-motion replays as this manager pushes that manager or perhaps gives him a piece of his mind. We can watch this one's heart break and the other's heart explode with joy. We can watch as a season is defined.

Seasons, for fans, used to be defined by being there, at the games. No more. Not any longer. Instead the season-defining moments as the year plunges towards 'squeaky bum-time', as the "cup-final rhythms" come into play, are seen on Sky, to the soundtrack of Martin Tyler's commentary. It used to be that we would go to the season-defining games thrusting through the turnstiles at the stadium, knowing we were at the very heart of the drama. Now the drama happens elsewhere. This is Jim White on Sky's split-screen coverage of the final matches of Premier League seasons, when the prizes are decided: "It was a nice demonstration of how Sky's technological advances had not simply enabled the delivery of the drama, they had enhanced it. In those pre-smartphone, Twitter-free days, in the stands information on critical developments elsewhere still came via a tortuous system of Chinese whispers, begun by those few who had thought to bring along transistor radios. On television you knew exactly what was happening as it happened. So not being there now meant being closer to the action than being there. How quickly the final day of the league season – and football in general – had become a television event."

Sometimes, league titles don't even get decided on the pitch. They get decided in pre- and post-match interviews – or so the media would have us believe. They get decided when, say, Fergie lands a knock-out blow and Kevin Keegan comes over all Kellogg's Honey Nut Loop-y in an interview, jabbing his finger and screeching about how much he would *love it*, thereby destabilising his team for the vital run-in.

The managers are absolutely central to the drama of the Premier League and they are eminently more watchable than a lot of the players. "Although players are given the leading roles, managers take the speaking parts," wrote Richard Williams in *The Guardian*. "When players, increasingly insulated from contact with the everyday world by their hugely inflated salaries, began to restrict contact with the media to bland interviews and brief post-match comments, the managers became the primary source of quotable material for the plots and subplots that animate the sports pages between matches.

"Managers learned to use interviews and obligatory press conferences before and after matches in a strategic way, exploiting the opportunity not only to celebrate success and present excuses for failure but to lay smokescreens or undermine rivals: Alex Ferguson versus Arsene Wenger, Wenger versus Jose Mourinho, Mourinho versus Manuel Pellegrini."

Mourinho said it himself. "When I go to the press conference before the game, in my mind the game has already started."

His press conferences are a masterclass in the art of Machiavellianism. As Jim White noted: "Before matches he would raise issues designed to get under the skin of a rival coach. One of his favourite tricks was to name the other side's team line up, the intention to cast doubt in his opposite number about his subsequent choice. (...) If it wasn't the coach, it was the referee or a rival player he targeted. There was not a word wasted in his deliberations: everything had meaning and purpose. It meant his press conferences quickly became major events; a source of drama, intrigue and controversy. Under his direction, Chelsea became the centre of the Premiership orbit, the story every reporter wanted to cover."

The Guardian's Daniel Harris has a more jaded view of the Mourinho show, describing a typical Jose Mourinho conference as containing "bathloads of bathos, panfuls of pathos and enough hubris to destroy a continent, along with the usual all-knowing narcissism and oblivious nihilism. Mainly, this was communicated through the medium of expressive snide."

But it is *still* more watchable than watching Wayne Rooney say "of course" over and over again, or your typical Premier League 'star' fudging his tenses.

At press conferences there often *are* no players. Occasionally a senior pro might rock-up and mumble the usual inanities, but mostly it is only Jose, taking on the opposition all on his ownio. What a hero.

The full make-up of Mourinho's Manchester United squad for the 2016-17 is as yet unknown but of the squad that completed the 2015-16 season under Louis van Gaal, only Wayne Rooney could challenge Mourinho in terms of celebrity. And the Wayne Rooney of 2015-16 is far removed from the Wayne Rooney of five or ten years ago.

At United, Mourinho will be *the man*, the big cheese, the big story. It is his reaction every media outlet will crave after every United game; it is his opinion every media outlet will seek out prior to the season's epic tussles.

Setting the tone

The great managers - the Super Coaches - set the tone for the clubs they manage. (And amongst the more traditional members of the Old Trafford hierarchy this has always been the main problem with Mourinho, during previous recruitment drives: the impression that the Portuguese might well *lower* the tone.)

In Mike Carson's *The Manager: Inside the Minds of Football's Leaders,* he discussed how Sir Alex Ferguson's Manchester United were "almost a direct expression of the manager's character." He described United as being "dependent (…) on the personality of Sir Alex" in order to succeed.

In order to illustrate his point, Carson quoted Paul Ince, who said: " 'When you sign for Manchester United, you want to play for Manchester United because for me it was the biggest club in the world. After about a year of being there I wanted to play for Alex Ferguson. In my eyes, he is Mr Manchester United.'"

During the fallow period following Ferguson's retirement, United have given the impression that they are still searching for an identity. David Moyes singularly failed to impress his own will, his own personality on the club, and indeed came out looking shit-scared at the scale of the task. He wasn't big enough for the club. Even Louis van Gaal - a *galactico* manager in his own right with a burgeoning trophy cabinet to show for three decades amongst the elite – couldn't impose his will fully. He met with resistance both from within and without. The fans never took to him; nor did the players.

Jose Mourinho acts like he is big enough for the job. He is box-office.

As Daniel Taylor wrote in *The Guardian* of Mourinho's first press conference as Red supremo, "Mourinho, much like Sir Alex Ferguson, can be a wonderful actor when the occasion demands it. (…) His first performance was (…) an impressive piece of theatre – he sounded, first and foremost, like a Manchester United manager – and a thin attempt to rewrite history didn't alter the perception that his new employers finally have the right man. Mourinho looked around him with the air of a man who already belonged. It was the aura of a man who considered himself the perfect fit. It felt like we were watching the Right One."

The Devil, after all, always has the best lines. And the devil had arrived.

They kept us waiting, all right. But now the waiting was over. Now the marketing machine would crank up into overdrive. And if you listened carefully, you could hear the cogs and wheels of the Old Trafford marketing machine grinding into life; getting ready to churn out Jose Mourinho shoe polish and Special One hair dye.

6

"THE APPOINTMENT SHOWS WHERE
THE CLUB'S PRIORITIES LIE – AND IT
ISN'T WITH THE FANS." (*THE
GUARDIAN*)
WHAT WE KNOW ABOUT MOURINHO
RUNS CONTRARY TO THE STORY
UNITED FANS TELL OURSELVES
ABOUT WHAT OUR CLUB *IS*.
HOW CAN THESE TWO STORIES - THE
GRAND NARRATIVE OF MANCHESTER
UNITED, AND THE 'JOSE MOURINHO
SHOW' - COME TOGETHER?

Manchester United fans believe – with an almost religious devotion - that the club is – to paraphrase the Barcelona motto – *more than just a club*. We're not like the rest: we're special ones. Not arrogant, just better. And we've the trophies to back it up:

we've won more top division titles than any other English club. But more than that we have our identity, our style. We're glamorous: we're the club of George Best after all. We've been known all over the world for our exciting, attacking play and our refusal to ever accept defeat. This identity was forged in the flames at Munich, where many of Sir Matt Busby's wonderful young team died – and Busby too, almost. The whole world fell in love with United as we – Phoenix-like – rose from the ashes; as we refused to go gentle into the good night. More recently, as a second young team began to hoover up trophies for the Reds – the famed Class of '92 - people have become jealous of United's success and the club has come to be one of the most hated in the land, but fans have always – until very recently - known what United *are*.

Over the past few years, the idea of what United are has become muddied. The Class of '92 have all now quit the game – even Ryan Giggs, who many thought might go on forever - and Sir Alex Ferguson has retired too. With them, the United way seems to have gone. And now, thanks to the Glazer regime, maybe United *are* just a football club. After all, recently, our transfer activity has come to resemble Manchester City's and Chelsea's. Real Madrid's too. And our marketing activity – a massive land-grab operation which spans the globe – is just like Madrid's also. Our playing style has to come to resemble Bayern Munich's, when they were managed by Louis van Gaal: it has become sterile. Nobody who went to Old Trafford last season would ever confuse the fare which was on offer as *glamorous*.

Van Gaal did at least blood young players, continuing a marvellous tradition within the club. The Dutchman, as Andrew Murray noted in *FourFourTwo* magazine, "gave first-team debuts to 15 academy graduates in his two seasons at Old Trafford, maintaining a truly remarkable statistic that a homegrown player has appeared in every United match-day squad since October 1937, comfortably more than 3000 games."

Marketing goons love to talk about unique selling points and key differentiating factors. The never-ending story of United's proud record in youth development is one we've been able to comfort ourselves with even as the club loses touch with some of its other traditions. We go right back to before even the Busby Babes, through Fergie's Fledglings and the Class of '92, to Marcus Rashford, Jesse Lingard, Cameron Borthwick-Jackson and Timothy Fosu-Mensah. And yet it is a story which many feel that the appointment of Jose Mourinho as manager will bring to a tragic end to. "Of all the criticisms levelled at Mourinho, his lack of long-term vision and hitherto unwillingness to promote from within are perhaps uppermost in people's minds," said Murray.

Mourinho attempted to deal with this criticism head-on during his very first press-conference as United supremo in July 2016, when he promised he wouldn't betray the Reds' proud youth development tradition. Indeed, he dismissed the claims about his own record in promoting youth as "one lie repeated many times" and then, in an almost Rafa Benitez-esque fact-rant, he talked – repeatedly – of the "49 players" he'd "promoted to the first team from academies" at his various clubs. "Some of them are big names, they are today Champions League winners or in the Euros, playing for national teams and 49 is a lot." The Portuguese even went as far as printing out a list of the names, which he offered as a hand-out to journalists, however, in true 'dog's eaten my homework, sir' style, it appeared someone had spilled coffee on it. He did, however, offer to send it out as an email instead.

The "49" did not stand up to much scrutiny however. As James Ducker noted in *The Daily Telegraph*, "almost half of them – 23 – made just one appearance under Mourinho with another 10 playing only two games for the Portuguese.

Most were packed off on loan or sold no sooner had they being handed their debuts. Just 14 of the players listed made more than five appearances under Mourinho."

You got the very real impression Jose was protesting too much.

Even those former players who tried to argue Mourinho's case for him seemed to have gotten hold of the wrong end of the stick. In Andrew Murray's *FourFourTwo* piece on Mourinho in the August 2016 edition of the magazine, he quoted Benni McCarthy, who won the Champions League under Mourinho at Porto. McCarthy said: "People say he doesn't like young players, but I disagree. We had so many young players at Porto, youngsters who became great players. At Madrid, Di Maria, Isco, Jese and Rafael Varane were all young."

Di Maria was 22 when he played for Mourinho at Real, and had been signed for £20 million. Isco didn't even play under Mourinho at Madrid: he was Carlo Ancelotti's first signing at the club, by which time, Jose was back at Chelsea.

The Marcus Rashford Question

But anyway, the proof of the pudding is always in the eating and it is actions which are supposed to speak louder than words. Alex Hess suggested that Jose Mourinho's second signing as United manager would almost immediately put the place of one of the young stars who'd risen to the fore under Van Gaal in jeopardy. When United signed the ageing superstar Zlatan Ibrahimovic, he wrote that Marcus Rashford's burgeoning progress: "could be stunted by his club's craving for attention. As Manchester United scramble to recover their status as England's No.1 club, it's no coincidence that their two major recruits this summer have been the planet's most famous coach and striker. There are plenty of footballing reasons behind the signings of Jose

Mourinho and Zlatan Ibrahimovic, of course, but we can rest assured that the club who currently boast 23 commercial partners across the globe may have seen a few non-footballing reasons too."

Those non-footballing reasons? Well, as Hess noted: "The year 2016 is (…) the first in which commercial deals will account for a majority of United's income. Sponsorship and merchandising makes up much of this, but so does the club's capacity to sell itself to would-be corporate partners who are simply seeking an audience. In this sense, the club's goal is nothing more, and nothing less, than profile. The more famous Manchester United are – the more people who tune in to watch them, the more circulation its players have on social media – the better the club can hawk itself to prospective associates, and the more money it can make. The club's owners, remember, are venture capitalists, not trophy collectors."

More than just a club? Not *even* a club these days – a *profile. A brand.*

"From this perspective," wrote Hess, "expensive short-term signings like Ibrahimovic (and Mourinho) are not in any way rash or ill-thought, but in fact perfectly sensible. They help make United the biggest story in football. Similarly, what could be more conspicuous and attention-grabbing than smashing the world transfer record to sign Paul Pogba, hottest property in Europe and burgeoning one-man brand? In that instance, spending crazy money would make perfect financial sense: a kind of inverse thrift."

"It's not a unique approach," he added, "Real Madrid have been doing something crudely similar for the past decade-and-a-half – but it is especially intriguing in the case of United, a club that prides itself (and sells itself) on misty-eyed notions of history, tradition and youth. This intrigue is even greater given the timing: United are currently seeing the emergence of their most exciting academy product in 20 years. It's still early days, but not too early to say that Marcus Rashford looks like the real deal – a player whose well-honed technique is fused seamlessly with a penchant for fearless dribbling and a poacher's instinct for sniffing out goals."

"In the recent past, Rashford's age, ability, playing style and local roots would have put him in the perfect position to be given a fair – even an overly fair – crack at establishing himself at United. Under the new order, the path may not be so clear, as Ibrahimovic's arrival demonstrates."

" 'We are continuing a long Manchester United tradition of bringing through our own talent," assured Ed Woodward at the end of last season, citing Rashford as proof. At the Dublin web summit in 2014, United's commercial director Richard Arnold boasted that "the new pope was announced the same day that Sir Alex Ferguson announced his retirement and we trended No.1 on Twitter"."

"We're directly in touch with 120 million fans," said Arnold. "Sixty million via Facebook; 264 tweets a minute. Fan engagement underpins everything we do. It drives sponsorship integration, which is a huge source of funds for us."

"It's important to note that the notions of profile and success should not be set in opposition. In fact, they generally align fairly well: Ibrahimovic is famous for being a sensational footballer, winning titles wherever he goes; Mourinho is famous because he is serial trophy-hoarder.

"United's own status as a commercial juggernaut is drawn directly from the success they have earned and enjoyed in the past. But whereas back then one was very much the bi-product of the other, nowadays success (as measured by trophies) is in danger of becoming little more than a happy offshoot to the real strategy.

"As for Rashford, his prospects are not helped by the fact that Mourinho has no track record of blooding youngsters for the sake of it. He will not pick the starlet simply to appease the spectre of Matt Busby.

"What will very much help Rashford's case, though, is the fact that Mourinho is interested only in winning football games – to the extent that he has turned pragmatism into a dogma – and Rashford himself is rather brilliant at football.

"Rashford's own excellence may be enough to carry him through, but the reality is that he's fighting against forces that did not exist for youngsters of previous generations.

"As far as Mourinho is concerned, Rashford's selection might often make more sense than some of his more commercially eligible team-mates, such as Memphis Depay, Wayne Rooney or even Ibrahimovic himself. Early signs are that he has a combination of pace, trickery and dependability that is unique within the United squad.

"But to look at it purely in these terms is to miss the bigger picture, which is that the club will by its very nature always be on the lookout for a statement signing – a player to ramp up the level of glitz, glamour and attention. Rashford, a quick, skilful attacker, is more likely than not to find his place threatened if and when they arrive. (There's a reason those periodic rumours linking United with Neymar – perhaps the most marketable player in world football – refuse to die.)

"Rashford's own excellence may be enough to carry him through, but the reality is that he's fighting against forces that did not exist for youngsters of previous generations. At this point we can take a moment to drink in the irony that it was David Beckham – famed product of the same youth academy as Rashford – that pioneered the modern-day incarnation of footballer-as-celebrity that has come so hellishly full circle with players like Neymar and

Ibrahimovic, who now stands in the way of Rashford's place in the United team.

"Perhaps, then, Rashford's best hope of establishing himself at United is to sport a mohican, hit the Northern Quarter in a sarong and hire an army of social media gurus to send his 'brand' spiralling into the digital stratosphere.

"Or perhaps he should just keep doing what he's doing. After all, much of the joy in Rashford's emergence has been its function as an antidote to the cynicism and corporate soullessness that increasingly defines top-level football, especially at the biggest clubs.

"Moreover, the nature of his arrival seems almost to have played in his favour: having sprung from obscurity, he's seemed liberated from the fame and scrutiny that weighs so heavily on his peers (not least during his brief England outings).

"If he's able to double down on that emergence and elbow his way to the forefront of United's setup under the new order of hits, shares and ratings, then that feelgood factor will only continue to soar. And besides, nothing draws in the viewers like a feelgood movie – right?"

The new story of Manchester United

All this talk of blooding young players is a smokescreen. The new story Manchester United tells the world is already very different from the one us fans still tell ourselves. Jose Mourinho doesn't have to go out in the Northern Quarter in a sarong in order to generate interest in the form of hits or to generate revenue in the form of newer, better commercial deals. That is the point of him. He is the obvious and only choice to be Manchester United manager.

Even now, just three years down the line, it seems very strange that United ever entrusted a job of such magnitude to someone like David Moyes. "Moyes," argued Barney Ronay in *The Guardian*, "was a sentimental, oddly literal kind of continuity appointment. United has been managed by Scots for 75 of the past 100 years (…), but Moyes was only ever the most flattering, rootsy Glasgow-centred Ferguson-Busby facsimile. It is Van Gaal, Jose Mourinho and the well-travelled elite of European management who represent continuity. Ferguson broke up, bought in and sold off teams on a similar scale to the itinerant big beasts of European football through his own successive United eras. He just didn't have to move house to do it."

Ferguson himself still seemed rather discombobulated by Moyes' (rather obvious in hindsight) failure at Old Trafford when discussing plans for his succession in his book *Leading*. "Life," he wrote, "is such that the best of theories, or the best of intentions, sometimes don't translate into practice. Believe me, the United board wanted nothing more than to select a manager who would be with the club for a long time. All of us knew the history of the club and the success and benefits that come from stable leadership. When we started the process of looking for my replacement, we established that several very desirable candidates were unavailable. It became apparent that Jose Mourinho had given his word to Roman Abramovich that he would return to Chelsea, and that Carlo Ancelotti would succeed him at Real Madrid. We also knew that Jurgen Klopp was happy at Borussia Dortmund, and would be signing a new contract. Meantime, Louis van Gaal had undertaken to lead the Dutch attempt to win the 2004 World Cup. We could obviously have taken the risk on a young manager who had not been tested, but eventually, as everyone knows, we selected David Moyes."

Moyes was the 'Chosen One', and then he wasn't. By the following season, United had been forced to look farther afield, for a bigger personality. Thus Louis van Gaal became United's first foreign manager in their history. Jose Mourinho, the second.

For a while it looked as though Louis van Gaal was big enough to succeed at Old Trafford, and certainly the media bought into the LVG 'story'. They built LVG up as a Mourinho-type figure upon whose every word they would hang. Journalists loved him – or at the very least were in awe of him. The media had craved a Mourinho type – controversial, outspoken, funny, arrogant, ridiculous – ever since Jose had left Chelsea back in 2007. The Mourinho who'd returned to the Stamford Bridge club in 2013 hadn't quite been the same. He'd been taken down a peg or three by his bitter experiences in Madrid. He returned worn-down, a little cowed, less arrogant. He wasn't so funny anymore (if anything he'd become a weak caricature of himself). And Fergie had also left a great, whopping hole when he'd retired from United. David Moyes proved unable to fill that hole in 2013-14. So the media were desperate to hang their hats on *somebody*.

Although LVG wasn't for everybody. Even while Louis van Gaal was enjoying the good times, Paul Wilson decided in a *Guardian* think-piece that although "Louis van Gaal presses all the right buttons for Manchester United now that they have joined the Super Coach circus after decades of doing things their own way" it was actually *Mourinho* they should have plumped for, a year previously when he was on the market after falling-out with practically everybody at Real Madrid (including, seemingly, himself). "Last summer, Mourinho's qualifications for the Old Trafford vacancy were clear. He too had won the league in different countries, taken two different teams to Champions League success, and as an additional bonus he had already proved himself a success in the Premier League. But he was overlooked because it was felt he would stick around for only three or four years before moving on. He was the restless type, would see himself as bigger than United, and he would make enemies and trouble along the way."

Instead United had opted for the known-quantity of David Moyes and got par for the Moyes course: seventh place.

But in the end, via a few U-turns, Mourinho arrived at Old Trafford anyway.

It didn't please everyone; far from it. Many match-going Reds felt the appointment went against everything Manchester United stood for. But that didn't bother the board. For it wasn't the match-going fan they were trying to please in appointing the Portuguese. Indeed, it would astound me if they even considered the opinion of the everyday, common-or-garden season-ticket-holder. Clubs like United are not answerable to their match-going fans any more. They are answerable to their owners and shareholders, and to the worldwide audience who tune in week-by-week to the TV coverage.

And clubs mean very different things to their worldwide fan-bases. "Some people are worrying that Jose Mourinho might mean the end of the Manchester United way," wrote Paul MacInnes in *The Guardian*. "They're fretting that fast-paced attacking football and the development of local talent might be a thing of the past. They're looking at the way an (admittedly unloved) manager (Van Gaal) was effectively sacked behind his back and are concerned about what that says about the club.

"These people are Manchester United fans and their opinions don't really matter. It may not be that every single United season-ticket holder is disenchanted but it seems likely that any person who is is a paying supporter. They're the ones who gorged on the Fergie years after all, but they are also themselves part of the tradition (…). Now they see their club becoming just another mega-brand and, what's more, one that chooses a former rival, a short-termist and a coach who shares none of their on-field values being chosen ahead of Ryan Giggs, a legend who has been with the club since he was 14 years old.

"But, like I said, these fans don't amount to much. That's because out there, beyond the turnstiles, are many millions more Man Utd (or Manchester or Man Yoo) fans who *do* want Mourinho in. Who *want* the unending drama that the Portuguese guarantees; the insults, the mind games, the histrionics. Oh and the trophies. Mourinho brings titles, and that's a fact. Millions of Manchester United fans won't settle for anything less."

The most recent TV deal for Premier League club means that the Premier League receives around five times as much for the rights to show Premier League matches worldwide than its nearest competitor, *La Liga* in Spain. And that includes Real Madrid and Barcelona. The two Spanish giants are eminently more watchable than most Premier League sides, and boast the two biggest footballing superstars in the world. And yet they *don't* promise the same drama as the Premier League.

"As football becomes less a sport and more a form of entertainment, drama matters," wrote MacInnes. "It's what persuades those millions of fans to pay for TV subscriptions, or buy replica shirts, or turn up at an Irish pub at 3am to get lashed for breakfast. These fans, just like the ones who pay to attend Old Trafford, feel an attachment to their chosen club. Just like the season-ticket holders, they hold strong opinions and they hold them genuinely. That their connection to the club is not geographical or familial, or even class-based (though that in itself would be highly unusual), is not their fault. Neither is the fact that their connection to their favourite team is a little less durable. It's the only way they know. The question for me is more what this means for the old fan, the physical fan. Once upon a time these supporters were the ones that kept their club afloat (and for the purposes of this argument, I'm talking Premier League fans here, a status all fans in whatever tier aspire to). Thanks to Sky and NBC and Continental and Gazprom this is no longer the case. They used to root a club in its local area, create a link that made them part of the community. That community is now a global one and it's rootless.

"What fans in the ground can do that supporters on the sofa in a onesie cannot is make a noise. They are still often described as the 12th man. But more often they might feel like a third wheel. When Newcastle fans see Moussa Sissoko turn it on for the TV cameras or Chelsea fans watch Eden Hazard emerge from a season-long slumber at the final possible opportunity to earn himself a slot on Leicester City's Miracle end-of-season documentary, they might wonder what value the atmosphere they create actually has. And yes Leicester are a glorious exception to this and yes you might think that proves the rule. While silent grounds are easily remedied in the edit suite, empty terraces are not. Shrinking attendances will provide bad optics, as they say in the PR biz, and hit the brand of both clubs and the league. Physical fans could vote with their feet and stop turning up in the expectation that clubs would drop prices to get them back in. But they could drop ticket prices to free and it wouldn't change the direction in which the game is going (though I'd love to see the crowd).

"Once the physical fan realises this, there's the chance of liberation. No longer is there the overwhelming need to pay astronomical ticket prices. No longer the requirement to waste your weekends and week nights travelling at inconvenient times to suit TV schedules. No need to deny yourself the half-and-half scarf because, you know, you feel you'd be letting the club down. No need to be stuck in a ground while you watch 90 minutes of conservative, scared-to-lose-out-on-all-this-money football. No need to drink weak lager ever again. With that liberty might come inner peace. Or at least enough money to punt out for Sky. The game is still for the fans, it's just a different type of fan now."

The Guardian usually reserves its editorial comment pieces for political happenings of great import. Everything else is frivolous. But when Jose Mourinho was made manager of Manchester United, the newspaper felt duty bound to comment. Maybe this was because the paper has its roots in Manchester (it started life as *The Manchester Guardian* after all), or maybe it was because the appointment was bound to get under the skins of many match-going Reds who already felt disenfranchised by the club they loved after the takeover by the Glazers. Or maybe it was because the appointment said a great deal about the state of elite level football today, and about Manchester United – this nation's greatest sporting institution – in particular. That is the interpretation I prefer, and it is the one which led me into writing this book.

"In the past," commented *The Guardian*, "a football club's primary purpose was to win games and trophies and attract fans through the turnstiles. Under Matt Busby and, later, Alex Ferguson, Manchester United set post-war benchmarks for that." But: Attracting fans to games is a secondary part of Manchester United's business plan. This year may be the first in which the majority of the club's income comes from commercial sources.

"As one commentary put it, the most valuable thing that Manchester United now sells is *not* the football it plays but the audience that the club can deliver for advertisers and commercial partners. Football fans like to imagine that their loyalty is what animates the club. That is no longer true, if indeed it ever was.

"That's why Mr Mourinho's arrival at Old Trafford is so resonant. Manchester United's grand self-image involves bringing on young British players and playing attacking football. Others may question that rose-tinted Mancunian view. But in any case Mr Mourinho is not interested in either of these things. For him winning is all. He is very good at it. He is also box office in his own right. But the appointment shows where any club's priorities lie — and it isn't with the fans."

7

"ONCE A BLUE, ALWAYS A RED?" CAN A MANAGER WHO IS SO RECOGNISABLY A BLUE BECOME A RED?

Chelsea fans used to sing Jose Mourinho's name to the tune of *La donna è mobile*. They still did sometimes, even after he left them twice. It remains to be seen whether they'll sing it again now Jose is at the helm at Old Trafford. Mind you, they did sing for Leicester City (and their ex-boss Claudio Ranieri) rather than their own team throughout their penultimate home game of the 2015-16 season so anything is possible.

La donna è mobile is from the Verdi opera *Rigoletto*. (And trust those West Londoners to sing opera.) It means 'The woman is fickle', or 'flighty'. And in many ways Jose Mourinho can be described as a fickle, or flighty boss. His positions have been defined, largely, by their short-termism.

Manchester United fans weren't alone amongst Premier League rivals in serenading the Portuguese with an alternative version of the song, but we were probably the loudest. We sang: 'fuck off Mourinho'. And we sung it with gusto.

Though Mourinho was popular, especially with the media, United fans weren't impressed with him. Not one bit. We didn't like his attitude and the often crass things he said. We didn't like the way he set his teams out. We didn't like how he splashed the cash. Mostly we didn't like it that his Chelsea team had won the Premier League title – a trophy most fans considered to belong to the Reds – two seasons in succession (in 2004-05 and 2005-06), apparently blowing United out of the water in the process.

In 2006-07 when United were back on track and breathing down Chelsea's neck we sang with increasing belief and, in the end, no little Schadenfreude, the following little ditty (to the tune of Walking in a Winter Wonderland):

Mourinho, are you listening?
You better keep our trophy glistening,
'Cause we'll be back in May to take it away,
Walking in a Fergie wonderland.

There are some Red fans I know still consider it one of the most joyous United songs of recent years. It was at once a statement of our renewed confidence in the team and our absolute determination that no *arriviste* team with its *arriviste* manager and shady owner was going to knock us off our rightful perch as England's best club for long. It was a sigh of relief, because in singing it, we were acknowledging that Mourinho's Chelsea were human after all - in the past couple of years the Stamford Bridge club had shown themselves to be veritable machines - and hence beatable.

The song was the fans' our way of sharing some of Fergie's fun; playing one of his famous mind-games. We're coming for you, we said, and Chelsea knees knocked, just as Blackburn knees had when Fergie mentioned Devon Loch and just as Kevin Keegan's *braincells* knocked when Fergie mentioned Leeds not trying against Newcastle and just as Rafa Benitez's chin had wobbled when he ranted about facts at Liverpool.

Another song intended to rile-up the Stamford Bridge faithful and which was sung up and down the land was the one about Chelsea having no history. But United had history with *Mourinho* all right.

When we were being generous we called him Maureen.

When we weren't, well, you can imagine.

During Mourinho's second spell at Chelsea I wrote an article for a fanzine regarding the vagaries of the managerial merry-go-round, comparing it with the TV (and book) series (and all-round cultural phenomenon) *Game of Thrones*. In the article I called Jose Mourinho "that puffed-up Targaryen dragon of spite and specialness".

How am I supposed to take that back now Jose Mourinho is the Manchester United boss,our supremo, our *numero uno*? How are we all supposed to forget what we sang?

Modern football makes hypocrites of us all, I suppose. It asks us to forget – if not forgive – many things. It asks us sometimes to take an airbrush to history. At United, we know all about the importance of history. It's what sets us apart from clubs like Chelsea. And yet...

And yet, sometimes you just have to hold your nose and get on with it.

I think to understand the extreme curvature of the U-turn Manchester United fans have got to make on Jose Mourinho, you have to go right back to the beginning. Actually, we might go back further than that. To the year *before* Jose's big-bang on the Old Trafford touchline as Porto manager, by which he announced himself to the English public.

Before that, we'd barely heard of him. But our Scottish cousins had, and he hadn't exactly charmed them.

The devil in Seville

Jose Mourinho exploded into the consciousness of Glasgow Celtic fans in May 2003. He was the manager of Porto, who would face the Hoops in Celtic's first European final for 33 years. Celtic had become the first British club to win the European Cup in Portugal with their famous Lisbon lions, all eleven of whom had been born within a 30-mile radius of Glasgow. Now they would be facing Portuguese opposition in the UEFA Cup final.

It is said that up to 100,000 Glasgow Celtic fans converged on Seville for the final. It was the largest mass-migration of British folk since the Second World War, for those of you who are interested in your history (maybe not Chelsea fans then). Some Celtic fans claimed 100,000 was actually an under-estimation. In fact, they reckoned, it was probably twice that. But then, they were seeing double by this point; had been before they'd even poured themselves out of their taxis at Glasgow Prestwick Airport; after a further two full days of incessant partying the Celtic fans could be forgiven for over-egging the pudding somewhat.

They'd come to see the last really great Celtic team; a team spearheaded by a truly great striker, Henrik Larsson, and managed by Martin O'Neill, who many Celtic fans believed a motivational genius. Gavin Berry in the *Scottish Mail Sport Extra* saw some similarities between the Celtic boss and his (then little known) Portuguese counterpart. He called Mourinho "O' Neill Mark Two".

Berry wrote: "He is the master of motivating his players, making them think they're better than they really are and always talking his team up. In return they will do almost anything for him."

As Celtic fans – and some Scottish journalists – would later contend, that *almost anything* included resorting to some of football's darkest arts. But before the final the Scottish media only had words of praise for Mourinho and his methods.

"Similarities between the FC Porto manager and his rival are uncanny," wrote Berry, "even to the point where his squad has many players rejected by other clubs or lingering in the reserves. That way players are hungrier and O'Neill did just that with Neil Lennon and John Hartson. The Irishman has since reaped the rewards. And that's the type of psychology which makes Mourinho the manager he is and has brought Porto so much success, including a possible treble this season. Midfielder Maniche was in the Benfica second string when Jose signed him and has now been called up to the national side, evidence of what can be achieved under Mourinho."

It was hot in Seville. Pitchside thermometers recorded temperatures of 35 degrees and above just prior to the evening kick-off. And it was hot on the pitch too. The first-half was tense and "punctuated by niggly fouls" (John Dillon in his *Daily Express* match report) before Derlei netted on the stroke of half-time for Porto. The Brazilian striker celebrated his opener rather exuberantly in front of the Celtic fans; something which was later blamed for what went on at half-time.

The re-start was delayed by a streaker who took it upon himself to take kick-off and hare down-field. He even managed to rattle off a shot at Porto 'keeper Vitor Baia before finally being hailed away by stewards. But, as Dillon noted: "it was, at least, an occurrence more in keeping with the party atmosphere than the mini-brawl between players which had erupted in the tunnel at half-time." Keith Jackson in *The Daily Record* noted O'Neill had to "throw himself in to pull his players (Balde and Alan Thompson) away from the flashpoint".

ANDREW J. KIRBY

Niggly fouls. Mini-brawls. Mourinho's tactics, it was clear, were to disrupt and frustrate Celtic. Rile one of their players into getting sent-off. But if that was the case, they didn't work immediately, for the Scots equalised within two minutes of the re-start through Henrik Larsson, the Swedish striker their fans knew as the 'King of Kings'.

The blue-touch paper had been lit in more ways than one. Six minutes later, Porto took the lead again, this time through the Russian midfielder Alenichev. But Porto could only hold their lead a further four minutes before Larsson again headed Celtic level. After such an antsy first-half, it was the fourth goal in twenty harum-scarum minutes. And after it, both O'Neill and Mourinho chose to tighten-up their sides. The last half-hour was a nervous wait until extra-time.

But in the additional half-hour, the Celtic centre-back Bobo Balde received his marching orders for a second yellow card – a lunging challenge which might have received a straight red - and at last Derlei found the crucial extra space to break Scots' hearts with a silver-goal winner five minutes from full-time.

Celtic fans were distraught; they felt as though they'd suffered a huge injustice, especially after the odyssey of their route to the final, and then playing so well in Seville. They felt it was a clear tactic on the part of Mourinho to instruct his players to lay a trap: lure one of the Celtic players into getting sent off.

Others without the green-tinted spectacles just thought that maybe Celtic didn't have the street-smarts to compete with Jose's team.

And besides, even the Scottish media (Keith Jackson in *The Daily Record*) admitted Celtic players were "almost too fired-up" during the early exchanges as the challenges flew in.

But Jackson's *Daily Record* colleague David McCarthy wasn't prepared to give Porto the benefit of the

190

doubt. He wrote of Celtic's brilliant, resilient display against "appalling adversity": Mourinho's Porto players, he contended, "were diving all night."

McCarthy, clearly as heartbroken as the supporters, went further: "Celtic's fans have been taunting the Rangers support for weeks about watching *The Bill* while they were in Seville. Little did they know they would spend the night in southern Spain watching a version of *Crimewatch*. Make no mistake, Porto are an excellent team. But the manner in which they played left a taste in the mouth more sour than anything a gallon of San Miguel the night before could muster."

"Porto were tricky," he added. "They were slick and surefooted. They had enough talent to resist resorting to ducking and diving around the penalty box. But they cheated anyway and it was a criminal waste of talent. Deco collapsed whenever he felt the breath of Neil Lennon on the back of his neck. Derlei (…) threw himself around like a rag-doll and Nuno Valente wasn't averse to a bit of play-acting whenever he charged down the left."

Mind you, McCarthy wasn't one for down-playing things – also in his piece he talked of how the only unsavoury aspect to the build-up to the match was the fact "so many spivs had made a fortune out of the Parkhead faithful's desperation to see the match." He described one, "a Cockney wide-boy" (though I have no idea how cockneys came to be involved, nor how McCarthy knew he was one, other than it fitted the story best) outside the ground "with a wad of match-tickets thick enough to choke a horse. Like some fly-by-night drug dealer he was flogging them for £500 a pop and he was getting plenty of takers from punters whose desire for their fix was greater than their need to hold on to their hard-earned cash."

And then, in one of those italicised sections which tabloids do so well and which the magazine *Viz* takes off so well; the ones which are supposed to let you know *here's the lesson folks*, he added: "It wasn't heroin he was dealing. It was hero worship and it was sickening to see him profiting so much."

The winning manager wasn't a fly-by-night, nor was he a spiv, and in the wake of the match Mourinho was keen to hit back at any suggestion of underhand tactics: "I'd prefer to ask whether the behaviour of the Celtic players was normal in your country. What Balde did to Deco in front of me could have ended his career. The referee didn't affect the result, in that there were no doubtful decisions, but I think Balde could have had a direct red for his foul and Thompson could also have seen a second yellow card on two occasions. The referee wanted to end the game with 11 against 11 and I think maybe he was a bit afraid to send anyone off. There was a lot of commitment in Celtic's game, commitment, toughness and aggression. I'm tempted to use another word - but I won't. We have given a great example to the world and those who love football and we have also made history by taking the UEFA Cup to Portugal for the first time ever."

But still, for many Celtic fans, they were left with a taste in their mouths more sour than last night's San Miguel. They wouldn't be the last to come out of a game with a Mourinho side feeling like they had to choke back the vomit.

Next, unfortunately, it was Manchester United's turn.

Left counting the Cost(inha)

The Red Devils were reigning Premier League champions. While Celtic and Porto had been navigating the latter stages of the UEFA Cup the previous season, United had been clawing back an eight point deficit from Arsenal thanks to Ruud van Nistelrooy's glut of goals, the imperial form of Paul Scholes in his pomp, and a defence which was the most parsimonious in the league (Rio Ferdinand, for whom

United had paid a then British record transfer fee, looked like an excellent purchase). Eight points behind in March, United won the title in May.

It was – astoundingly – their eighth Premier League title in eleven seasons and they'd bolstered the squad some too, prior to another tilt the Champions League crown in the 2003-04 season. World Cup-winning midfielder Kleberson was brought in, as was the American goalkeeper Tim Howard. French speed-merchant David Bellion was bought from Sunderland. Eric Djemba-Djemba, the midfielder so good they named him twice arrived also, from Nantes.

Unfortunately, none of the new signings proved to be upgrades on what the Reds already had. Kleberson might have been an Ed Woodward-style imposter; surely he couldn't have won a World Cup; surely he wasn't even *Brazilian*. Eric Djemba-Djemba proved too fond of the Manchester nightlife. Bellion was fast, but didn't look like he'd ever kicked a ball before. And Tim Howard... well, maybe he proved to be just a little bit unlucky. Certainly he was doing very well in between the sticks at United, thank you very much, until the clash against Mourinho's Porto. That game pretty much ended his United career. But for English football as a whole it would have far bigger consequences.

There was, however, one unqualified success amongst United's pre-season signatures. The young boy United brought in from Portugal as a direct replacement for the Madrid-bound David Beckham did not bad in the famous number 7 shirt, eh? Yeah, Cristiano Ronaldo was all right.

But in 2003-04, he was still very young. He was just 19 at the time of the last-16 tie against Porto, and as usual in crucial Champions League away games Ferguson preferred to trust his more experienced performers, especially given the hostile atmosphere which awaited

Ronaldo – a former Sporting Lisbon player – at Porto's Estadio do Dragao.

They could unleash Ronaldo later in the tournament, couldn't they? After all, things seemed to be going all kinds of smoothly for United that year. United had been on easy street during the group stage. They progressed comfortably to the round of 16 following five wins out of six in a Group E which included Stuttgart, Panathinaikos, and Celtic's bitter Glasgow rivals, Rangers. The aggregate score of the three home ties against that trio was ten goals to nil to United.

Reds fans were confident United would breeze past Porto too. UEFA Cup winners or no, the last time we'd faced them, we'd thrashed them 4-0 in one of the all-time best European nights under the lights at Old Trafford. The draw, we felt, had been relatively kind to us. We could have pulled one of the Italian giants, Juventus or Milan. We could have pulled Bayern Munich, or Real Madrid. Instead we got Porto. All we needed to do was get a decent result – possibly an away goal – out there, and then get them back to Old Trafford, where we'd dispatch them with ease.

Well, United did get an away goal. And though the result wasn't great, it was certainly no disaster. Certainly it was retrievable at the Theatre of Dreams. Or so we thought.

The first-leg of the tie was played on 25th February 2004. Utility man Quinton Fortune gave United an early lead – and a precious away goal – but his fellow South African Benni McCarthy – a replacement for Celtic's conqueror Derlei – equalized for Porto on the half-hour with a sumptuous goal. Cristiano Ronaldo came on as a 76th minute substitute for Louis Saha, but two minutes later McCarthy netted his second. As United chased an equalizer of their own, captain Roy Keane was sent-off for a late challenge on Porto goalkeeper Vitor Baia.

After the game, Fergie made like David McCarthy of the *Daily Record*. He didn't go so far as accusing Mourinho's players of cheating, but he did insist Baia made the most of Keane's contact and his actions had gotten the United man sent off. Ferguson said: "The goalkeeper made more of it than he should have done. Certainly he stood on the lad but I don't know whether he could have got out of the way. I can understand why the linesman flagged but the keeper made a meal of it There was no malice in the incident, it is not Roy's style to do anything like that."

Alf Inge Haaland, amongst others, might disagree with that.

But certainly the Glaswegian was spitting feathers about the decision. He confronted Mourinho at the final whistle. Mourinho shrugged him off, but came out fighting in the ring of his own choice: the post-match press conference.

He said, calmly: "I understand why he is a bit emotional."

And then he waited a beat, two, before he applied the upper-cut; the punch-line: "You would be sad if your team gets as clearly dominated by opponents who have been built on 10% of the budget."

Things got more niggly still. Mourinho demanded Ferguson apologise in full for his comments about Baia. "Ferguson told me in the tunnel that he thought Vitor had made the most of it," he said. "But again, I understand why he is a bit emotional. He has some top players in the world and they should be doing a lot better than that."

The Portuguese, however, would not be drawn on claims Ferguson had refused to shake hands with him after the game. Perhaps he already knew how important ritual, routine and tradition were to English football – the handshake, "the fabled glass of wine, the *deus ex machina* of all phoney deference" (*The Guardian's* Daniel Harris) - and particularly to Ferguson.

Mourinho's gibes aside, the other blow to the solar-plexus which United and Fergie were forced to take was the fact the talismanic Roy Keane would miss the second-leg.

Mind, Keano might not have *lasted* the second-leg such was the gamesmanship on display from Porto at Old Trafford. United fans hadn't seen anything like it. David McCarthy would have had a field day. Defenders Costinha and Ricardo Carvalho – who we'd see more of under Mourinho at Chelsea – niggled and spoiled at every turn. Alenichev and Maniche time-wasted. And to the rogue's gallery of divers named and shamed in the *Daily Record* after the UEFA Cup final – Deco and Nuno Valente - could be added one name. The most unsteady on his feet of them all: Carlos Alberto de Jesus. Think an unholy combination of current equivalents Sergio Busquets, Pepe, and Ashley Young all rolled into one package.

The Brazilian is an interesting historical anomaly. He was to many as exciting a prospect as Cristiano Ronaldo back in 2003-04 and certainly he one of the key figures in Porto's run to the final of the Champions League that year, even scoring the opener in the final against Monaco. However 2003-04 was to be his one and only season in the sun. Eventually, homesick and out-of-sorts, he moved back to Brazil having played only 22 matches in all competitions for Porto.

But boy did he make an impact during that last-16 tie and boy could the lad dive: pikes, triple-pikes, tucks, somersaults. The lad had it all. And he showed his full array of talents on the pitch at Old Trafford on the evening of 9th March 2004, in front of 67,029 witnesses who were baying for his blood.

However, in the end, Carlos Alberto would prove only a footnote. As would the actions of his cronies. For the real headline action of the evening – the stuff which would have the faithful at the Theatre of Dreams howling at the injustice of it all – took place off the green-sward and on the touchline. Make no mistake the real scoundrel of the piece for United fans was Jose Mourinho; the arch-villain of them all. Carlos Alberto *et al* were only his minions.

That wasn't to say there wasn't drama on the pitch – there was: the game was steeped in dramatic tension – but in the end, the most powerful image was Mourinho, sprinting and sliding down the Old Trafford touchline, "catapulting himself into the eye of the football world" (Scott Hunt for *Mancunian Matters*). For that was the image which spoke louder than a hundred thousand words of newsprint and which launched a million new Premiership narratives. In its own way, the power of that image and the impact of it on English football could only be compared with Cantona's Selhurst Park kung-fu kick, with Brian Kidd and Fergie leaping about on the pitch after Steve Bruce's Fergie-time winner against Sheffield Wednesday, and – yes – later, Sergio Aguero securing the championship for Manchester City by netting in the last-knockings of the last match of the 2011-12 season. "For when Francisco Costinha struck for Porto in the last minute (and inspired that extravagant celebration) he not only dumped Manchester United out of the Champions League, but help change the face of football."

"It was audacious. It was arrogant. It was attention seeking. It was Mourinho."

In an alternative, sliding-doors reality, one in which United had *not* seen Paul Scholes' goal incorrectly chalked-off for offside (had the lino not flagged, Scholes and United would have had their second of the night, and they'd have been cruising; maybe fans might have laughed at the antics of Carlos Alberto *et al*) the Reds would have won the game no question. And then maybe gone deep in the competition. With Scholes at the height of his powers – the type of form which prompted Zinedine Zidane no less to call him "undoubtedly the greatest of his generation" – and Van Nistelrooy as lethal as any other striker in Europe, who knows, United might have gone on to the final in Gelsenkirchen – certainly they'd have given each of the other semi-finalists a game (Monaco, Deportivo La Coruna and a pre-Mourinho Chelsea). Maybe they'd have even won it. And if it had been Manchester United's name carved onto that famous trophy and not Porto's, then maybe nobody on British shores - aside from the usual European football hipsters – would have known Jose Mourinho's name.

If Porto hadn't won at Old Trafford, Scott Hunt asked: "Would Mourinho have been made Chelsea manager? Would the football world ever have really known the name Mourinho? That is impossible to say, but when the Portuguese danced down the Old Trafford turf, he made the world take notice. He has done the same ever since."

Incidentally, this wasn't the first time the landscape of English football had been changed so enormously off the back of a Champions League tie at Old Trafford, and not because of anything United had achieved. It wasn't even the first time in the new millennium. Roman Abramovich, of course, was seduced into the idea of owning his own football club after witnessing United beat Real Madrid 4-3 (but lose on aggregate) in 2003. He bought Chelsea just four months later. Maybe in hindsight Fergie should have gone 4-5-1 in that match and tried to scrape through by keeping it tight at the back. Maybe that way we'd never have seen the like of the oddball Russian and his billions (and maybe that way the precedent would never have been set: maybe we'd never have then seen the Abu Dhabi guys converging on Manchester City, either).

No: United fans wouldn't have it that way. Not if it meant sacrificing the club's philosophy. Not if it meant playing 4-5-1.

But we're talking *what ifs* and *what might have beens*. What did happen was Mourinho. As "a result of that game the Portuguese became a big deal. His unfancied Porto side had knocked out European giants Manchester United in their own back yard. Not only that but they would go on to win the Champions League that season, thrusting Mourinho up to the top table of the European game."

And into the history books.

History books wouldn't record *how* Mourinho's Porto won it, but football is not all about facts and figures; fans memories do not turn on the grist of statistics; the cogs and wheels of them are wound to the pitches and rhythms of matches. As such, like the Celtic fans before us, we would remember Carlos Alberto (even though he only played 22 matches, and probably many *Portuguese* fans don't recall much about him) and we would remember his dives and his rolls. Boy; that lad could roll almost the full length of the pitch. And most of the time he'd barely even been breathed upon. We would remember how Porto played. "They were entirely defensive in both legs, diving and cheating their way through. Credit to them, it worked, but it certainly wasn't kind on the eye," wrote Scott Patterson, in his Republik of Mancunia fanzine.

Mourinho's Chelsea machine

Even before the Stamford Bridge club *sold your arse to a Russian* (as the tasteful little number went), United fans' affectionate nickname for Chelsea was *rent boys*. Yeah it wasn't very grown-up, but *football* isn't very grown-up. For a while though, Roman Abramovich's purchase of Chelsea FC and his subsequent appointment of Jose Mourinho as manager had United fans putting away our childish things. Our fancies: sport was no longer something wild and untameable. It was something to be trapped and killed. We'd been forced to face a new reality, to admit the Arcadian past – those halcyon early Premier League years under Fergie – were exactly that: the past. Chelsea had come onto the scene and they'd rewritten the rules of the game; changed everything. We'd just have to grow up, be adult about it, and admit that yeah, money spoiled everything. Football was no longer the game we'd grown up loving. It was something else.

In the previous section I talked – childishly - about alternative realities. What would have happened if the linesman had not raised his flag on that Scholes goal, if Mourinho had not had the chance to perform his glory-dance on the Old Trafford touchline?

What would have happened if Roman Abramovich had not bought Chelsea?

We'll never know. Fate turns on the moments which seem the most insignificant; the closing of a sliding carriage door when you're dashing for the last Metro home; selling a corporate seat – the hottest ticket in town – to a Russian bloke who lived in London for a Champions League clash. In hindsight, the bods in corporate should have told him we were sold-out. But then, part of growing-up is also admitting to your own faults and United have *never* been able to turn down flashed cash.

And so Roman Abramovich *was* in Manchester to witness Manchester United entertain Real Madrid at Old Trafford on 23rd April 2003 in a Champions League quarter-final. And entertain they did. Both sides. It was a rip-roaring, skill-laced, star-studded affair and United won the game 4-3, though Real Madrid would progress on aggregate scores. That Madrid side contained Raul (the Spaniard who no less than Alex Ferguson had once deemed the best player in the world, Zinedine Zidane (the Frenchman who everyone else thought was), and the Brazilian Ronaldo (who scored a hat-trick on the night, and was applauded off the field by the faithful at the Theatre of Dreams). United's line-up was no-less stellar. Certainly they included the world's most-*famous* footballer in David

Beckham, alongside "pricey imports like Ruud van Nistelrooy and Juan Sebastian Veron."

For the football fan, watching the game is all about *being there, at the ground.* Sometimes we watch history unfold; sometimes we'd rather watch paint dry. But we're there all the same. Supporting. Television, ticket prices, kick-off times and growing-up have changed how we watch football. Now, Sky has made it all about being there, in your armchair, with your Sky remote. Consuming. For the oligarch, football has always been about consuming. It's been about training your sights on a game, then shooting it, both barrels. Displaying its head on your wall like a trophy.

In his book *Premier League: A History in Ten Matches* Jim White talked of how this "clash between the world's two most followed clubs, sides fabled for their attacking verve (…) was the tie everyone wanted to attend, a must-see event for every big-game hunter."

And not just must-see; must-*have.* Abramovich had seen the magnificent lions, that journey of giraffes, the teeming herds of zebra out in the wild, on the African savannah, and now he wanted more. He wanted to *own* them. He'd got the bug. After the game he enquired – tentatively - as to how easily he could purchase Manchester United. But United were a Plc. There were stumbling blocks; not least tracking down every shareholder and asking them to sell their shares. And in the end, the oligarch wanted to live in London, where there was a growing presence of mega-rich Russian exiles. London, not this *Manchester,* whatever it was: was it a safari park?

In the end, he plumped for Chelsea.

He bought the 'Chelsea Village' for £18 million from Ken Bates and then bought out the other stakeholders with quick dispatch. "He also took responsibility for the club's debt," said Jim White, "immediately paying most of it back to the banks, converting it into soft loans to himself. Within four months of seeing that game in Manchester he now owned a football club in the Premiership. Chelsea was his. The total bill – including paying off the debt – was £140 million."

And the spending wouldn't end there. Now he needed the players; the stellar names to fill the Chelsea roster: the Ronaldos, the Rauls, the Beckhams of this world. Stuff the lions and the giraffes and the zebra. Abramovich wanted to make like Dickie Attenborough (a famous Chelsea pensioner before his death) in *Jurassic Park*. He wanted to be able to say: "Yes, we have a T-Rex."

Abramovich wanted instant success. Trophies (actual trophies, ones which required silver-polish and not just heads to display on the wall). He knew only one way of ensuring this happened: money.

"In effect," wrote Jim White, "what Abramovich had done was take the idea first made flesh by Jack Walker (at Blackburn Rovers) – that money could buy the Premier League – and inflated it to fit the pricier parameters of the competition as it entered its second, ever more financially muscular, decade. Where Walker had done it for tens of millions, the price of entry had doubled in less than ten years. This was now a seriously rich man's game. An oligarch's game."

To back up his point White mentioned in passing the Reading owner John Madejski, and his attempts to sell his majority shareholding in the club. In a newspaper interview which was tantamount to taking out a full-page ad, he said: "'The brand is getting stronger all the time and if there is a billionaire who wants a nice accessory down the M4 then come and talk to me. (…) I'll listen to sensible offers. But from billionaires only. Millionaires need not apply.'"

Billionaires *did* apply, and they did so against all received wisdom. There is a famous idiom that goes a little something like this: how do you make a small fortune? You start out with a large fortune and you invest in a football club. (And you can imagine the stuffy old suits under the moose- and deer-heads in an exclusive Mayfair club spitting out their caviar as they LOL at that one. Slapping each other on the back. 'Say, what was that Boris? A football club? How do I get me one of those?') But then, the super-rich – and even some dentists – are willing to pay exorbitant amounts and risk plastic-surgery-perfected life and limb to go *off reservation* into the African wild (where the authorities can't see you but maybe the lions can) in the hope that they might see a leopard or maybe a rhino. Then shoot the bastard right between the eyes and pose for a photo, legs astride it as it takes its shuddering last breath.

The best description I have ever read of this risk/reward conundrum the billionaire investor faces when taking on a football club was written by Barney Ronay in *The Guardian*. He acknowledged: "the basic inanity of the billionaire himself, a creature whose existence is essentially the complete opposite of sport, with all its ragged edges and imperfections. Whereas the billionaire lifestyle is pegged out around a notion of absolute certainties, a sense of being continually replete, recumbent on a giant mattress made of veal, helicoptered from triple-glazed pyramid to glass-walled enormo-drome. To the billionaire, sport, with all its glorious uncertainty, is something to be tamed and killed, machine-gunned with money, until even the grandest football club begins to resemble some stretched and burnished trophy wife, muzzled beneath a paste of high-end slap and stitch."

When Abramovich first took over at Stamford Bridge he took on a team which was stuffed with "ragged edges and uncertainties". As such, he allowed the then manager Claudio Ranieri to spend a cool £111 million on new players in 2003 alone. But the Premier League refused to be "machine-gunned with money". Not that season anyway. Instead it was "tamed and killed" by Arsene Wenger's Arsenal Invincibles. This feat, Abramovich decided, wasn't achieved because Wenger had, over time, built a fantastic team dripping with talent like Thierry Henry and Dennis Bergkamp. It was achieved because *Chelsea* hadn't spent enough money yet. And hey, how would Wenger like a job?

At the end of the season, Ranieri went on his merry way. But even before he'd gone, Abramovich was casting his net far and wide, trying to bag a "trophy wife" successor. *The Sun* might be an abhorrent institution but they are very good at *catching out* other abhorrent institutions: they plotted the 'sting' operation which caught out Chelsea's (ex-United) Peter Kenyon meeting 'discretely' with the then manager of the England national side, Sven Goran Eriksson.

But eventually Abramovich found the answer to how best navigate the risk/reward conundrum: he plumped for Jose Mourinho. "Young, dynamic, good-looking, comfortable in half a dozen languages but especially fluent in football, the man who had first become involved in the game as Bobby Robson's interpreter and assistant at Barcelona in the 1990s was identified by Abramovich's sources as a manager who could not only build a football team, but could also create a dynasty."

Hindsight is, of course, a wonderful thing. Even if the sights on your big-game rifle are absolutely perfect, the billionaire can't see as clearly as we can now, looking back. Could Mourinho really create a dynasty? That's certainly debatable. He's now developed a reputation as a specialist, able to deliver the short-term fix, the short-cut to the title. But back in 2004-05, Mourinho was a different animal, and it seemed he'd be around for a long time.

In the previous passage I talked about how the image of Mourinho darting down the Old Trafford touchline changed everything. It was worth a hundred thousand words. But, as we were soon to discover, Jose Mourinho's words weren't half bad either. In his very first press conference, he "created his own fanfare" (Scott Hunt:

Mancunian Matters. Come on, we all know the words by now, don't we: "I think I am a special one." Back then though, the phrase hadn't become stale, hackneyed. Back then it was music to the ears of Chelsea fans and Premier League marketing goons. What's more, even the decidedly cynical English press liked the sound of this new lion's roar.

For Mourinho, right from the very start, from the B of the Bang, it was game on. We hadn't even settled into our seats yet. But it wasn't only in the media arena Mourinho was to steal an early march on his rivals. No, according to Jim White:

"Even as he refashioned the team to his liking, Mourinho spent the summer ahead of his first season studying, studying and studying again his new working environment. And one thing he noted was the number of times other managers referred to the Premiership title as a marathon, not a sprint. He sensed a degree of complacency in the observation; he saw that there was almost an acceptance of errors and defeats early in the season because they might be rectified later. Under Ferguson, Manchester United, for instance, were renowned as sluggish starters, never seeming to hit peak performance until after Christmas, often falling to spectacular defeat in the autumn before going on to win the title the following spring. As far as Mourinho understood mathematics, however, three points won in August are worth as much as three gleaned in May. So his approach would be different: he would get his team to sprint from the start. Hit the ground running, charge to the top of the table and stay there, disappearing over the horizon before his opponents had woken up to the threat they posed."

This tactic – sprinting out of the blocks like Usain Bolt and staying there - worked to such a degree that Sir Alex Ferguson was later forced to admit that in subsequent seasons he and his coaching staff re-thought Manchester United's entire pre-season training regime in response to this new threat from Chelsea. United traditionally started slowly, and their training was geared up to ensure there was plenty left in the tank for the run-in. No more. Now everybody had to follow the pace-setters' lead and they had to sprint for the whole marathon.

But it wasn't the only ace Mourinho had up his sleeve. He had, of course, *loadsamoney*. Abramovich wanted to shower Mourinho with his golden riches. He offered to buy him Zidane, Shevchenko, Beckham. Maybe a T-Rex. Certainly the whole nine-yards. But Mourinho's response was, according to Jim White: "'No, (...) to win everything you only need one superstar: me.' It was a riposte that neatly summarised the new man's approach. (...) Mourinho had failed to make the grade as a player. Instead he dedicated his considerable intellect to mastering the art and science of coaching. (...) A trained teacher, his real genius lay in team-building. Not for him success through the simple expedient of employing superstar players. As he had done at Porto, he sought to create an impregnable dressing-room culture that would elevate the talented to the level of the untouchable."

That's not to say the Portuguese was parsimonious during his first close-season as Chelsea boss. Far from it: over summer Mourinho secured the signatures of no less than five players whose price-tags were above the £10 million mark (amongst them Didier Drogba, and Ricardo Carvalho and Paulo Ferreira, who both joined from Jose's former club Porto). These days reserve full-backs can shift for around £10 million, but at the time, these were headline-making signatures and transfer fees. He signed stars, then, but this was anything but the scattergun approach Abramovich himself might have favoured.

The Russian-Portuguese revolution which was taking place at Stamford Bridge was a cause for concern for many Manchester United fans. Especially given the fact our own team was very much in transition (and in this case transition really was a euphemism: this was by some distance the worst United squad in Premier League era). Scott Patterson noted in the Republik of Mancuina fanzine: "With Roman Abramovich's money and the current Champions League-winning manager, the fear for United fans was that the rule of west London would be indefinite."

Manchester United signed Alan Smith from relegated and financially wrecking-balled Leeds. Though Smith was a workhorse his signing, when set against the incomings at Chelsea, was hardly inspiring. It was hardly the signing to get us back on track, back on our perch; the continuation of our dynasty ensured.

The Premier League fixture computer did its job, ensuring that Mourinho's Chelsea regime would begin in dramatic fashion with a home clash *against* United. Right from the off: the clash everyone wanted to see – the undisputed kings of the Premier League against – Arsenal notwithstanding - the pretenders to their crown. It would be an indication as to how far the balance of power had already shifted, thanks to Abramovich's money. And it would also be a good early test of Mourinho's men.

The game was anything but dramatic. Eidur Gudjohnsen scored what proved to be the winning goal after 14 minutes, after which Chelsea mostly protected what they had; a job which, given the paucity of the United starting XI on display (one which included the likes of Liam Miller, Eric Djemba-Djemba, Quinton Fortune and the aforementioned Smith (who missed a very good headed opportunity) they found pretty easy.

In fact, in 2004-05 Chelsea found *everything* pretty easy, or at least they made it look that way. After beating United in their opening match they didn't look back, just as Mourinho had predicted. But they didn't let up. They *kept* sprinting. And it demoralised their rivals. Chelsea looked like a machine.

"By the spring of 2005," wrote Jim White, "the principal sense (…) was that what was being witnessed was the start of something huge. Chelsea were re-writing the Premiership rulebook."

The League Cup rulebook too. Not for Mourinho the resting of star players and blooding the youth, as Sir Alex Ferguson and Arsene Wenger habitually did in this competition. Instead the Portuguese played pretty much his full strength XI right from the off, intending to blitz the opposition and blaze a trail through the tournament. His first trophy in England couldn't come quickly enough as far as he was concerned. It didn't matter *which* trophy it was.

They met United at the semi-final stage, and though the Reds thought they'd done enough, drawing 0-0 in the first-leg at Stamford Bridge, and assuming another Old Trafford big finish, instead Chelsea won out 2-1 in the second-leg. Damien Duff scored the winner late on with a 50-yard cross from a free-kick which looped into Tim Howard's net. It was the latest in a long line of bloopers for the American stopper, going right back to his boo-boo against Mourinho's Porto when he missed the ball on a late centre, allowing Costinha to stoop to score (and Mourinho to ham it up on the touchline).

Chelsea would go on to beat Liverpool in a thrilling final. John Arne Riise appeared to have won the game for Liverpool with the quickest goal ever in a League Cup final, and the Scouse fans barracked Mourinho incessantly throughout the game until, close to the end, when their skipper Steven Gerrard slipped-up, scoring a late own goal to take the game into extra-time. Mourinho celebrated the goal by raising a finger to his lips and shushing the Liverpool fans, and for that he was sent to the stands. Forced to watch the drama of the additional half-hour on TV. Drogba, then Kezman seemed to have made the game safe for Chelsea, but the (long-forgotten) Antonio Nunez pulled one back for Liverpool to ensure a nerve-wracking finale for the Portuguese. He needn't have worried; Chelsea clung on to win.

Chelsea always clung on to win. They were machine-like in their efficiency. And though United fans had enjoyed the devilment Mourinho had shown in shushing the Liverpool hoards – we'd have loved to have done the same ourselves for sure – and there was a sense that this symbolic image was a message to *all* of the old order: there was a new sheriff in town and fans might do well to pipe down and take their medicine.

And just over two months after the League Cup final, on 10th May 2005, United fans were forced to swallow their bitterest pill yet. That day, the United team had to form a guard of honour for their Chelsea counterparts, applauding the Blues onto the pitch at Old Trafford in recognition for their winning the league (leaving United in their dust, back in third place). Chelsea went on to beat United 3-1, thus setting a new Premier League points record of 94. Despite Van Nistelrooy's early opener, Tiago, Gudjohnsen and Joe Cole soon silenced the crowd at the Theatre of Dreams. Chelsea were breaking all sorts of records and sweeping our team away, in front of our eyes, in devastating fashion. It was a terrible watch. Despite the presence of young tyros like Ronaldo and Wayne Rooney within the Red ranks, the game (and what had preceded it) made us fear for the future. We could – almost – excuse our opening day defeat to Chelsea at the Bridge. We'd fielded a weakened team. We were used to the United machine taking some time to work up through the gears. But *this*. Well, it was something else.

Chelsea had secured the title two weeks previously, again in the north-west. On 30th April they'd gone up to the Reebok Stadium – the venue at which another capital club's Premier League dreams had gone up in smoke two years earlier, when Arsenal blew a two goal lead and also the title – to face a final test of their mettle. But Chelsea were made of sterner stuff than Arsene Wenger's mob had been. It wasn't the famous 'wet, windy night' in the north-west but in the end the Blues turned Sam Allardyce's battlers into a damp squib. In the end Chelsea cruised to a 2-0 win, thanks to a Frank Lampard double. It was some statement.

Jim White heard it, loud and clear: "What was happening on the Bolton pitch and in the dressing room afterwards (where Chelsea redecorated the place with Champagne) did seem like the birth of a new dynasty. A skilfully manipulated juggernaut that would brook no opposition, Chelsea were the new kings of the Premiership orchestrated by a genius of a coach."

Going forward, how on earth were United going to compete?

It was a depressing time to be a Red all right, and two days after the humiliation of that guard of honour at Old Trafford, things got decidedly worse. The parasitic Glazer family bought United, foisting all kinds of debt upon the club in the process. While there were doubts about the moral character of Chelsea's owner, he was at least a benefactor, willing to splash his own cash on behalf of the club. Our own owners were something else. "It was a dreadful time for the club and the supporters," wrote Scott Patterson in the *Republik of Mancunia* fanzine, "and Mourinho's Chelsea became synonymous with it."

Indeed they did. And over summer Mourinho's squad only got stronger as he again raided the Abramovich piggy-bank to bring in three more big-money buys: from Manchester City he captured the diminutively-sized but loftily-rated Shaun Wright-Phillips (for £21 million); from Athletic Bilbao he took Asier del Horno for £12 million (some going for a full-back); and from Lyon, Michael Essien. Essien came in for £24 million, and was Chelsea's club-record signing. The Blues had beaten off Manchester United to acquire him and this too was a statement. The best players now wanted to go to Stamford Bridge and *not*

Old Trafford. It wasn't just the money – though that helped – it was the promise – nay, *guarantee* - of silverware.

Make no mistake about it Michael Essien was a beast. Nicknamed 'the Bison', his buccaneering running-style, his box-to-box power, and his excellent tackling made him the complete central midfielder: surely he was the heir apparent to Roy Keane at Old Trafford. Keane was still at United when the Ghanaian signed for Chelsea, but was aging and had become injury prone. It was obvious the Reds would have to replace him sooner rather than later. But Abramovich's pockets were deeper than the Glazers' and Mourinho got his man. Three months later, Keane took his rage against the dying light of his powers out on the wrong man. He and Fergie fell out – to date they have still not made up – and Keane's position became untenable. He left the club by mutual consent and the beast who should have replaced him was instead tearing up trees at Chelsea.

Michael Essien wasn't the first player to choose the Chelsea 'project' over United's history and grandeur. The PSV forward winger Arjen Robben might have become the Red Red Robben were United not gazumped right at the last by Roman Abramovich's Chelsea. John-Obi Mikel had actually signed for the Reds and posed with the famous red shirt before Chelsea intervened. Amid rumours of "kidnapping and brainwashing" (Balls.ie) Mikel claimed he'd never wanted to sign for United at all and in the end he got his wish to play for Chelsea instead... once the Blues had stumped up £16 million in compensation to United.

Nor was Essien the last player to plump for the Blues rather than the Reds. Indeed, Chelsea's gazumping of United began to occur nearly every summer. There was Michael Ballack in 2006, Eden Hazard in 2012, Cesc Fabregas in 2014, and Pedro in 2015. But missing out on Michael Essien was the one that hurt the most. Hamstrung by the Glazer's unwillingness (and inability) to enter into a bidding war with Abramovich, they lost out on one of the most dominant midfielders of a generation.

This kind of signing by Mourinho's champions showed which way the wind was blowing, and to United fans, it stank. The balance of power had shifted. Not only were Chelsea blowing us out of the water in terms of their spending power, they were also blowing us away on the pitch. In 2005-06, Scott Patterson noted, "Chelsea won the league again, this time thanks to a 3-0 victory over United at Stamford Bridge."

The defining image of that game was not a guard of honour, nor was it Mourinho shushing the crowd. It was instead United's young hero, and one of our twin bright lights for the future, Wayne Rooney limping out of the game with a metatarsal injury.

United limped to defeat, and to distant second place..

"With United tipped to plunge in to decline," wrote Scott Patterson, "following in the footsteps of their hated rivals Liverpool, Chelsea were on the rise, and it was painful. With no other teams able to challenge them, it felt like Mourinho would have another 10 titles before he left the country."

The wheels start to come off the perfectly-oiled machine

It seemed like nothing would get in the way of the Chelsea juggernaut. It had – it was assumed - the best driver, in Jose Mourinho; the best engine, in his expensively-assembled squad; and the wheels of it were greased by Roman Abramovich and his seemingly never-ending pile of dough. Chelsea already had two Premier League titles in the bag. Ten more would surely follow.

But that nightmare scenario reckoned without three things. Firstly it ignored the fact United had a pretty good driver of their own, in Sir Alex Ferguson; a men who'd won the lot and was hungrier than ever to win *his* 'glistening' trophy back in May. Secondly it reckoned without the further development of the young, talented squad Fergie was putting together at Old Trafford, and in particular those twin tyros Cristiano Ronaldo and Wayne Rooney. Thirdly it reckoned without the spanner-in-the-works which was Chelsea's owner's meddling. Roman Abramovich's spending might have *made* Chelsea, but it also had a great deal to do with their *unmaking*. Certainly it was a large contributory factor in their never fulfilling their promise to become a dynasty-proper. (Instead they'd become a short-termist's club with a short-termist's vision: there was no continuity.)

The perfect storm of those three things came to a head in the 2006-07 season. Mourinho's Chelsea empire began to crumble, to tear apart at the seams at the very moment a new, resurgent United offered for the first time a coherent challenge to Mourinho's Chelsea hegemony. And the very fact Mourinho had to fight off challenges to his own authority from without as well as from within meant there was only ever going to be one winner: Sir Alex Ferguson's horse.

But at the time United fans did not have the benefit of hindsight. At the time, it seemed very much like business as usual in the summer of 2006. The Reds had, as Scott Patterson noted in the *Republik of Mancunia* fanzine, "sold Ruud van Nistelrooy and didn't replace him, only adding Michael Carrick to the squad that had previously finished second, miles behind Chelsea. In contrast, Mourinho added Ashley Cole, Michael Ballack and Andrey Shevchenko to their title-winning side."

The new signings were A-list all right. Ballack was the captain of the German national team. Acquiring Cole's signature was an even bigger coup, seeing as though he came over from Arsenal, where he'd been a mainstay of the Invincibles team of 2003-04 and was widely regarded as one of the best young English talents in the game. In one fell swoop not only had Mourinho strengthened Chelsea's cause, but he'd also weakened the hand of one of his main rivals for the coming season.

But despite all that, Shevchenko's was the stand-out name on the Blues' summer shopping-list. Deified at Milan, where he was the second most prolific striker in the history of the club, he'd won the Ballon d'Or as recently as 2004 and was thought of as one of the best strikers in world football. In buying Shevchenko, Chelsea had finally entered the *galactico* market. In buying Shevchenko, Chelsea had surely secured the final piece of the jigsaw which would see them not only dominate English but also European football.

And yet, within 'fortress' Stamford Bridge Andrey Shevchenko the straw that broke the camel's back. And in time, the misfiring Ukrainian would come to be seen as the ultimate white elephant.

He was a destabilising force.

Back in 2004 Mourinho had told Abramovich he wasn't interested in expensive baubles with which to decorate his tree. He wanted team players above *galacticos*. Mourinho's attitude hadn't changed. *Roman Abramovich's* had. Abramovich had fallen in love with football because of that wonderful Manchester United-Real Madrid clash in April 2003. That was how he wanted to see *his* Chelsea teams play. And sure, he was fine with Chelsea hoovering up trophies during the first two Mourinho-led seasons of his tenure by playing the win-first, play-second stuff the Blues had served up. But now he was itching for fantasy, for the icing on the cake, and Abramovich wasn't prepared to wait. Not many billionaires are renowned for their patience.

And so Shevchenko came in behind Mourinho's back, and no matter how many times Jose tried to claim the contrary, nobody believed him. Mourinho's relationship with the owner – which was already tense due to Abramovich's parachuting in Frank Arnesen as sporting director - was at an all-time low. Suddenly the position of the Portuguese as the boss of the footballing side of the club was open to some debate.

Still, if Shevchenko hit the ground running, if he maintained his form which had seem his decorated with the Champions League, *Scudetto*, and Ballon d'Or trophies during his seven years in Italy, everything would be rosy in the end. But the problem was he didn't. Sheva struggled, and badly. By the end of the season he'd netted only four times in the Premier League and he was as out-of-sorts as another, later Abramovich trophy-purchase – Fernando Torres - would be.

Mourinho, of course, hadn't trusted Shevchenko right from the off, and he began to drop the Ukrainian for crucial games, most notably in the Champions League semi-final against Liverpool at Anfield, where Sheva didn't even make the bench, much to the chagrin of Abramovich.

For the first time Mourinho began to show signs of stress. For the first time life in the Premier League wasn't a breeze for the Portuguese. He became snappy, snide, in press conferences. His gibes began to get further and further below the belt. He did not like being out of control and he did not like losing. This was to be Mourinho's first season without a league title win in five years and he didn't take it well. And his tension transmitted itself to the Chelsea team. In the end, and "against all odds, United won the title convincingly" (Scott Patterson).

Chelsea went down bitterly, full of recrimination. As the season went down the pan, things got increasingly sour for Jose. "Mourinho's behaviour as United beat Chelsea to the 2007 title was cranky and classless," wrote

Samuel Luckhurst, in the *Manchester Evening News*. "He accused Cristiano Ronaldo of a lack of education and could not bring himself to say United were the better team."

The dig at the 21-year-old Cristiano Ronaldo – who was fast-becoming a United legend in the vein of previous great number sevens like Beckham, Cantona, Robson – went down particularly badly with Reds fans. It came in response to Ronaldo's suggestion that Mourinho didn't know how to admit his own failings. And it was, as Scott Patterson wrote "one of the earlier indicators to show Mourinho has no boundaries. For a grown man to publicly attack a young lad for having a difficult upbringing" was going too far.

Chelsea did beat United to win the 2007 FA Cup, in the first final to be played at the newly rebuilt Wembley Stadium. They'd also retained the League Cup. But the domestic cups were scant compensation. The Premier League and Champions League were where the best were tested, and in both competitions Chelsea had been found wanting. United won the Premier League by six points, outscoring the Blues by 19 goals (the uneducated and badly brought-up Ronaldo bagging 17 of them). The previous season Chelsea and United had scored the exact same number of goals, so that was some swing. As was the points difference: United had finished runners-up to Chelsea in 2005-06 by eight points. In one year, they'd made up 14 points on the Blues.

The end of the line for Mourinho at the Bridge

Chelsea may have lost their on-field superiority by the end of the 2006-07 season, but behind the scenes things were going from bad to worse for Jose, particularly in the case of his relationship with the owner.

Cracks had started to show during the controversy over Anders Frisk - which we saw in Chapter 4 ('A United manager wouldn't do that') – which ended up with a referee having to hang up his whistle after receiving death-threats, UEFA effectively accusing Chelsea of lying, and Chelsea refusing to appeal the decision to fine Mourinho (which left Mourinho feeling all kinds of sulky – he didn't feel he'd been granted the full support of the club. In order to assert more control over the Mourinho 'earthquake', Roman Abramovich further complicated the hierarchy of the club by appointing the Israeli Avram Grant as director of football, notionally above Mourinho in the pecking-order. The Portuguese was particularly upset that Grant was also awarded a seat on the club's board.

Now Jose's nose had really been put out of joint, and a wounded Jose Mourinho is like a cornered animal. He came out fighting. That is his default status in times of crisis, as we later saw at Real Madrid. But it was all futile.

It was a fight he could never win.

As early as September 2007, despite establishing a new record of 64 consecutive home league matches without defeat, Mourinho was on decidedly shaky ground. After a string of poor results including defeat against Aston Villa and a goalless draw against Blackburn Rovers in the Premier League, another home bore-draw this time against the Norwegian minnows Rosenberg in the Champions League was the nadir. Stamford Bridge was barely half-full for that game and Abramovich, whose expectations had been heightened and his ambition sharpened by that famous swashbuckling Manchester United-Real Madrid clash in front of a packed Theatre of Dreams, had had enough. Enough of the histrionics. Enough of the dull, win-above everything else football. Enough of Mourinho's Chelsea not being Ferguson's Manchester United.

Mourinho left by "mutual consent" on 20th September to nobody's surprise. None other than Avram

Grant stepped up to replace him, and, maligned as the Israeli's spell at the helm of the Stamford Bridge club was, he would lead Chelsea to the final of the Champions League, which was one step further than Mourinho had managed during his tenure (he'd managed three successive semi-finals). Grant's Chelsea went on to be bested by Manchester United in Moscow, on penalties.

And so, Mourinho was gone and the moratoriums for his reign at Chelsea could begin. Wherever he pitched up next, we hoped he wouldn't be allowed within a hundred miles of Old Trafford, even if Fergie did eventually concede defeat to the ageing process and retire. A winner he might be, but Mourinho was not a likeable person and his behaviour often bordered on the unacceptable.

Scott Patterson wrote in the *Republik of Mancunia* fanzine: "He was a man I liked to begin with, the 'breath of fresh air' the Premiership needed, but between his lies and low rent behaviour, the air became rancid and stale. The football his teams play is not good enough for United, simple as that. The players he buys (unless the top players around Europe who all big teams were after, but Chelsea could afford to outbid everyone on e.g. Michael Essien, Michael Ballack etc.) are not good enough for United, simple as that. I don't want the likes of Ben Haim, Sidwell, Boulahrouz, Kezman, Ferreira, Pizzaro etc. at United! You might say Fergie has made his errors in the transfer market, which he has, but nothing close to scale we're working with when looking at Mourinho. Don't forget he was there for just three years! Mourinho's total spending was £225.76 million, yet in his last season, when he should have created something close to the perfect squad, they were eight points behind United on the day the title was won. He's not special, he never was, and he certainly isn't capable of taking on the job at United!"

Absence makes the heart grow (slightly) fonder

There is no doubt that if Jose Mourinho had somehow contrived to make another Premier League club his destination of choice after his (first) departure from Chelsea, United fans would have hated him just as much as they had when he was Blues boss. There is also no doubt that Jose Mourinho would have given United fans *cause* to hate him that bit more.

But as it was, the Portuguese pitched up at Internazionale next and over the next couple of seasons, perhaps because we weren't having the Jose show rammed down our throats every day by the English media and perhaps because we could view him at one remove, at a club who weren't a rival or even a threat to us, our feelings towards him softened somewhat. We couldn't bring ourselves to forgive what he'd said and done, but maybe, just maybe, in time we could forget.

Winning helped, of course, and Mourinho did a great deal of that at Inter. In his first season, Mourinho reminded us all what a truly brilliant manager he was once you got past all the bluster and bravado, by bagging the *scudetto* by a whopping ten point margin.

Losing helped too. United beat Mourinho's Inter in the first knockout round of the Champions League (2-0 on aggregate) in 2009 and the Portuguese seemed to bend over backwards to make it known he both admired and respected the Reds. Which was nice.

At the time United were defending their Champions League crown following their victory in Moscow against Chelsea, the team Mourinho built. Not only that, United were back on their perch as champions of England (and the world). And Jose cut an uncharacteristically humble figure during the build up to, and in the wake of, the clash. After a stale-mate at San Siro in the first leg, the return leg at Old Trafford was all set up to be a classic – after all, Inter boasted the Swedish maverick Zlatan Ibrahimovic up front - but the Reds showed their class and won through thanks to a headed goal in each half from Nemanja Vidic and Cristiano Ronaldo. The soundtrack to the evening was the boisterous United fans belting out: "You're not special any more" to Jose, who looked all kinds of lonely on the touchline he'd once jigged down.

United marched on to their tenth UEFA Champions League quarter-final in 13 seasons and there were serious hopes they might become the first team since AC Milan in 1990 to retain Europe's premier trophy. (Those hopes were only dashed in the final, in Rome, when the Reds lost 2-0 to Barcelona.) Mourinho had other fish to fry. His Inter side hadn't won a European crown since 1965 let alone retained one.

Mourinho's Nerazzuri had been beaten by Sir Alex Ferguson's Red Devils, then, but there were no histrionics from the Portuguese. He did not lose badly, as he had when Fergie's side beat his Chelsea mob to the Premier League title in 2006-07. Indeed, even in 2006-07 - those ill-judged comments about Cristiano Ronaldo aside – Mourinho had never made things *personal* with United, or with Ferguson. Not like he had with his rivals at Arsenal and Liverpool (Wenger and Benitez).

The glasnost between Fergie and Mourinho had actually begun almost as soon as any beef started between them. In the aftermath of the United-Porto Champions League clash in 2004, the storm in a teacup which was the missed handshake at the end of the first-leg in Porto, and Fergie's pointed accusations that the Porto stopper Baia had made the most of contact to get Keane sent off, might have boiled over into something far more treacherous, especially given the circumstances of the Reds defeat: Scholes goal being controversially disallowed for offside; Mourinho's crowing jig on the touchline after Costinha's late, late winner. Such stuff lifetime grudges were made of, and Sir

Alex Ferguson for one held a grudge - and cultivated it - as lovingly as he might have held a new grandchild; Mourinho the same.

But the two managed to somehow set their differences aside; that brouhaha about the missed handshake would become only a footnote in history. "Following the rancour surrounding Porto and United's tumultuous Champions League ties, Mourinho and Ferguson began to bond. The United manager entered the away dressing room to congratulate Porto on their aggregate win over United, a gesture that was alien to the Iberian Mourinho," wrote Samuel Luckhurst, of this extraordinary turn-around.

Patrick Barclay, in his biography of Sir Alex, goes further: "After Porto had prevailed at Old Trafford, there was pandemonium in their dressing room. 'You would have thought we had won the World Cup,' said Mourinho. 'And then there was a knock on the door. It was Alex, with Gary Neville. As they came in, everybody fell silent, respectful. The party stopped. The party was over. And, as Gary Neville went round shaking hands with my players, Alex shook hands with me and said that, after the press conference, I was invited to come to his office for a drink. What a special person it was, I thought, who would do anything to win but, if he lost, still do that. At that moment I made a decision. It was that, if I ever came to England, I would follow this example.'"

There are plenty of opposing managers, of course, who would take issue with Mourinho's words, and we'll come to them later, but with Fergie, after that match Jose made (mostly) like Uriah Heep. He was ever so humble. Jose called Alex 'Boss' and after a league clash in 2005, "they shared a bottle of wine and Mourinho said he hoped United would beat Arsenal in the FA Cup final." (Luckhurst). But there was a sense Mourinho was merely humouring Ferguson's Godfather-like status within the Premier League hierarchy. Right up to the moment the old man staggered back to his feet and wrested the Premier League trophy out of Mourinho's grasp, Jose thought of Sir Alex as "a very nice person doing the job the best he could" (as quoted from Sky's Goals on Sunday show). After all, as Luckhurst wrote: "United's steady decline had already begun, in contrast to nouveaux riche Chelsea, and Mourinho effectively took pity on Ferguson, mainly because United were not competitors."

And then they were, and it all fell apart for Jose at Chelsea.

But actually, when you look back on it, the worst of Jose's barbs and insults, the most crass of his behaviours, were reserved for the other guys, the guys who hadn't quite made it to Silverback, Alpha-male status in the Premier League 'group' like Fergie had. No, when Mourinho bared his teeth and beat his chest, he was generally confronting the Betas: Arsene Wenger, Rafael Benitez. And when Mourinho took on those guys, he was also taking on guys who'd had a crack or two in their time at Sir Alex.

There was a sense of: my enemy's enemy is my friend.

There was a sense of... well, sometimes we thought Mourinho took it too far. But mostly, it was pretty funny hearing Mourinho taking swipes at the guys we'd come to loathe at rivals like Arsenal and Liverpool. It would have been classless and graceless had a United manager done it, but yeah, at one remove. Go for it, Jose!

Fighting talk with Fergie's former foes

Many a Premier League manager had tried – and failed – to take down Sir Alex Ferguson. And in doing so, mostly, they fell into the Glaswegian's cleverly-laid traps. Mostly, Ferguson swatted away the 'mind-game' challenges of his rivals; he saw them off. Made them blubber or gibber, and then slink off into the night. But there was a sense in the mid-noughties that these constant attacks on Sir Alex's Silverback status had weakened him; tired him out. His United teams of this vintage also came across tired. Certainly they weren't as vicious in their desire to win as earlier incarnations of the Red Devils had been. Rivals smelled blood.

But then, into the breach, like the number two in a tag-team; enter stage-left Jose Mourinho, here to wage war with Ferguson's former foes.

And how. As Samuel Luckhurst wrote: "Mourinho appears to despise Arsene Wenger and his lacerating put down of Rafael Benitez – and his wife – must have had as many United fans in raptures as Chelsea supporters. Mourinho does genuinely abhor those individuals, however this was made possible by becoming Ferguson's ally."

Mourinho's put-downs were pithy. They were withering. And they were as seized upon as hungrily by the media as his comments about his own specialness (maybe more so, given the desire to frame Premier League matches, seasons and even *decades* as *mano a mano* duels between managers). Perhaps most famously, the Portuguese responded to Arsene Wenger's claim that rival Premier League managers were playing down their title chances in 2014 because they "feared to fail" by dubbing the Arsenal boss a "specialist in failure". He added: "If I do that in Chelsea, eight (trophyless) years, I leave and don't come back."

(He was even more crass in his remarks on Wenger nine years earlier in 2005, infamously calling the Frenchman a voyeur: "He likes to watch other people. There are some guys who, when they are at home, have a big telescope to see what happens in other families. He speaks, speaks, speaks about Chelsea." Wenger's retort? "He's out of order, disconnected with reality and disrespectful. When you give success to stupid people, it makes them more stupid sometimes.")

But the war of words United fans most relished was the one which was established between Jose Mourinho and Rafael Benitez. It seems incredible to believe now, but once upon a time, Mourinho said the following of his adversary: "My friend Rafa Benitez hasn't come to England just to visit; he's here to make Liverpool a winning team again."

But maybe that was the point. His "friend" *did* make Liverpool a winning team again (in cup competitions at least) and often at the expense of Chelsea.

Soon, they were sworn enemies; they couldn't even bring themselves to shake hands at games.

The seed for the enmity blew in on the breeze which came through the open summer transfer window on successive summers between 2004 and 2006. Every year, Mourinho's Chelsea tried to lure Liverpool's captain and talisman Steven Gerrard to the Bridge. Though Gerrard had his head turned – he was desperate to win a Premier League winners' medal and knew he stood a better chance with the Blues; and he was bang-on with that assessment as it later proved – he always backtracked at the last. But the constant wrangling had a destabilising effect on Liverpool Football Club, and Benitez didn't like that and he didn't like Mourinho throwing his weight around, trying to make off with the Liverpool fans' darling. And so, the seed had been sown.

It germinated during that testy League Cup final encounter which Chelsea edged 3-2 after extra-time. And it was then hot-housed during a series of Champions League clashes during the mid-noughties; blossoming at last into a rivalry at least as intense as the one between Arsene Wenger and Alex Ferguson, and certainly one which blew hotter for longer.

Every season between 2005 and 2009 Mourinho's Chelsea and Bentitez's Liverpool were drawn together in the Champions League: once in the group stage, but more regularly in the latter stages of the competition, including three semi-finals and one quarter-final. By the time the third, and fourth meetings between this pair had been drawn, it began to look as though the balls were sticking. Or else the draw-masters were using were hot-balls (copyright: fair-play's own Sepp Blatter). By the fifth meeting, it looked like some huge cosmic joke, though who the ultimate *victim* of the joke was remained unclear.

Yet although it was fun watching both teams kicking lumps out of each other, and developing that same brand of snarling hatred for each other as they both traditionally reserved for us – the pair were our major rivals then, don't forget: there was no Manchester City (well, there was, but not as we know them now); Chelsea, with Abramovich's petrodollars greasing the wheels, were hoovering up league titles at United's expense; Liverpool, well, they were Liverpool – still, there was one, whopping great downside, and that was the fact one of *them* had to be the winner. And one of them, in grinding their opponent to the dust, would take one step closer to a Champions League crown which we'd long hoped would elude both of them.

We didn't want Chelsea to win because of the *nouveau riche* nature of the club. We didn't want them to simply be able to go out and buy a trophy we'd worked so hard to attain back in 1999. We didn't want players like John Terry to get their mucky paws on a medal. We couldn't bear it if Jose Mourinho became a self-fulfilling prophecy. And wasn't it nice a team from our nation's capital had (until Chelsea lucked into winning the competition in 2012) never won the ultimate continental honour?

A big fat zero, when Manchester had two (make that three in 2008), when *Nottingham* had two, and when even Birmingham had one.

Liverpool, of course, had four (five in 2005 as the fans ceaselessly reminded their United counterparts, *fiving* the digits of their hand outwards, in our general direction). They were the most successful English side in the European Cup. And although United were closing in on, and would eventually overtake their league title haul of eighteen, in Europe, they thought they were the kings.

Which really stuck in the craw…

Mainly, United fans wanted Liverpool to lose. At all costs. But we didn't like Chelsea either. Mainly, United fans turned off our tellies. Let fate - ghost goals, plastic flags on seats, stupid petty arguments between two particularly petty managers, snide fouls, diving, *all* of that - take its course. Concentrate on the real joy of European football, which, to our mind, was seeing *our own team* compete against a proper continental team, *not* one we faced week-in, week-out, in English league competition.

But there it was: and boy there were fireworks. There was pettiness.

It was very much he said/ she said.

After Luis Garcia's controversial 'ghost goal' helped Liverpool knock Chelsea out of the Champions League in 2005 Mourinho said: "You can say the linesman's scored. It was a goal coming from the moon or from the Anfield Road stands."

Benitez responded, tit-for-tat: "To me, Arsenal play much better football (than Chelsea). They win matches and are exciting to watch. Barcelona and Milan too. They create excitement so how can you say Chelsea are the best team in the world?"

After another meeting, this time in the FA Cup, Mourinho sniffed: "Did the best team win? I don't think so. In a one-off game maybe they will surprise me and they can do it. In the Premiership the distance between the teams is 45 points over two seasons." He also refused to shake the hand of his opposite number.

Benitez couldn't resist coming back: "We have *our* special ones here, they are our fans, who always play with their hearts."

Even after Mourinho left Chelsea, he felt the need to stick his oar in regarding Benitez. "How many championships has Benitez won since he joined Liverpool? None," Mourinho said. "And how many names were suggested by the press to replace him? None."

Eventually Benitez *was* replaced at Liverpool, but the war-of-words continued, proving that it transcended the traditional Blue-Red divide and crossed over into something deeper, and more personal. Benitez took charge of Inter in 2010, succeeding Mourinho – who had won the treble the previous season – at the San Siro. The Spaniard told the Italian press: "There's the coaches, first Mancini, then Mourinho and now me, and I hope to win more than them. We could win six trophies this season." Benitez had barely been able to spit out the name Mourinho.

Mourinho cracked his knuckles, let a wry smile play upon his chops, and predicted: "One thing is for certain. Benitez won't do better than me. Another thing is also true that should he lift the Intercontinental Cup, he will have only won two games compared to my 13. Therefore it will be my trophy and not his."

And of course, when Internazionale *did* win the Intercontinental Cup in 2010, Mourinho was quick to comment: "I expected at least a thank you for the success that I gave him. Ask all the Inter fans what they think of me and him."

The pair crossed-over again in 2013, when Mourinho took over from Benitez at Stamford Bridge, where the Spaniard had 'enjoyed' a spell as Interim Manager. Mourinho was asked whether he would like to comment on Chelsea under Benitez. Of course he would. "I watched every game (…) in the last year. (…) Mental. Not tactical. Nothing. Mental. Afraid to assume. Afraid to go. Afraid to say we want to win, we can win."

Benitez sniffed: "Mourinho talks a lot about a lot of people, but I prefer to talk about facts." (Yes, we know that Rafa: so does Sir Alex.) "At Liverpool, with a squad half of the value of Chelsea, we twice knocked his Chelsea side out of the Champions League."

Benitez was at Real Madrid now. His dream job, but one in which he'd have to face enough battles within the club, let alone from without. And then there was Barcelona. And so it came to pass that his *wife* (Montserrat Seara) made the terrible mistake of getting involved in the squabble. "Real are the third of Jose Mourinho's old teams that Rafa has coached," she joked in an interview published by the Galician newspaper *La Region*. "We tidy up his messes! If you think about it, of course you end up crossing-paths. There are only a few world-class clubs out there."

Mourinho, smelling blood in the water, was quick to pounce on Montserrat's throwaway comment. In a press conference in America, following a pre-season friendly win for Chelsea against Barcelona, he chose not to talk about the game he'd just witnessed at all. Instead, he went out on the attack. "The lady is a bit confused, with all respect," he said. "I'm not laughing, because her husband went to Chelsea to replace Roberto Di Matteo and he went to Real Madrid and replaced Carlo Ancelotti. The only club where her husband (actually) replaced me was at Inter Milan, where in six months he destroyed the best team in Europe at the time.

"And for her also to think about me and to speak about me, I think she needs to occupy her time, and if she takes care of her husband's diet she will have less time to speak about me."

It was probably the lowest Mourinho has stooped in terms of personal criticism of his rivals, and it is probably best *we* leave it there – the barrel well and truly scraped - as far as the Benitez-Mourinho duel is concerned. But even without his Spanish rival at the helm, Mourinho still seemed to have a particular fondness for beating Liverpool. He celebrated wins against them more emphatically than he did wins against any other team. He found it easy to get under the skins of Liverpool fans (and thus endear himself – a little – to their United counterparts.

One game in particular is memorable.

Sunday 27th April 2014. Anfield. Liverpool were making their first serious bid for the Premier League title. Actually, *sod* the Premier League; if Liverpool won the league it would be the first time since 1990 – the old First Division days – that they'd won England's top-flight and proved themselves the best team in the country. Scouse fans were getting giddy, especially after they beat title rivals Manchester City at Anfield, meaning it was all in their hands. If they won every game they'd be champions. Their mantra, as they kept on racking up the points, game after game - Liverpool had won 11 games on the bounce (and their unbeaten streak stretched to 16 matches) – was: *we will not let this slip now*.

For United fans, Liverpool clambering back on their perch was unthinkable. Unbearable. It really seemed like Liverpool *wouldn't* let it slip. They had the momentum; the luck. Their players were on hot-streaks: Luis Suarez (yeah, him) was on fire. Steven Gerrard, the captain and talisman, was making this season into his last crusade to win the big one that had eluded him throughout his career. Ever since he'd turned down Chelsea in the mid-noughties, it had been a case of *look at what you could have won,* and United fans had delighted in reminding him that even such luminaries as Luke Chadwick, Darren Ferguson, Roy Carroll, Darron Gibson, and Michael Owen had more Premier League medals than him.

More than that, United had been forced to wait out *26* years of hurt between 1967 and 2003 when *we* didn't win the top-flight. 26 years during which time we had to watch Liverpool walk away with trophy after trophy, building up their haul to a seemingly insurmountable 18 championships. We'd enjoyed our own moment of sun ever since 2003, and it had been very nice to see Liverpool lurking in our shadow, smarting at the fact we overtook their 18 and took it up to 20. But Liverpool now looked as though they were getting back on the horse after only *24* years. That wasn't fair. We wanted them to suffer for – at least – 26 years, just as we had to.

And so, on that day, Sunday 27th April 2014, we were all Chelsea fans.

We willed Chelsea to go at Liverpool, put them to the sword. But they didn't. Mourinho was too canny for that. Still, it was painful to watch as the Blues sat back and let Liverpool have the ball. It seemed as though a Liverpool goal was surely only a heartbeat away; they were encamped in the Chelsea half after all. All it would take was a lucky break, a slip-up.

But Chelsea held firm. Resolute. They were absolutely determined, and that determination was instilled in them by Mourinho. Though Chelsea were *mathematically* in the championship race, even Mourinho knew they were out of it, and given that they had a Champions League semi-final in the coming week, they could have been forgiven for going easy. Indeed, it had been suggested prior to the game that Mourinho would field a weakened side. But instead he parked the bus and his hard-working Chelsea team frustrated Liverpool at every turn.

"Liverpool's attempt at a trademark fast start failed in the face of a wall of blue shirts, with the visitors' five-man midfield sitting deep to protect their back four," wrote Chris Bevan for the BBC Sport website. "Chelsea were keen to disrupt the home side's flow in other ways too, taking their time over set-pieces from the first minute onwards to visibly frustrate Liverpool's players as well as annoying their fans. (…) Mourinho was producing another tactical masterclass."

Still, it looked like the best United (and Chelsea, and Manchester City) fans could hope for was a draw. Chelsea simply couldn't get out of their own half.

But then, in injury time at the end of the first half, under no challenge at all, captain and talisman Steven Gerrard did what he said they must not do. He let it slip. He received a pass from Sakho inside his own half and took his eye off the ball, possibly already dreaming about the Hollywood pass which would ensue from his much vaunted left-foot. Perhaps he was already imagining the ever-hungry Luis Suarez haring onto that pass and giving Liverpool the lead. Perhaps he was already imagining how the Premier League winners' medal would taste when he bit it, Olympian-style.

Ah but Stevie! Beware tempting fate!

Gerrard miscontrolled and then slipped, trying to get it back. Demba Ba picked his pocket and ran, "unopposed towards the Kop before coolly slotting the ball past Simon Mignolet".

"The Liverpool fans chanted Gerrard's name at half-time," wrote Bevan, "but, try as he might with a succession of long-range shots, their usually inspirational skipper could not make amends for his mistake."

Actually, Gerrard became more of a hindrance than a help; his all-consuming desire to be the rescuer, the hero, Liverpool's Roy of the Rovers stopping the team from building any proper attacks. He would have never gotten away with it in a Mourinho team. Jose would have hauled him off after his first pot-shot from miles away.

Time ticked by. Allen nearly scored with a volley. Suarez came *this* close to equalising in the last minute, only for reserve goalie to pull off a spectacular stop to keep the

Anfield mob at bay. And then, in injury time, Chelsea broke and scored again; the former Liverpool man Fernando Torres, who'd hardly been an unqualified success at Chelsea raced clear and with no Liverpool defender in sight seemed certain to net himself. It was a procession. But then, into the picture flashed Willian, quicker than Bolt. Torres, who'd maybe had too much time to think about scoring and probably now feared he'd miss, squared to the Brazilian. 2-0. Game over bar the shouting.

The shouting, mainly, came from Mourinho. There he was at the final whistle, beating his gilet-clad chest in front of the Chelsea fans, letting out a barbaric yawp of triumph which said everything we needed to know about how he felt about United's rivals from just down the M62. Liverpool let it slip again in the next game at Palace, throwing away a three goal lead to draw 3-3. But the damage had really been done at Anfield, by Chelsea. By Jose. Manchester City went on to win the league, and you have no idea how much it hurts me to write that. But one thing I can do is thank my luckies I didn't have to write *Liverpool went on to win the league* instead. Now that would have been *agony*.

Jose, you sense, would feel almost the same way.

So, about that U-turn then…

At the start of this chapter, I talked about the U-turn all United fans have been forced into making on the Jose Mourinho question. The question which is, baldly: can a manager who is so recognisably one of our bitterest rivals' men become a Red? Can fans accept him now? Well, we can because we have to. But that doesn't mean we've been allowed to rest easy. Since the appointment of the Portuguese many of us have been forced to eat our words and wash them down with a pint of liquidised humble pie.

"Chelsea, Manchester City, Liverpool and Arsenal fans, and others, have taken to social media over the past few days (since the appointment) and are on the rampage. Who knows how many hours they've collectively spent searching through the timelines of United fans, trying to find incriminating tweets where they've previously said something negative about Mourinho, but it's not an amount of time that anyone could be proud of," noted Scott Patterson on the Republik of Mancunia website.

"The conclusion of their hard work is that United fans have changed their minds on the manager. It may be hard to believe, but United fans used to think one way a few years ago, and now they think something else. It's quite a remarkable find really, given that, judging by the hysterical reaction, they are the first group of human beings to ever change their opinion."

Maybe under different circumstances, we might have stuck to our guns, protested the appointment on both moral and footballing grounds. But who else could the club have employed? Ed Woodward might be a colossal bungler, but even a stopped clock is right twice a day and he was (mainly) correct when he described Mourinho as: "quite simply the best manager in the game today". (If you're still doubtful of that, I explored the veracity of that claim in another chapter.) And sure, the club *could* have held on to Louis van Gaal, who had after all, just secured the first silverware for United since Sir Alex Ferguson's retirement. But Van Gaal had missed out on Champions League football, and there was constant griping from the fans regarding the style of football he chose to play. The identity of *his* United wasn't right, just as it wasn't right under David Moyes.

But the rot set in even before that.

The following is taken from *The Secret Footballer's Guide to the Modern Game: Tips and Tactics from the Ultimate Insider,* by the Secret Footballer: "Teams struggling with their identity, struggle, in turn, to achieve what they should be achieving on the pitch. (…) In truth, the problems at Manchester United began before David Moyes took the job, thanks to a chronic lack of investment in the playing squad by Sir Alex Ferguson. (…) Consider this: in the 2013-14 season, Manchester United fielded fifty-two different line-ups with no two the same from one game to the next, and they played fifty-two games. If that isn't an identity crisis then I don't know what is.

"The identity of the club under Sir Alex Ferguson was such that Manchester United didn't change for anyone; his players were continually being told they were the best. (…) The juxtaposition between the mind-set of what was largely the same group of players under Ferguson and Moyes is stark. Before the Liverpool game at Old Trafford David Moyes said, 'Their league position suggests that they are ahead of us and they possibly do come here as favourites,' and after the Manchester City game which United lost 3-0 at Old Trafford Moyes was quoted as saying, 'We have played a very good side playing at the sort of level we are aspiring to.' Let me tell you how those comments went down with the players: 'We would never have heard anything like that from Sir Alex, absolutely never; we were always the best and if we weren't then it was never our fault. For the first time, the players were being told that they were inferior to other teams, it wasn't a happy time for anyone.' Moyes changed the identity of the club and Manchester United went from a team that had the confidence to attack teams home and away to a team that were set up not to lose."

Mourinho is a strong character and he will imprint his identity on the club. It might not be the pristine, whiter-than-white character many desire, but it will be a winning one. To ignore the Portuguese, as the board did when Ferguson retired, would have been a huge dereliction of duty on the part of the robber-barons, debt-peddlers and greed-merchants who own the club and the clearest indication yet that the powers that be are not interested in winning, more in signing up 'brand partners' and new consumers (not fans) across the globe.

"United fans aren't now pretending that Mourinho is the perfect solution, or talking about him as if he's a saint," said Scott Patterson, "but it surely doesn't need much explaining to understand why they would be pleased the former Chelsea man is their manager, and Van Gaal isn't.

"When United fans really hated Mourinho, their team had just been blunged close to £1 billion in debt, while Abramovich was buying players for Chelsea like it was going out of fashion. United fans had enjoyed the luxury of having the same manager for close to three decades, one who valued youth and played attacking football. Of course United fans didn't want Mourinho back then, a manager who only ever spent a few years at a club, never gave youth a chance, and whose football was far more pragmatic.

"Given a choice between Ferguson and Mourinho, United fans would pick Ferguson every time, but that's not their choice today. Things change.

"Having endured one season of David Moyes and two seasons of Louis van Gaal the option of Mourinho is obviously an upgrade. Being pleased that Mourinho is the manager, and the two previous managers aren't, doesn't mean that United fans are *en masse* forgetting all his misdemeanours. It's still not on that he lied about that ref, or tried to belittle Ronaldo for not having a wealthy upbringing, or stuck his thumb in someone's eye socket, or treated Carneiro in an appalling way, or was guilty of an almost endless list of other embarrassing actions."

We won't forget Mourinho's connections with Stamford Bridge either. And neither will Chelsea fans forget him. Mourinho maintains god-like status at Stamford Bridge. (Mind you then again, the racist John Terry is still considered 'a ledge' by them.) Chelsea fans' reaction to their hero pitching up at Old Trafford has been largely mixed, but Celia, from the Chelsea Supporters' Trust told me that: "in general I think most wish him well except for when in direct competition with us."

Of course, Mourinho isn't the first person whose name is intrinsically linked to one of our rivals who has made the switch to Old Trafford. Elite-level football is by its very nature a transient beast. Though true fans never change who we support players and managers switch allegiances regularly, even after kissing the badge. Even in the good old days it was the same: one of the two most revered figures in United history - Sir Matt Busby - played for both Liverpool and Manchester City. Eric Cantona played for Leeds United. And we loved both of them. Hell, United even boast a former Chelsea player within the ranks of the playing staff Mourinho will inherit: Juan Mata. Mata was hugely popular amongst Blues fans and although his transfer to United hasn't been an unqualified success, he is still well-liked by Red Devils fans too.

But maybe that is because Mata is a nice guy, you say. Maybe that is because he never said nasty stuff about United when he was at Stamford Bridge. Jose Mourinho isn't a particularly nice guy and he *has* said nasty stuff about United in the past. The Portuguese was handed a five-grand fine in 2005 after accusing United players of diving in the League Cup semi-final first leg at Stamford Bridge. He said: "Sir Alex was very clever, if you can say that, at half-time by putting some pressure on the ref. In the second half it was whistle and whistle, fault and fault, cheat and cheat."

And that is just the tip of the iceberg.

However, as we have seen, he said nasty stuff about *everyone*. And actually, he went easier on United than with the rest; Wenger's Arsenal and Benitez's Liverpool in particular.

The truth is, as that sage of football my Dad says, with Mourinho we are going to have to "hold our noses" but "enjoy the ride".

For now, as Scott Patterson wrote, United fans will: "focus on Mourinho's positives (…). They will talk about the treble he won at Inter, or the 121 goals his Real Madrid side scored when they won the league in 2012—an average of over three goals a game—because that's the natural reaction for any set of fans when a new manager is signed or a new player is brought in."

We know "it's likely Mourinho will make an idiot out of himself when again entering those infamous mind games with Arsene Wenger or Pep Guardiola, or will play tactics in big games that the fan-base would rather he didn't, or get fined for something he says or does when United lose. He will probably only stay for a few years, then it will all implode and they'll be back to square one. But at least the club will have someone in charge who is qualified for the job, unlike Moyes, and won't send the fans to sleep at Old Trafford, unlike Van Gaal."

Another thing we know: Jose Mourinho is a contrarian. "If everyone is saying he won't play the academy players, after Van Gaal gave 15 youth players their debut in two years, and mockingly claim Marcus Rashford will be sent out on loan, you can presume Mourinho will do the opposite. If people claim that United will play boring and defensive football, you can guess that Mourinho will set up his team on the opening day of the season to go all-out attack."

That's how he rolls.

"In two seasons time, United may very well be just where they are now, or worse," concluded Patterson. "Let's not forget how badly Mourinho defended the title with Chelsea. Even Moyes did a better job, which says a lot. But chances are United supporters will enjoy watching their team play more than they have done over the past season, they will likely see them compete to win the title again, and for a lot of fans, that's worth the downside of having Mourinho as the manager.

"The objectives have changed, reality has sunk in and fans have warmed to their new manager. There isn't another Ferguson, but Mourinho resembles the legendary manager much more than Moyes or Van Gaal do. United fans have been brought down to earth over the past three years, so their reaction to Mourinho's appointment is obvious and completely justified.

" 'I think I prefer to forget the last three years,' Mourinho said at his unveiling. United fans couldn't agree more and they are now desperate to see what their manager can do to add to their history books in the seasons ahead."

We're desperate, and we're also – guardedly – excited.

We've taken a look, sighed wistfully, and then bought into the identity Mourinho will imprint upon us. Ben Greenwood from T-34 Limited, who sell an excellent array of unofficial United merchandise including some particularly excellent tee-shirts, told me that in the wake of Mourinho's selection as the new United supremo, "Mourinho tees have accounted for 9% of total sales since their launch on 26th May. The 'Special One' version is currently the second most popular of all tees on the site."

He added: "We'd say this level of sales has been pleasantly surprising given the negativity towards him, even in the face of acceptance it was probably the only move we could make as a club."

There you go: *acceptance*. That seems to be the general mood amongst the United fans. But don't just take my word for it. In the next chapter, a number of fans from various walks of life give their own views on Mourinho.

I believe that fans - generally - are willing to forget (if not forgive) Jose, with the caveat that it means winning.

8
"I FEEL BEING MANAGER OF UNITED THESE DAYS IS NOT JUST ABOUT THE ABILITY TO BRING SUCCESS ON THE FIELD BUT TO HAVE A MASSIVE MEDIA PRESENCE THAT WILL APPEAL TO THE CORPORATE SIDE OF THE BUSINESS."
FANS GIVE THEIR VIEWS ON THE APPOINTMENT OF JOSE MOURINHO.

Mike Hopkins, Season Ticket Holder: "He might win us a trophy but let's face it, he's a bell end of great magnitude."

Ben Greenwood, T-34 Limited (T-Shirts United – unofficial United merchandise): "We backed Mourinho's appointment at Old Trafford – he's the best man for the job and though we have reservations about his commitment to youth development, his style of play, and just how long he might stay, we're hopeful that, having been everywhere else and done his thing, he might now be willing (and able) to change his ways slightly to fit United without sacrificing his winning touch."

Eoin Donaghy, Contributor to fanzine *United We Stand:* "Mourinho's not the man for me. I understood the concerns about appointing Ryan Giggs, but I would have given it to him anyway because I'm a dreamer. The rewards would have been worth the risk. What was the point of grooming Giggs to be Louis van Gaal's successor and going on about a mythical 'Man United way' if, when it came down to it, it all went out of the window in favour of a short-term dividend.

What's the worst that could have happened under our greatest-ever player? We might have gone a few more years without a league title, perhaps? Boo fucking hoo. It's only been three years since the last one, not fucking 23. Giggs as the manager would have given us something pure – something that was ours and ours only, not something bought off a shelf.

But here we are, sitting in the big-top. Mourinho's poisonous Machiavellian ways are our future now. So let's get on with it."

Bryn Meredith, Season Ticket Holder: "I feel being manager of United these days is not just about the ability to bring success on the field but to have a massive media presence that will appeal to the corporate side of the business.

Unfortunately for us fans the ability to make money and a profit outweighs the desire for trophies on the field therefore having a manager and in effect a 'leader' who will constantly be 'quotable' and possess an ego that causes him to act out all his eccentricities with impunity provides ample opportunities for media exploitation which in turn keeps our club prominent to all our sponsors and worldwide fan base.

From a football point of view I feel is strength is to unite a team into having an 'us and them' mentality whereby the players play for each other and manage to win games in adversity. He demonstrated this at Chelsea, Inter and Madrid only falling down at Chelsea the second time around because some of the players there have bigger egos than him (Fabregas, Hazard, Costa to name but three).

Other than Wayne Rooney (sadly in decline) we do not have any 'superstars' anymore... Most are new to the club and even if he keeps the majority I am confident he will build a strong team spirit with a never say die attitude.

His appointment was inevitable in my view due to his coaching history but more importantly due to his 'presence' in the media.

I am excited about the new season and look forward to a more direct and pacey style of play but anticipate I will be disappointed at times."

Sam Sharp, Manchester United fan: "I think we've been too spoiled by the Fergie era. Over those years we convinced ourselves that it was the long term loyalty to one manager that caused our repeated successes, rather than the other way round. Things have changed now, and despite reservations about his enormous uber-ego he'll certainly attract new players, hopefully play them in the right positions, and increase our chances of silverware."

Tony Parker, Manchester United fan: "I envisage this a short-term solution. There's still some ground work to be done; a number of players who, whilst they may be reasonable (in fact, good) at another club, are not United class or style. Being honest, I'm not a fan of Lingard's, and for the life of me struggle to see why Valencia and Young have to be first choice full-backs. However, with Shaw on the mend and some potential talent LVG gave us glimpses of I do believe JM may be the person to shape and develop a new team/squad. Some sensible buys required. Courage too, which he has in abundance. I think we must accept it won't be cavalier, Fergie-style, and it definitely won't be *go out and enjoy yourselves* Busby-style."

Ray Kirby, Season Ticket Holder: "I was always very prejudiced against Mourinho. The seminal touchline dash at the Porto match should never have happened. We were comfortably the better team: Scholes' 'offside' goal was a shocking decision, would have made it 2-0 and decided the match: Tim Howard should have ignored the indirect free-kick in the last minute.

At Chelski Mark 1, he just had more money than anyone else. His behaviour, whilst at first entertaining, soon became rather boring and made him eventually a caricature of himself.

Similarly at Real Madrid. Real did also knock us out of the Champions League with a decision re. Nani only marginally worse than the Scholes' goal error (and only marginally better than Clattenburg's ludicrous non-punishment of Vardy for his assault on Rafael).

As regards Chelski Mark 2, his behaviour towards the team doctor remains unforgivable (unless there is another story not in the public domain). And it did all go catastrophically and inexplicably wrong.

But:

Porto did win the Champions League - a superb achievement.. His management of Inter's Champions League successes and the Chelski Mark 2 win at City were magnificent. And he clearly wanted the United job - witness his behaviour, and comments, after the Real match at Old Trafford.

Above all, he is a 'big' enough personality, for good and ill.

Only a man of this stature could conceivably have successfully followed Fergie. The job is just too big. For that reason I wanted him to be appointed three years ago when David Moyes got the job. When LVG replaced Moyes it was clear the Dutchman was 'big' enough and arrogant enough too. Ideally I would have liked LVG to stay on now. He has shipped out so many sub-standard players. But too many of their replacements have been sub-standard as well: or if good enough, rarely fit enough.

So, on balance, another change was probably inevitable. And in these circumstances let's get the best, enjoy the fun, hold our noses on occasions, and above all.... win."

Alexandra Jonson, Barcelona Fan: "To start with I think Jose Mourinho is an incredible tactical coach and he's done some incredible things, with Porto, Chelsea, Inter etc. However, sadly, there is another side to Mourinho as well - one I'm not particular fond of. That being his childishness. I believe his petulance may have ruined his career somewhat.

He always wants to be the centre of attention and if someone - according to him - has done or said anything he considers out of order towards him, he wants revenge. And along the way it seems like revenge has taken over and become the main motivation for him, all the time. It's become almost toxic in some ways; he just needs to find problems or someone who wronged him.

And I do believe it has changed him. There are people who worked with him when he was an assistant in Barcelona, who describe him as someone who was very close to the players and had a great relationship with them; who cared about others. When they see him on TV today they say it's not the same person as they once got to know.

Just look what happened in Chelsea in his second spell there: he made enemy of pretty much everyone working around the squad and the players too. He gives the impression of a child that doesn't get the attention he wants and therefore does everything to get it. Frankly, it's a development that has been really sad to see, because behind everything he truly is an amazing football coach one we have all been missing out on for the last couple of years because he has focused on all the wrong things.

The relationship between him and FC Barcelona in general is a quite a fraught one. Mourinho first came in contact with Barça when Bobby Robson was appointed head coach back in 1996. Mourinho was his assistant but acted also as his translator, though as journalists would soon to realise, he spiced Robson's words up with his own opinions.

Overall Mourinho became the link between Robson and the journalists. During his entire stay as assistant (he continued under Louis Van Gaal too), Mou had a strong relationship both with the Catalan media as well as the players. For instance him and a certain Josep Guardiola would have long tactical discussions, and back then they actually enjoyed talking to each other. So - in short - Mourinho was very well liked in Barcelona and especially among the players and the journalists. Then he went out in the world and became a fantastic coach.

It all started to go wrong when he first returned to Camp Nou as Chelsea manager for a Champions League game in 2005. Mourinho accused Frank Rijkaard of making a visit to the Swedish referee Anders Frisk's dressing room at halftime. The Portuguese went on and complained to UEFA and soon after Frisk announced his retirement after receiving death threats from fans over the issue.

When the clubs again met each other in 2006, Mourinho accused 17-year-old wonder boy Lionel Messi of diving and when Chelsea scored, he provoked Barca fans with a knee-slide celebration along the Camp Nou touchline.

Then came 2008. Barcelona decided to part ways with Frank Rijkaard and was looking for a replacement. While Mourinho now a successful manager was looking for his next great opportunity and he had already decided it was going to be Barcelona.

But his relationship with the Barça fans – which had taken a wrong turn after the incidents in 2005 and 2006 - made the club's board unsure if he was the right pick. Yet he also had a lot of admires at the club (Sandro Rosell for instance wanted the job to go to the Portuguese) and a meeting between Barcelona directors and Mourinho took place in the spring of 2008 in Lisbon.

Jose desperately wanted to impress them and after the meeting he was convinced he had been chosen ahead of Pep Guardiola - the other contender for the job. But when he was rejected, with no clear notification from the Barcelona directors for many weeks, there was a burning feeling of betrayal.

Guardiola, who never coached a professional football team before, got the job ahead of Jose Mourinho a Champions League winning coach. It hurt, and it hurt a lot. From that day on Jose Mourinho went on to detest both Barcelona and Guardiola.

Next time he returned to the Camp Nou would be with Inter Milan, and with some great tactics but also with a lot of luck (Barcelona had a Bojan Krkic goal wrongly disallowed for offside goal, which, had it have counted would have taken them through), he managed to knock Guardiola and Barcelona out of the Champions League.

Ahead of the encounter all Mourinho did at his press conference was talk about Barcelona and Guardiola, trying to paint them up as the big villain, while he almost seemed to have forgotten about his own team.

After the final whistle at the Camp Nou, he ran around taunting the Barcelona supporters in the stands. Victor Valdes, the Barcelona 'keeper who'd been at the club since he was ten-years-old, couldn't stand seeing Mourinho taunting the fans of the club he loved in a moment in which he knew they were suffering just as much as he was, so he leaped upon Mourinho to try to make him stop. Mourinho just laughed and continued. Were it not for the interventions of Pique and Puyol, who dragged Victor away, it would have made for a very ugly incident indeed.

So when Jose Mourinho signed for Real Madrid his relationship with Barcelona and its supporters was already horrible. In Madrid his goal was obvious from the start: he focused more on bringing Guardiola and Barcelona down than he did on trying to make Madrid the best. That was also his biggest mistake and the reason he never truly succeeded.

To be honest, I do believe Jose Mourinho could be a success at *any* club if he just focuses on the football. Because he is that good. However with Josep Guardiola so close by and in a rival team he will have a very difficult time doing so. So no I don't believe he'll be a success at Man U: there will be too much of his time going to how to destroy Pep rather than how to make United win.

In short I believe Josep Guardiola is Mourinho's biggest Achilles Heel; not because of Pep being better but because of Mou not being able to focus on the right things when Pep is close by."

CONCLUSION

On Friday 5th August 2016, I finally finished proof-reading this book and sent it off to my publishers, Endeavour Press, in order that they could begin the publication process. It had been our aim to get the book out to coincide – as closely as possible – with the first rounds of fixtures in the 2016-17 Premier League season. I then closed up my laptop and spent a lovely Saturday at my niece's fifth birthday party with my kids, not allowing myself to think about football and in particular about that sometimes very childish man, Jose Mourinho.

On Sunday 7th August, Mourinho's Manchester United played their first 'competitive' fixture, and won their first trophy – the Community Shield, at Wembley. After a relatively quiet game a Mourinho signing, Zlatan Ibrahimovic, leaped like a salmon to head a late winner - in off Kasper Schmeichel's post - to beat Premier League champions Leicester City 2-1. Mourinho's winning-mentality already paying off? Well, maybe. But it wasn't much of a performance. It was still very stodgy in parts and not much different from the fare served up under Louis van Gaal. Certainly it wasn't enough for me to email the publishers come Monday in order to request the manuscript back in order that I could make some last-minute alterations.

That did happen, but it was nothing to do with the Community Shield.

What prompted me to request my manuscript back as hastily as United fans wanted our trophy back after Mourinho had taken it away for a couple of seasons in his first spell at Chelsea was the statement we'd all been waiting weeks for. The Reds had broken the world-record transfer-fee in bringing back the 23-year-old central-midfielder Paul Pogba from Juventus. It was a box-office signing to match the club's previous box-office signings in the summer of 2016: the veteran striker Zlatan, and the manager Jose Mourinho. It was a signing which spoke to everything I've written within these pages, and said so much about the state of Manchester United, and of Premier League football, today. United got Mourinho and the conclusion of that was United got Zlatan and Pogba. Therefore, I had to include it in *my* conclusion.

"Manchester United will not see themselves as mugs for paying a world record fee to buy back a player who was on their books four years ago", wrote Paul Wilson in a *Guardian* piece entitled 'Manchester United's signing of Paul Pogba proves they are still box office'. "Instead, their marketing men can present the purchase of Paul Pogba, who signed a five-year deal late on Monday night, as evidence of the club's enduring power and prestige. United are not in the Champions League this season, but they have ensured, by adding Pogba to a box-office cast that includes Jose Mourinho and Zlatan Ibrahimovic, they remain more interesting than many clubs who are. That's showbiz, in which United have a specific role to play. Outbidding Real Madrid is at least as important to them as outperforming Leicester City."

United stumped up a fee of around £89 million to secure Pogba's signature. Sir Alex Ferguson had let the Frenchman go on a free-transfer. That was some hit United had to take on him. And although there were some commentators who questioned the wisdom of such a splurge - mainly those who quibbled about the size of the fee were rival managers; traditional Mourinho foes such as Arsene Wenger at Arsenal, and new ones such as Jurgen Klopp at Liverpool: Jose was swift to call them out on their quibbles, calling such behaviour as commenting on another club's business as "unethical" - most were sensible enough to see the fee paid as "in tune with the times".

Anyway, the size of the fee didn't really matter. The football transfer market at the elite level works on supply and demand, and United demanded a high-quality midfielder, and, thanks to their many global partners, their sponsorship and TV deals, and Jose Mourinho's presence they could go out and (finally) get him.

"Pogba, in fairness," wrote Wilson, "is more than just a glamour signing who shows that United, and the Premier League, are wrestling some pulling power back from European rivals, notably Spain's swoonsome hunks. This is a trophy recruit who could also help land trophies. Indeed, the fact he is every bit as image-conscious as United could help give more substance to his status; the size of the fee is unlikely to be a millstone around the neck of a player who, like Cristiano Ronaldo before him, has always believed he has what it takes to become the greatest and seems reinforced by others' confirmation."

Wilson concluded that no matter how much United had paid, the Reds had still secured a good deal: "Although they have set a new benchmark for expenditure, their readiness to win a major title is questionable. But Pogba's arrival certainly makes them stronger and more intriguing, which makes his purchase good business."

That is the way football works nowadays. Above all else, be intriguing. Make for a good story.

Jose Mourinho's road to Old Trafford has been a long and winding one. His journey has taken him hop-scotching across the continent as he awaited the job he wanted above all others. But finally he is here. Maybe he should have arrived earlier, as a direct successor to the Godfather, Sir Alex Ferguson, but instead he – and *we* – had to wait a little longer as our stock sunk lower. "What *then* would have been a match made in heaven," wrote Hitesh Ratna in his editorial to the August 2016 issue of *FourFourTwo* magazine, "is now a marriage of convenience, as two giants look to restore their reputations. Will it all end happily ever after?"

Well, we'll be lucky if we ever get as far as the seven-year-itch, we know that much for sure. But it'll sure make for compulsive – box-set; box-*office* - viewing.

"United have lost their way and it is too early to know whether Mourinho on his best behaviour will be a guide back to the sunny uplands or a new turn in the wrong direction," wrote Paul Wilson. "But it is going to be a ride. Next season we will mostly be talking about Madchester again. Anything seems possible, from *I Am The Resurrection* to *Bye Bye Badman.*"

BIBLIOGRAPHY - BOOKS

Leading, by Sir Alex Ferguson with Michael Moritz, Hodder & Stoughton, Tuesday 22nd September 2015

The Game of Our Lives: The Meaning and Making of English Football, by David Goldblatt, Penguin Books, Thursday 5th March 2015

The Secret Footballer's Guide to the Modern Game: Tips and Tactics from the Ultimate Insider, by the Secret Footballer, Guardian Books, Tuesday 4th November 2014

Jose: Return of the King, by Harry Harris, John Blake Publishing, Thursday 4th September 2014

The Numbers Game: Why Everything You Know About Football is Wrong, by Chris Anderson and David Sally, Penguin Books, Thursday 5th June 2014

The Manager: Inside the Minds of Football's Leaders, by Mike Carson, Bloomsbury, Thursday 8th May 2014

Fear and Loathing in La Liga: Barcelona vs Real Madrid, by Sid Lowe, Yellow Jersey, Thursday 26th September 2013

Premier League: A History in 10 Matches, by Jim White, Head of Zeus Books, Thursday 26th September 2013

I am Zlatan Ibrahimovic, by Zlatan Ibrahimovic, David Lagercrantz, and Ruth Urbom, Penguin, Thursday 5th September 2013

I Am The Secret Footballer: Lifting the Lid on the Beautiful Game, by The Secret Footballer, Guardian Books, Thursday 23rd

August 2012

Football - Bloody Hell!: The Biography of Alex Ferguson, by Patrick Barclay, Yellow Jersey, Friday 14th October 2010

Commonsense Direct & Digital Marketing, by Drayton Bird, Kogan Page, Fifth edition, 2007

Manchester United: The Betrayal of a Legend, by Michael Crick and David Smith, Pan Books, Wednesday 1st August 1990

BIBLIOGRAPHY – ARTICLES

'Manchester United's signing of Paul Pogba proves they are still box office', by Paul Doyle, in *The Guardian*, Monday 8th August 2016

'Giving a toy to a child and then taking it straight back,' by Nick Miller, for *The Guardian's 'The Fiver'*, Monday 8th August 2016

'Premier League 2016-17 preview No4: Chelsea', by Paul Doyle, in *The Guardian*, Wednesday 3rd August 2016

'"I'm not afraid of the consequences of my decisions," by Andrew Murray, in *FourFourTwo* magazine, August 2016

'FourFourTwo's 50 Best Football Managers in the World 2016: No.4, Jose Mourinho', by Alex Hess, on Four Four Two.com, Friday 29th July 2016

'Euro 2016: a bloated tournament where dour defence eclipsed the fairytales' by Barney Ronay, in *The Guardian*, Monday 11th July 2016

'Jose Mourinho suggests he could be the Right One for Manchester United', by Daniel Taylor, in *The Guardian*, Wednesday 6th July 2016

'Local boy Marcus Rashford is battling Manchester United's club values, as well as Ibra', by Alex Hess, on Four Four Two.com, Wednesday 6th July 2016

'Axes grinding and bile bubbling,' by Daniel Harris, for *The Guardian's 'The Fiver'*, Tuesday 5th July 2016

'The 49 players that Jose Mourinho promoted from academies, and why his list does not stand up to scrutiny', by James Ducker, in *The Telegraph*, Tuesday 5th July 2016

'Jose Mourinho unveiled as Manchester United manager: 'I want everything'', by Jamie Jackson, in *The Guardian*, Tuesday 5th July 2016

'Eva Carneiro: The shame of Chelsea, a club who were ready to drag Carneiro's name through the mud', by Ian Herbert, in *The Independent*, Wednesday 8th June 2016

'Got something to smile about Eva? A day after Chelsea issue their grovelling apology and settle for a reported £5million the former first team physio is beaming' by Emma Glanfield, in *The Daily Mail*, Wednesday 8th June 2016

'Mourinho accused of being bad employee at Eva Carneiro employment tribunal', by Anthony Jepson and Matt McGeehan, Monday 6th June 2016

'Why It's OK For Man Utd Fans To Change Their Minds About Jose Mourinho' by Scott Patterson, for *Umaxit.com*,

Monday 30th May 2016

'José Mourinho more of a risk for Manchester United than three years ago', by Paul Wilson, in *The Guardian (Sportblog)*, Saturday 28th May 2016

'Why new manager Mourinho is lifting Manchester United's share price', by David Reid, for CNBC.com, Friday 27th May 2016

'Mourinho: Real Madrid weren't happy with what I said after United game!', by Scott Patterson, for *The Republik of Mancunia*, Friday 27th May 2016

'After-shave and napkin rings – Mourinho's image rights delay United appointment', by Guardian Sport and Agencies, Thursday 26th May 2016

'Jose Mourinho dividing opinion among Manchester United's global fanbase', by Paul MacInnes, in *The Guardian (Sportblog)*, Tuesday 24th May 2016

'Jose Mourinho just the man to shake Manchester United out of their torpor', by David Hytner, in *The Guardian (Sportblog)*, Tuesday 24th May 2016

'Eric Cantona: 'I love Jose Mourinho but he is not Manchester United'', by Owen Gibson, in *The Guardian (Sportblog)*, Tuesday 24th May 2016

'The Guardian view on the changes at Manchester United: football's changed priorities', *The Guardian Editorial*, Monday 23rd May 2016

'Mourinho has been auditioning for the Manchester United job since 2009', by Samuel Luckhurst, in the *Manchester*

Evening News, Saturday 21st May 2016

'Premier League clubs admit to meeting over changes to Champions League', by Owen Gibson, in *The Guardian*, Wednesday 2nd March 2016

'Jose Mourinho in quotes: a legacy of jibes, boasts and putdowns', by Jamie Grierson and Nadia Khomami, in *The Guardian*, Thursday 17th December 2015

'7 Transfer Targets Who Chose Chelsea Over Manchester United', by Mikey Traynor, for Balls.ie, Wednesday 19th August 2015

'Jose Mourinho hits back with jibe about Rafa Benitez's weight,' by Steve Brenner, in *The Guardian*, Wednesday 29th July 2015

'Football's technical area lets managers strut their stuff upon the stage', by Richard Williams, in *The Guardian*, Friday 13th February 2015

'Marks And Spencer Is Bringing Back Its Food Porn Adverts', by Louise Ridley, in The Huffington Post, Tuesday 2nd September 2014

'6 Easy Tips on How to dress like Jose Mourinho', by Alex Scott, on *The Idle Man*

'Louis van Gaal the right man at the wrong time for Manchester United', by Paul Wilson, in *The Guardian*, Saturday 19th July 2014

'Holland's World Cup win over Spain wasn't the return of Total Football - Louis van Gaal has created something new' by Jonathan Liew, in *The Telegraph*, Saturday 14th June 2014

'Louis van Gaal: Manchester United turn to an anti-Moyes disciplinarian', by Barney Ronay, in *The Guardian*, Monday 19th May 2014

'Liverpool 0, Chelsea 2', by Chris Bevan, for BBC Sport.co.uk: Football, Sunday 27th April 2014

'A decade on: How Jose Mourinho made his mark on Manchester and changed face of football forever' by Scott Hunt, for Mancunian Matters, Sunday 9th March 2014

'Jose Mourinho 'cried' after being overlooked for Manchester United job' by Guardian Staff, in *The Guardian*, Thursday 26th September 2013

'Mourinho's "young eggs" – don't believe the hype', by Andrew Kirby, in the Republik of Mancunia, Friday 20th September 2013

'Manchester United 0-0 Chelsea,' by Phil McNulty, BBC Sport, Monday 26th August 2013
'The antihero in popular culture: Life history theory and the dark triad personality traits', by Peter K. Jonason; Gregory D. Webster; David P. Schmitt; Norman P. Li; and Laura Crysel, Review of General Psychology, Vol 16(2), Jun 2012, 192-199

'Superman Beckham's fond farewell as Spider-Man Terry spreads magic dust', by Barney Ronay, in *The Guardian*, Friday 17th May 2013

'Holders United head through to quarter-finals', by Simon Hart, UEFA.com, Thursday 12th March 2009

'Mourinho May Return... But Never To United', by Scott

Patterson, for the Republik of Mancunia, Monday 20th October 2008

'Mourinho mocks Ferguson', from BBC Sport: Football, Wednesday, 25th February, 2004

'Larson's twin-strike all in vain, by John Dillon, *Daily Express*, Thursday 22nd May 2003

'Astonishingly Sevill-iant', by David McCarthy, *The Daily Record*, Thursday 22nd May 2003

'So Costly: Porto cash-in on red card for Celts ace Balde', by Keith Jackson, *The Daily Record*, Thursday 22nd May 2003

'Porto boss is O'Neill mark two', by Gavin Berry, Scottish Daily Mail, Wednesday 21st May 2003

'The Human Face of Football,' by Monty Smith, in *New Musical Express*, Saturday 12th May 1979

ACKNOWLEDGEMENTS

Ten years ago if you'd told me I'd be writing a book on Jose Mourinho in 2016 I'd have laughed. Asked: what next, a volume on Steven Gerrard? I hated Mourinho back then - and yes, I know hate is an ugly word, and one I encourage my children not to use, but still *Mourinho?* He was a hateful man. He behaved in a hateful way. He *inspired* hatred.

You might agree with the author Laurie Halse Anderson: "A book is like a sausage. You love the end product, but you don't really want to know how it's made." I won't bore you, but the process of planning, researching, and writing a book takes a lot of time and energy. The author is forced to spend a great deal of time in the company of their subject. For me to have even considered spending a book-length amount of time with Jose Mourinho would have seemed inconceivable to my younger self. Me and Mourinho? Nah… Not unless I was writing some kind of 80,000 word take-down character-assassination on the man, it simply wouldn't work. Well, either that or some catastrophe must have taken place; the entire football world turned on its head. Then, maybe, I might have considered it.

In the past decade the entire football world *has* turned on its head. Manchester City are a big club. They have won trophies. Who'd have thunk it. Sir Alex Ferguson has retired. Again: inconceivable. Manchester United finished seventh in a Premier League campaign, and twice in the past three years have missed out on a Champions League place. Who are you kidding?

Jose Mourinho is – mostly – just the same as he was back then, though. Spiky. Arrogant. Unlikable. And yet, love or loathe him, he is now the man most associated with the current Manchester United. *He* is our identity. Suck it up, boys.

The other thing about Jose is he is a winner. He's

proved it time and again.

This is one deal with the devil which the Red Devils board (mostly devils themselves) have made.

In the process of writing this book I've had to confront a number of harsh truths and I've done a lot of wrestling with my own soul and my morals. I supported United for many reasons – mainly because my Dad did, and I loved the romance of the stories he used to tell. I supported United because of the prestige of some of the players (Robson, Whiteside, and Olsen back then) and the slightly crumbledown grandeur of Old Trafford. I didn't support them because they were winning, because they weren't back then. But I did love the glory of those FA Cup wins in 1985 and 1990.

That United isn't the United of today, and this is hard to accept. We're not even the United of 1992-93, when we won the first ever Premier League trophy and sung along to Queen. We're not even the United of 1999, and our fantastic treble. We're different.

A lot of that is down to Ferguson retiring. He *became* Manchester United during his tenure, much as I fear Mourinho might now, if the media has their way. But a lot is also down to our owners, those leaches the Glazers. And it is down to the way that bloated monster the Premier League keeps growing.

United have reaped the profits from the Premier League era, and we have been highly successful in the competition. But at the same time, the club has been taken away from us, the match-going fans. The club doesn't answer to us any more. It answers to a global fan-base now. It answers to the official snack-partners in Asia or to the banking partners in Nigeria.

For them, Jose Mourinho was the only choice. He is a brand. He is box office.

For us, well, if Jose Mourinho was the answer then perish the thought what the question might have been.

But yeah, in all honesty we know the question. It was: do we still want to enjoy European nights at Old Trafford (and not of the *Diet*, Thursday-night Europa League variety, the full-fat Champions League); do we want to return to the very pinnacle of English football? And if we're being brutally honest with ourselves we do. If only so we don't become another Liverpool, basking in past glories. If only so we don't slip any further behind Manchester City.

Suck it up, boys.

We are where we are and it is what it is. Jose Mourinho's massive ego has been installed at Old Trafford. In his first home league game as United boss, he will face the Sir Alex Ferguson Stand. I hope this teaches him about the benefits of the long-term over the short. Looking his shoulder will be the Sir Bobby Charlton Stand. I hope this teaches him some humility. In the crowd, us, the fans. I hope we teach him what it really means to be a Red.

But in turn I hope Mourinho teaches the current – and future – crop of United players what it is to be hungry to win, to be absolutely desperate to do so. I hope he whispers in Anthony Martial's ear that he has it in him to be the best player in the world in a few years' time if he keeps working, just like Jose did with Frank Lampard. I hope he encourages the development of Marcus Rashford, whose debut Old Trafford goals I was present to witness, just a few rows (and a corporate box balcony) away from Wayne Rooney, who didn't look like he knew whether to laugh or cry. I hope he attracts new, stellar names which will make us purr.

I hope.

And there have been some times over the past three seasons when watching United has seemed a pretty hopeless pursuit.

In this process of writing this book, I've had the pleasure of speaking with a number of seasoned United fans who were more than happy to share their own views on the appointment of Mourinho and what it means for the club we love. They are just as conflicted on the matter as I am, and just as wearily accepting. But some are hopeful too. I'd like to thank Tony Parker, Bryn Meredith, Mike Hopkins, Sam Sharp, Ben Greenwood at T-Shirts United (check out t34.co.uk for their full range of tees), and Ray Kirby.

The last name on that list is my Dad; in a roundabout way, it's his fault I've written this book in the first place. And he'll also be its number one cheerleader, as he has been with all of my other United books. He'll also be the most brutally honest about Mourinho's regime at Old Trafford, and those who sit around him in the crowd in the N49 section will be more pleased than most if Mourinho's United achieve success and play well in achieving it. That way they won't have to suffer the dogs abuse Dad yells out to the players at the top of his voice when they aren't performing to the high standards we have traditionally seen from those who fit the famous United shirt.

I'd also like to thank the fans of opposing teams whose opinions I've canvassed, from Alexandra Jonson (Barcelona), to Celia (from Chelsea Supporters' Trust). They've been able to provide a more balanced view than my own impassioned one.

And finally, I'd like to thank the great wealth of wonderful football writing I've quoted from over the course of these pages. From Sid Lowe to Scott Patterson; your work makes me as jealous as opposing fans used to be of United's flair and panache.

When I quoted Laurie Halse Anderson, the contributions of the other writers and fans to this book have been all the good parts. If you find a piece of gristle which gets stuck between your teeth, consider it mine.

It only remains to say that I hope you have enjoyed this book. I hope it has given you food for thought. I hope it has come at a subject which is already so well-known to have become almost clichéd, and made it new.

But most of all I hope Mourinho's United make us happy,

Andrew J. Kirby, 2016

ALSO BY THIS AUTHOR:
Fergie's Finest: Sir Alex Ferguson's First 11, by Andrew J Kirby, Endeavour Press Ltd. 8th May 2013
Search for it on Amazon

Sir Alex Ferguson was one of the greatest football managers of all time. Over 26 years in charge of Manchester United, his passion for winning and tactical flair made them the most successful club in the Premier League. Under his guidance, United won an eye-watering 38 trophies, including 13 league championships.

But who were the greatest players of the Ferguson era? Over 185 players debuted for United under Ferguson and more than 200 players wore the red jersey for Fergie. They included legends of the modern game from David Beckham to Ryan Giggs, from Roy Keane to Bryan Robson, and from Eric Cantona to Cristiano Ronaldo.

But which were the Greatest Eleven? Is Robin Van Persie the greatest striker? Or Ruud Van Nistelrooy? Was Paul Scholes the best player in the heart of the midfield? Or Bryan Robson?

In this fascinating study, Andrew Kirby selects the ultimate 'Team Fergie'? With interviews from football writers and former players, this book considers the leading contenders for each position in Sir Alex Ferguson's First Eleven.

It is the one book that every Manchester United fan - and indeed every football supporter - will want to read.

ALSO BY THIS AUTHOR:
The Pride of All Europe: Manchester United's Greatest Seasons in the European Cup, by Andrew J Kirby, Endeavour Press Ltd, 23rd June 2014
Search for it on Amazon

Manchester United was the first English team to make the foray into the European Cup, participating in the tournament despite the express disapproval of the Football League.

They were also the first English winners of the trophy.

Over the years, United's European adventures have spanned tragedy – the 1958 Munich Air Disaster – and triumph – three European Cup wins – and have provided no shortage of memorable stories.

Despite United being only the eighth most successful club in the competition's history, the United name is irrevocably linked to the European Cup.

This book explores the reasons why.

With interviews from fans, personal anecdotes and excerpts from football archives, this book looks back at the history of the club and their greatest – and worst – moments.

'The Pride of All Europe' celebrates Manchester United's triumphs in European football, concentrating on ten key stories from the twenty-five seasons and six decades the club has participated in the Europe's premier competition, interspersed with brief, first-hand fan accounts of those fabled United "Euroaways."

In this detailed study, Andrew Kirby dissects the rich history of Manchester United in Europe.

This is the one book that every true Manchester United fan ought to read.

ALSO BY THIS AUTHOR:
Louis van Gaal: Dutch Courage, by Andrew J Kirby, Endeavour Press Ltd, 4th August 2015
Search for it on Amazon

When unveiled as Bayern Munich manager in 2009, Louis Van Gaal remarked, "I am what I am; self-confident, arrogant, dominant, honest, industrious, innovative."

Former players have described him as "scary", as a "volcano". The former Barcelona president described him as "the devil himself". At Bayern, they said he "vaangalised" their team.

And yet at the same time, he is "warm-blooded". He openly admits: "I cry almost every day. There's always something that touches me." Barcelona's Xavi says of him: "People see him as arrogant and aloof but he's really not."

'Dutch Courage' separates the man from the myths.

This Dutch master has been the head of some of the greatest dynasties in European football - Ajax, Barcelona, Bayern Munich, and Manchester United - as well as the boss of the Netherlands national team (twice).

This biography, by the bestselling author of Fergie's Finest, brings the Van Gaal biography up to date.

'From Ajax to Man United, via Bayern Munich, Andrew J Kirby plots the rise of this indomitable, complex figure with verve and great insight. This book is exhaustively researched, and offers great psychological insights into the man, as well as the world of football. A must-read for fans of United, and those of us interested in this colossus of football.' - Guy Mankowski, author of 'How I Left the National Grid'.

ANDREW J. KIRBY

Printed in Great Britain
by Amazon

24897927R00155